In giving us a history of America and the Protestant church, Jemar Tisby has given us a survey of ourselves—the racial meanings and stratagems that define our negotiations with one another. He points courageously toward the open sore of racism, not with the resigned pessimism of the defeated but with the resilient hope of Christian faith. The reader will have their minds and hearts pricked as they consider just how complicit the church has been in America's original sin and how weak a word *complicit* is for describing the actions and inactions of those who claim the name of Christ!

THABITI ANYABWILE, pastor, Anacostia River Church

With clinical precision, Jemar Tisby unpacks the tragic connection between the American church and the countless historic iterations of American racism. Readers are served well by Jemar's refusal to minimize the horror of this history or sanitize the church's hands from its complicity. For this reason and many others, *The Color of Compromise* is an appropriately discomforting volume for such a time as this. May it be referenced and heeded as a prophetic warning for decades to come.

TYLER BURNS, vice president, The Witness

If you want to understand why we remain mired in racial unrighteousness, you need to read this book. Its pages radiate not just historical but also moral insight, as Tisby shines a light on to the dark places of American church history. *The Color of Compromise* tells the truth—and only the truth will set us free.

HEATH W. CARTER, associate professor of history, Valparaiso University, author, *Union Made*

The Color of Compromise is essential reading for American Christians. By telling the brutal history of white Christians' deliberate complicity in racial oppression, Jemar Tisby confronts the church with its own past. But his is not simply a story of condemnation. If racism can be made, it can be unmade, he reminds us. "There can be no deep disappointment where there is not deep love," Martin Luther King Jr. once wrote. Tisby's book is a labor of love and, ultimately, a work of hope.

KRISTIN DU MEZ, professor of history and gender studies, Calvin College

Each individual and society is a compilation of what has come before them, whether they own this notion or not. Tisby's thoughtful work reminds us that you can run from, deny, or remix it, but history will find you out. The American church's history of wanting to hold holiness in one hand and racial stratification in the other has seeded a deeply corrupted tree. The book causes us to examine the implications of the historical trajectory of our theological influences. Yet this book, with the same intensity that it offers historical truth, provides grace. If race can be constructed, racism can be deconstructed. In Christ's name, it must be!

CHRISTINA EDMONDSON, dean for intercultural
student development, Calvin College

Christianity in the United States has had problems for centuries as it concerns racial injustice, and most American Christians need what can only be described as remedial education when it comes to understanding the abusive racist history of our faith tradition. In *The Color of Compromise* Jemar Tisby courageously challenges some of our long held collective assumptions and whitewashed accounts of rationalized racism for the church in America. With a thoroughly researched and detailed examination of archival documents and literary sources, he compels readers to focus on hard truths, addresses the realities of American Christianity's past, and does so in a well-reasoned and lovingly direct writing style. Upon reading this book, one will come away having to reconsider how individuals who proudly boast of a Christian way of life in America continue to do so at the expense of others. As a historian and a Christian, Tisby presents truth with accuracy but also with much love and humility. If it is true that those who fail to learn from history are doomed to repeat it, then this book is a timely must-read for any Christian seeking justice and mercy, as we learn how problems in American Christianity's past could lead to solutions in our future.

ALEXANDER JUN, professor of higher education, Azusa
Pacific University, author, *White Out* and *White Jesus*

Reconciliation doesn't happen without truth telling. Jemar takes us on a historical journey laying out the racial complicity of the church. It's difficult to understand the complexities of the history of racial oppression in America; one must begin to identify the intentional and unintentional blind spots many have. Jemar calls the church to face its tragic history in an effort to build a new future and to save it from repeating past mistakes. The foundation of reconciliation begins with truth. Tisby encourages us to become courageous Christians who face our past with lament, hope, and humility. History is imperative to understanding the present. *The Color of Comprise* gives us an aerial view of our past with hopes of a Christian awakening. This is a must-read for all Christians who have hopes of seeing reconciliation.

LATASHA MORRISON, founder and president, Be the Bridge

With the incision of a prophet, the rigor of a professor, and the heart of a pastor, Jemar Tisby offers a defining examination of the history of race and the church in America. Comprehensive in its scope of American history, Tisby's data provides the full truth and not a sanitized version that most American Christians have embraced. Read this book. Share this book. Teach this book. The church in America will be better for it.

SOONG-CHAN RAH, Milton B. Engebretson Professor of Church Growth and Evangelism, North Park Theological Seminary, author, *The Next Evangelicalism* and *Prophetic Lament*

In *The Color of Compromise*, Tisby reveals the role that racism has played in the American church and how that has manifested in policy making. Those following the relationship between white evangelicals and President Trump need to know that this union was a long time coming—even before the rise of the Moral Majority, led in part by the late Jerry Falwell, father of one of Trump's most vocal evangelical supporters, Jerry Falwell Jr. Tisby's book gives the historical context that is often missing from the conversation about how so many black and white Christians can be described as theologically conservative but vote so differently on Election Day. *Compromise* helps the reader understand that Martin Luther King Jr.'s assessment—that Sunday morning is the most racially divided hour in America—rings true today and manifests in the voting booths when Christians express their deeply held convictions.

EUGENE SCOTT, reporter covering identity politics for *The Fix* for *The Washington Post*

Some American evangelical Christians are often confused and sometimes frustrated by all the talk surrounding white supremacy and American Christianity. Some think that racism and its deleterious intergenerational, personal, psychological, social, institutional, and systemic effects are of the past and too often exaggerated in the present or that in a certain way

American Christianity was somehow immune to this national spiritual and moral pathology. In *The Color of Compromise*, Jemar Tisby has provided an account that reminds some of us and informs others of the sad demonstrably historical fact that the American church intentionally perpetuated racial injustice socially and politically while attempting to undergird all of this theologically. The claim itself will no doubt make some uncomfortable. We must nevertheless come to grips with these realities. Others may even become defensive, yet this response must be resisted. For those who care about the collective witness of the American church, it is necessary that readers journey with Tisby through this treacherous landscape of American church history. This sordid history should not be hidden, downplayed, or explained away. It must be confronted. There cannot be a way forward without a profound truth telling. This is exactly what *The Color of Compromise* does. Those who are deeply concerned about the witness of the American church must read this book and pass it on to others. By looking back, *The Color of Compromise* pushes us to look forward to live out a courageous Christianity that is authentically grounded in the gospel of Jesus Christ.

PATRICK SMITH, associate research professor of theological ethics and bioethics, Duke Divinity School, senior fellow, Kenan Institute of Ethics, Duke University

The Color of Compromise presents an irrefutable and haunting historical survey of white evangelical churches' complicity with racism and white supremacy. Tisby invites the reader to answer this question: What is the color of compromise? The answer is red, politically and literally, as the blood of black women and men—slain by the wickedness of white supremacy and antiblack racism vis-à-vis the altar of complicity—continues to pour out.

EKEMINI UWAN, public theologian

Jemar Tisby has written a concise history of the way white supremacy wrapped itself in Christianity in the American story, compromising the gospel for the sake of money and power. This slaveholder religion is with us still, adding fuel to the fire that threatens to consume the institutions of our common life. To face the truth this book illuminates is to see that it didn't have to be this way—and that, by God's grace, there has always been a prophetic tradition calling us to confront the compromise and be born again.

JONATHAN WILSON-HARTGROVE, author, *Reconstructing the Gospel*

THE **COLOR** OF **COMPROMISE**

THE TRUTH ABOUT THE AMERICAN CHURCH'S COMPLICITY IN RACISM

JEMAR TISBY

ZONDERVAN

The Color of Compromise
Copyright © 2019 by Jemar Tisby

ISBN 978-0-310-59726-1 (hardcover)

ISBN 978-0-310-59727-8 (ebook)

ISBN 978-0-310-59730-8 (audio download)

Requests for information should be addressed to:
Zondervan, *3900 Sparks Dr. SE, Grand Rapids, Michigan 49546*

Scripture quotations are taken from the Holy Bible, New International Version®, NIV®. Copyright © 1973, 1978, 1984, 2011 by Biblica, Inc.® Used by permission of Zondervan. All rights reserved worldwide. www.Zondervan.com. The "NIV" and "New International Version" are trademarks registered in the United States Patent and Trademark Office by Biblica, Inc.®

Any internet addresses (websites, blogs, etc.) and telephone numbers in this book are offered as a resource. They are not intended in any way to be or imply an endorsement by Zondervan, nor does Zondervan vouch for the content of these sites and numbers for the life of this book.

Published in association with the literary agency of Wolgemuth & Associates, Inc.

Cover design: RAM Creative
Cover photography: Everett Collection Historical / Alamy Stock Photo
Interior design: Kait Lamphere

Printed in the United States of America

18 19 20 21 22 23 24 25 26 27 28 29 /DHV/ 15 14 13 12 11 10 9 8 7 6 5 4 3 2 1

To Janeé and Jack

CONTENTS

FOREWORD

On July 4, 2016, as my social media feeds filled with images of American flags and friends' backyard barbecues celebrating America's independence, I took to Twitter and posted a picture seven African Americans picking cotton in a field with the following caption: "My family on July 4th 1776."

While the tweet received more than 15,000 retweets and 23,000 likes, there were numerous tweets frustrated by the fact that I chose to post such an image and caption on the day celebrating America's independence. One follower questioned my patriotism; another accused me of making every issue a race issue instead of a gospel issue. From where I sat, I was simply telling the truth about our country's complicated, imperfect history on a day when people were celebrating a simplistic, incomplete narrative about our country.

Though those responses frustrated and grieved me, they didn't surprise me. My work as a black hip-hop artist with an audience in white evangelicalism has shown me the tension that exists between black and white America, specifically when it comes to the history of the white evangelical church in America.

That's why I'm excited that this book by my friend and brother Jemar Tisby is in your hands. Throughout its pages, Jemar carefully surveys the history of the white church in America and its complicity with racism. As a student of history, he's careful with stories and data, seeking to let history speak for itself by boldly telling the truth and helping us connect the dots between events over the past 400 years of our country's history.

In a time when discussions grow heated quickly and narratives clash as black and white American Christians think about and discuss our country's racial history and its ongoing implications, Jemar's book challenges us to consider the history that has shaped us.

As Christians, when we read the Bible, we recognize that events that happened thousands of years ago are still relevant today. We also see that Scripture never hides the ugly parts of history when it comes to the people of God. The Bible reveals David's adultery, Jonah's selfishness, and Peter's failure of faith. Just as we can't take out the parts of the Bible that we don't like or that make us uncomfortable, we can't celebrate the shining moments of the American church's history and then ignore the shameful aspects of that history. We either fully acknowledge the entire history or dismiss it all. The truth about humanity's heritage turns a mirror on our souls and pushes us to recognize who we truly are and who we are not.

Jemar challenges us to take history seriously and account for it. My brother has done his due diligence in researching and understanding the history of the evangelical church in the United States. He has carefully collected historical records, interviews, and stories and then organized that history in a way that helps us see how the travesty of racism in and from the church deeply impacts our politics, churches, neighborhoods, schools. The account is sobering and challenging

Fortunately, Jemar doesn't simply leave us on our own to figure out next steps. Along with the bleak, heart-wrenching account of the past, he offers thoughtful, constructive action steps we can take to pursue justice and reconciliation in our communities, churches, and country.

Education should lead to informed action, and informed action should lead to liberation, justice, and repair. Through reading this book, we realize that if we built the walls on purpose, we need to tear down the walls on purpose. This demands political, social, and personal action that cuts through theological and political lines. It requires us to hold our Bibles with clarity and strength while correcting our country's broken systems, such as mass incarceration and police brutality.

We live in a country centered around whiteness that disregards how the image of God is on magnificent display in nonwhite bodies (and histories and theologies, etc.). If we don't take responsibility for what has happened in America, we're not willing to see the image of God throughout the world.

Jemar has done a service to the church through this book. He has traced our country's wicked, racist history and demonstrated how the church has been complicit in that work. Understanding the past isn't simply an end in and of itself; it's also a means to an end. Through understanding our history, we can look to the world around us with new eyes and see ways we can move forward with focus and intentionality to make right what has been wrong so that justice will "roll down like waters, and righteousness like an ever-flowing stream."

Lecrae

CHAPTER 1

THE COLOR OF COMPROMISE

Four young girls busily prepared for their big day. It was September 15, 1963, the day of the "Youth Day" Sunday service at Sixteenth Street Baptist Church in Birmingham, Alabama, and the girls, along with the other young people of the congregation, would spend the next few hours singing songs, reciting poems, praying, and giving encouraging messages in front of hundreds of beaming parents. The girls—Addie Mae Collins (14), Denise McNair (11), Carole Robertson (14), and Cynthia Wesley (14)—had just finished Sunday school and were in the church basement making final adjustments to their white dresses when the bomb exploded.[1] The blast, which killed all four girls and injured at least twenty others, left a hole in the floor five feet wide and two feet deep. It decapitated Cynthia. Her parents could only identify her body by her feet and by the ring she was wearing.[2] A newspaper report at the time indicated that all of the church's stained-glass windows had been destroyed except one. That window depicted "Christ leading a group of little children. The face of Christ was blown out."[3]

Three days later, an integrated crowd of thousands of mourners gathered at Sixth Avenue Baptist Church for a funeral for three of the girls. So many attended that the mass of people spilled out of the sanctuary and into the street.[4] The cover of this book shows the scene of the funeral.

Before the funeral, on the day after the bombing, a young, white lawyer named Charles Morgan Jr. delivered a lunchtime speech at Birmingham's all-white Young Men's Business Club. Of course, he had heard about the tragedy in his city, and this lifelong southerner jotted down some words about racism and complicity that would prove to be a turning point in his life.

Reflecting on the events he said, "'Who did it? Who threw that bomb? Was it a Negro or a white?' The answer should be, 'We all did it.' Every last one of us is condemned for that crime and the bombing before it and a decade ago. We all did it."[5]

Morgan recognized that no matter who had physically planted the dynamite, all the city's white residents were complicit in allowing an environment of hatred and racism to persist. The acts that reinforced racism happened in countless common ways. Morgan explained, "The 'who' is every little individual who talks about the 'niggers' and spreads the seeds of his hate to his neighbor and his son. The jokester, the crude oaf whose racial jokes rock the party with laughter."[6]

Morgan also recognized that Christians bore as much responsibility as anyone for the state of race relations in city. "It is all the Christians and all their ministers who spoke too late in anguished cries against violence." He then asked a series of rhetorical questions for his listeners to ponder. "Did those ministers visit the families of the Negroes in their hour of travail? Did many of them go to the homes of their brothers and express their regrets in person or pray with the crying relatives? Do they admit Negroes into their ranks at the church?"[7]

Some white Birmingham residents did not receive Charles Morgan Jr.'s speech well. Though many hurled death threats at Morgan personally, the threat that most disturbed him listed every place his wife and son had been on a recent Saturday. Morgan soon closed his law practice and moved elsewhere to engage in a long career of civil rights law.[8]

Although many people from Birmingham and beyond expressed outrage at the murder of these four black girls at church, Morgan's point stands out—the most egregious acts of racism, like a church bombing, occur within a context of compromise. The failure of many

Christians in the South and across the nation to decisively oppose the racism in their families, communities, and even in their own churches provided fertile soil for the seeds of hatred to grow. The refusal to act in the midst of injustice is itself an act of injustice. Indifference to oppression perpetuates oppression.

History and Scripture teaches us that there can be no reconciliation without repentance. There can be no repentance without confession. And there can be no confession without truth. *The Color of Compromise* is about telling the truth so that reconciliation—robust, consistent, honest reconciliation—might occur across racial lines. Yet all too often, Christians, and Americans in general, try to circumvent the truth-telling process in their haste to arrive at reconciliation. This book tells the truth about racism in the American church in order to facilitate authentic human solidarity.

In this book you'll read about the American church's sickening record of supporting racism. Many would prefer this history to remain locked away and hidden. But Martin Luther King Jr. gave an important rationale for shining a light on injustice, despite the pain it may provoke. "Like a boil that can never be cured so long as it is covered up but must be opened with all its ugliness to the natural medicines of air and light," he wrote, "injustice must be exposed, with all the tension its exposure creates, to the light of human conscience and the air of national opinion before it can be cured."[9] King's words apply to racism in the church. The festering wound of racism in the American church must be exposed to the oxygen of truth in order to be healed.

Although activists have achieved a remarkable amount of racial progress at great cost, racism continues to plague the church. One of the reasons churches can't shake the shackles of segregation is that few have undertaken the regimen of aggressive treatment the malady requires. It seems like most Christians in America don't know how bad racism really is, so they don't respond with the necessary urgency. Even when Christians realize the need for change, they often shrink back from the sacrifices that transformation entails.

This book is about revealing racism. It pulls back the curtain on the ways American Christians have collaborated with racism for centuries.

By seeing the roots of racism in this country, may the church be moved to immediate and resolute antiracist action.

CHRISTIAN COMPLICITY WITH RACISM

While many Christian traditions and other religions have varied and valuable narratives, Protestants, especially evangelicals, have written some of the most well-known narratives of racism in the United States. Other religious groups, such as white Catholics, have certainly contributed to racism, but the narrative that unfolds in the following pages focuses on Protestant churches. Methodists, Baptists, and Presbyterians all have a central, sometimes repressive, place in the story of race in America. No matter which faith tradition or denomination is at the forefront of discussion, racism extends across sectarian lines.

What do we mean when we talk about *racism*? Beverly Daniel Tatum provides a shorthand definition: racism is a system of oppression based on race.[10] Notice Tatum's emphasis on systemic oppression. Racism can operate through impersonal systems and not simply through the malicious words and actions of individuals. Another definition explains racism as *prejudice plus power*. It is not only personal bigotry toward someone of a different race that constitutes racism; rather, racism includes the imposition of bigoted ideas on groups of people.

In light of these definitions, it is accurate to say that many white people have been complicit with racism. Although there have been notable exceptions, and racial progress in this country could not have happened without allies across the color line, white people have historically had the power to construct a social caste system based on skin color, a system that placed people of African descent at the bottom. White men and women have used tools like money, politics, and terrorism to consolidate their power and protect their comfort at the expense of black people. Christians participated in this system of white supremacy—a concept that identifies white people and white culture as normal and superior—even if they claim people of color as their brothers and sisters in Christ.

White complicity with racism isn't a matter of melanin, it's a matter of power. Other nations have different dynamics. Whether society is stratified according to class, gender, religion, or tribe, communities tend to put power in the hands of a few to the detriment of many. In the United States, power runs along color lines, and white people have the most influence.

Historically speaking, when faced with the choice between racism and equality, the American church has tended to practice a complicit Christianity rather than a courageous Christianity. They chose comfort over constructive conflict and in so doing created and maintained a status quo of injustice.

Given the history, *complicity* is a weak word for describing how American Christianity has often interacted with race. As historian Carolyn DuPont describes it, "Not only did white Christians fail to fight *for* black equality, they often labored mightily *against* it."[11] Complicity connotes a degree of passivity—as if Christianity were merely a boat languidly floating down the river of racism. In reality, white Christians have often been the current, whipping racism into waves of conflict that rock and divide the people of God. Even if only a small portion of Christians committed the most notorious acts of racism, many more white Christians can be described as complicit in creating and sustaining a racist society.

WHAT A HISTORICAL SURVEY IS AND ISN'T

Before jumping into the waters of history, it's important to acknowledge the limitations of a book like this one. Every book is an introduction, an invitation to further study. This is especially true with a historical survey.[12] A survey covers a large amount of historical territory quickly. It gives readers a sense of the historical patterns and how they have changed or persisted over time. Yet surveying the history of the American church and racism leaves no doubt that race has exerted an undeniable influence on the way Christianity has developed in this nation.

At the same time, a survey focuses on breadth instead of depth.

A high degree of selectivity goes into a historical survey, and more gets left out than put in. So it should come as no surprise that important leaders, events, and stories may not even get mentioned in this book. This is not to say that the facts left out are unimportant; it is merely an indication of what can be accomplished in a single volume. This book is a doorway into the endless hallways and chambers of American history and makes no claim to be a comprehensive treatment of race and the American church.

The Color of Compromise focuses on prominent figures, precipitous events, and well-known turning points in American history. These stories serve as an entry point to a deeper study of the host of local people and lesser-known narratives with significant historical and social importance. But even though most of history's precipitous events hinge on the actions of numerous people at the grassroots level, certain individuals and their actions symbolize broader movements and sentiments. Widely recognized people, such as George Whitefield and Billy Graham, are highlighted not because their voices matter most but because their stances represent larger cultural trends.[13]

This book focuses on the black-white racial divide in American Christianity. Of course, there are many other intractable conflicts along racial and ethnic lines. These various schisms have their own unique stories and dynamics. It would be impossible to do them all justice in a single volume. Yet justice for one group can open pathways for equality to other groups.[14] The principles outlined in this book, when applied to other racial and ethnic conflicts, can help lead to greater understanding and positive change.

Even though a survey approach poses several limitations, it also offers the opportunity to see long-term trends and change over time. Throughout this journey several themes dot the horizon of history. One notable theme is that white supremacy in the nation and the church was not inevitable. Things could have been different. At several points in American history—the colonial era, Reconstruction, the demise of Jim Crow—Christians could have confronted racism instead of compromising. Although the missed opportunities are heartbreaking, the fact that people can choose is also empowering.

Christians deliberately chose complicity with racism in the past, but the choice to confront racism remains a possibility today.

Another theme this survey reveals is that racism changes over time. Skin color is simply a physical trait. It is a feature that has no bearing on one's intrinsic dignity. As the following chapters show, people invented racial categories. Race and racism are social constructs. As society changes, so does racism. Racist attitudes produced different actions in 1619 than they did in 1919 or 2020. The malleability and impermanence of racial categories help explain how the American church's compromise with racism has become subtler over time. History demonstrates that racism never goes away; it just adapts.

WHY WRITE ABOUT RACISM AND RELIGION?

Martin Luther King Jr. said, "There can be no deep disappointment where there is not deep love."[15] This study is not about discrediting the church or Christians. I love the church. My concern for the church and for the well-being of its people motivates my exploration of Christian complicity in racism. The goal is to build up the body of Christ by "speaking the truth in love," even if that truth comes at the price of pain.

The church has not always and uniformly been complicit with racism. The same Bible that racists misused to support slavery and segregation is the one abolitionists and civil rights activists rightly used to animate their resistance. Whenever there has been racial injustice, there have been Christians who fought against it in the name of Jesus Christ. Christianity has an inspiring history of working for racial equity and the dignity of all people, a history that should never be overlooked.

The black church, in particular, has always been a bulwark against bigotry. Forged in the fires of racial prejudice, the black church emerged as the ark of safety for people of African descent. Preachers and leaders in the church saw the truth of the gospel message even as slaveholders and white supremacists distorted the message to make more obedient slaves. Black churches looked to the exodus of the

Hebrews from Egypt as a model for their own exodus from American slavery. Black Christians saw in Scripture a God who "sits high and looks low"—one who saw their oppression and was outraged by it. Through the centuries, black people have become the most religious demographic in the United States. For instance, 83 percent of black people say they "believe in God with absolute certainty" compared to 59 percent of Hispanics and 61 percent of whites. Additionally, 75 percent of blacks say "religion is very important" to them compared to 59 percent of Hispanics and 49 percent of whites.[16] Through their religious heritage, black people have passed on a tradition of struggle, liberation, and rejoicing to every generation. Black Christians have played a vital role in shaping the history of America, and they have much to share with the church universal.

But the examples given in this book do not present a positive picture. The focus is mainly on racist acts and actors. This emphasis is purposeful. American Christians have never had trouble celebrating their victories, but honestly recognizing their failures and inconsistencies, especially when it comes to racism, remains an issue. All too often, Christians name a few individuals who stood against the racism of their day and claim them as heroes. They fail to recognize how rarely believers made public and persistent commitments to racial equality against the culture of their churches and denominations. Jumping ahead to the victories means skipping the hard but necessary work of examining what went wrong with race and the church. That can lead to simplistic understandings of the past and superficial solutions to racial issues in the present. *The Color of Compromise* undoes the tendency to skip the hard parts of history and directs the reader's attention to the racist realities that challenge a triumphalist view of American Christianity.

WHY *THE COLOR OF COMPROMISE* MAY BE HARD TO READ

The long history of racism reveals that certain people will object to the very premise of this book. The notion that racism has colored the character of the American church for the past four hundred years will seem incomprehensible to some. As a result, they will voice strenuous and, typically, very public opposition to the claims that racism, especially in its systemic and institutional manifestations, has shaped the church. These individuals are often Christians themselves, but they are not uniformly white; such attitudes cut across the racial and ethnic spectrum.

The people who will reject this book will level several common objections. What stands out about these complaints is not their originality or persuasiveness but their ubiquity throughout history. The same arguments that perpetuated racial inequality in decades past get recycled in the present day. Critics will assert that the ideas in *The Color of Compromise* should be disregarded because they are too "liberal." They will claim that a Marxist Communist ideology underlies all the talk about racial equality. They will contend that such an extended discussion of racism reduces black people to a state of helplessness and a "victim mentality." They will try to point to counterexamples and say that racists do not represent the "real" American church. They will assert that the historical facts are wrong or have been misinterpreted. They will charge that this discussion of race is somehow "abandoning the gospel" and replacing it with problematic calls for "social justice." After reading just a few chapters, these arguments will sound familiar. These arguments have been used throughout the American church's history to deny or defend racism. Other books more pointedly respond to the ways people attempt to explain away or deflect claims of racism.[17] In this book the stories themselves tell the tale of racial oppression. It is up to the reader to determine whether the weight of historical evidence proves that the American church has been complicit with racism.

You may have trouble reading *The Color of Compromise* for different reasons. Your issue may not stem from opposition to the notion that racism pervades the American church; instead, you may have to grapple with learning a narrative that contradicts much of what you have been taught since childhood. Ideas about people who have been cast as heroes of the faith, concepts about systemic injustice and historic patterns of oppression, alternatives to political conservatism as the only Christian way, insights into the reality of black suffering—learning this information will likely take time to absorb and process. No matter your level of education about race and the church, you may need to pause from reading to reflect or recover emotionally. Such a response is only natural in light of the long and deflating history of Christian compromise with racism.

Reading *The Color of Compromise* is like having a sobering conversation with your doctor and hearing that the only way to cure a dangerous disease is by undergoing an uncomfortable surgery and ongoing rehabilitation. Although the truth cuts like a scalpel and may leave a scar, it offers healing and health. The pain is worth the progress.

Finally, for some of you, news that the American church has often been complicit in racism is not news at all. You have known for a long time that a version of Christianity has bought into bigotry. You may even have written off Christianity, or at least evangelicalism, as a whole. What readers like this may find difficult about *The Color of Compromise* is that very rarely do historical figures fit neatly into the category of "villain." Many individuals throughout American church history exhibited blatant racism, yet they also built orphanages and schools. They deeply loved their families; they showed kindness toward others. In several prominent instances, avowed racists even changed their minds. Moreover, despite the American church's complicity in racism, black Christians have forged a faith of their own. Christianity has been an engine for black progress even as others co-opted the faith to buttress white supremacy. Studying history forces people in the present to view people in the past as complex and contradictory figures.

The goal of this book is not guilt. The purpose of tracing Christian complicity with racism is not to show white believers how bad they are. It is simply a fact of American history that white leaders and laity made decisions to maintain the racist status quo. Even though the purpose of this work is not to call out any particular racial group, these words may cause some grief, but grief can be good. In 2 Corinthians 7:10, Paul says, "For godly grief produces a repentance that leads to salvation without regret" (ESV). This kind of grief is a natural response to the suffering of others. It indicates empathy with the pain that racism has caused black people. The ability to weep with those who weep is necessary for true healing.

Though the work of racial justice is difficult and will never truly end in this life, God has provided a colorful portrait of the goal. In a cosmic case of beginning with the end in mind, God pulls back the curtain of eternity to provide a glimpse of future glory. Revelation 7:9 says, "After this I looked, and there before me was a great multitude that no one could count, from every nation, tribe, people and language, standing before the throne and before the Lamb." In that heavenly congregation, we will finally see the culmination of God's gathering a diverse people unified by faith in Christ. We will not all be white; we will not all be black. We will surround the throne of the Lamb as a redeemed picture of all the ethnic and cultural diversity God created. Our skin color will no longer be a source of pain or arrogant pride but will serve as a multihued reflection of God's image. We will no longer be alienated by our earthly economic or social position. We will not clamor for power over one another. Our single focus will be worshiping God for eternity in sublime fellowship with each other and our Creator.

This picture of perfection has been bequeathed to believers not as a distant reality that we can merely long for. Instead, the revelation of the heavenly congregation provides a blueprint and a motivation to seek unity right now. Jesus taught his disciples to pray, "your kingdom come, your will be done, on earth as it is in heaven" (Matt. 6:10). Christians have been mandated to pray that the racial and ethnic unity of the church would be manifest, even if imperfectly, in the present. Christ himself brought down "the dividing wall of hostility" that separated humanity from one another and from God (Eph. 2:14). Indeed, reconciliation across racial and ethnic lines is not something Christians must achieve but a reality we must receive. On the cross when Christ said, "It is finished," he meant it (John 19:30). If peace has been achieved between God and human beings, surely we can have greater peace between people of different racial and ethnic backgrounds.

THE IMPERATIVE FOR IMMEDIATE ACTION

Although our eternal peace is secure, a diverse but unified body of Christ will only come through struggle in this life. A survey of the history of racism and the church shows that the story is worse than most imagine. Christianity in America has been tied to the fallacy of white supremacy for hundreds of years. European colonists brought with them ideas of white superiority and paternalism toward darker-skinned people. On this sandy foundation, they erected a society and a version of religion that could only survive through the subjugation of people of color. Minor repairs by the weekend-warrior racial reconcilers won't fix a flawed foundation. The church needs the Carpenter from Nazareth to deconstruct the house that racism built and remake it into a house for all nations.

By surveying the church's racist past, American Christians may feel the weight of their collective failure to consistently confront racism in the church. This should lead to immediate, fierce action to confess this truth and work for justice. Then, perhaps, Paul's words to the Corinthians might ring true for today's church: "As it is, I rejoice, not because you were grieved, but because you were grieved into repenting" (2 Cor. 7:9 ESV).

Progress is possible, but we must learn to discern the difference between complicit Christianity and courageous Christianity. Complicit Christianity forfeits its moral authority by devaluing the image of God in people of color. Like a ship that has a cracked hull and is taking on water, Christianity has run aground on the rocks of racism and threatens to capsize—it has lost its integrity. By contrast, courageous Christianity embraces racial and ethnic diversity. It stands against any person, policy, or practice that would dim the glory of God reflected in the life of human beings from every tribe and tongue. These words are a call to abandon complicit Christianity and move toward courageous Christianity.

CHAPTER
2

MAKING RACE IN THE COLONIAL ERA

The colonial museum in Williamsburg, Virginia, features exhibits detailing the earliest English settlements in North America. Plaques explaining the conditions for Africans in colonial Virginia hang on the walls. One display explains the process by which those Africans became slaves for life. The heading reads, "Key Slavery Statutes of the Virginia General Assembly," and cites a law enacted in September 1667.

On the question of whether baptism would render slaves free, the Virginia General Assembly decided, "It is enacted and declared by this Grand Assembly, and the authority thereof, that the conferring of baptism does not alter the condition of the person as to his bondage or freedom." This statute encouraged white enslavers to evangelize their human chattel since baptized slaves would not be freed. In the words of the assembly, "Masters, freed from this doubt, may more carefully endeavor the propagation of Christianity by permitting children, though slaves, or those of greater growth if capable, to be admitted to that sacrament."

The Virginia General Assembly, made up of Anglican men, had been compelled by public pressure to address whether baptism rendered slaves free. It had been longstanding custom in England that

Christians, being spiritual brothers and sisters, could not enslave one another. Yet the economy of the European colonies in North America depended more and more on slave labor. So plantation owners discouraged the enslaved from hearing the Christian gospel and receiving the sacrament of baptism. They did not want to lose their unpaid labor and diminish their profits. At the same time, missionaries exerted pressure on the slave owners to evangelize their slaves.

The Virginia Assembly took the initiative to enact a new law. Despite the established tradition, the assembly decided that baptism would not confer freedom upon their laborers. Instead, these Africans would remain in physical bondage even after their conversion. Missionaries, ministers, and slaveowners encouraged African Christians in America to be content with their spiritual liberation and to obey their earthly masters.

The assembly enacted its law concerning enslaved persons and baptism in the seventeenth century. The law predated the existence of the political entity now known as the United States of America. It was enacted more than 100 years before the Declaration of Independence and more than 120 years before the "founding fathers" drafted and ratified the Constitution. Looking at the history of colonial Virginia uncovers the reality that racism in the church has been a problem from the very first moments of European contact in North America.

To grasp how American Christians constructed and cooperated with racism, one has to realize that nothing about American racism was inevitable. There was a period, from about 1500 to 1700, when race did not predetermine one's station and worth in society. This is not to say that racism did not exist; it surely did. But during the initial stages of European settlement in North America, the colonists had not yet cemented skin color as an essential feature of life in their communities. Race was still being made.

This chapter outlines the early days of European contact with indigenous peoples and the first days of African slavery in North America.[1] It shows how individuals and groups who had power chose dividends over dignity and made America a place where darker-skinned people occupied a limited and inferior role in society. Through a series of immoral choices, the foundations were laid for race-based stratification. Yet if people made deliberate decisions to enact inequality, it is possible that a series of better decisions could begin to change this reality.

EUROPEAN CONTACT WITH NORTH AMERICA

After about two months of sailing, Columbus and his bedraggled crew stumbled onto the shores of the Americas in 1492. Of course, Columbus and his men did not walk onto uninhabited land. When they arrived, they found a place vibrant with flora and fauna as well as sophisticated communities of indigenous people who had dwelled there since before written memory. Columbus's band was not even among the first Europeans in North America. Centuries earlier the Scandinavians made landfall on the northern Atlantic coast in a failed colonization project.[2] Instead, Columbus's arrival represented the beginning of an era of European colonization, motivated by profit and predicated on unpaid labor.

Race has been so inscribed into American society that nowadays it is hard to imagine another reality. But in the early decades of European contact with North America, the racial caste system had not yet been developed. Race is a social construct. There is no biological basis for the superiority or inferiority of any human being based on the amount of melanin in her or his skin. The development of the idea of race required the intentional actions of people in the social, political, and religious spheres to decide that skin color determined who would be enslaved and who would be free. Over time Europeans, including Christians, wrote the laws and formed the habits that concentrated power in the hands of those they considered "white" while withholding equality from those they considered "black."

The racial attitudes that underlay these ideas formed over time. From the colonial through the Revolutionary eras, the racial caste system remained malleable and uneven. European contact with the indigenous peoples of North America and the importation of Africans to the continent posed questions about how to organize society, and no one had preestablished answers.

Yet while the contours of American society after European contact had not yet been decided, the explorers still arrived with preformed ideas about the inherent superiority of lighter-skinned (that is, more European-looking) people. One of Columbus's early letters back to Spain compared indigenous and European physical features. "As regards beauty, the Christians [Europeans] said there was no comparison, both men and women, and that their skins are whiter than the other [indigenous people]. They saw two girls whose skins were as white as any that could be seen in Spain."[3] Europeans evaluated the people they encountered in North America based on how similar they were to themselves. This is a common human response when interacting with other groups, but the description in Columbus's letter reveals that colonists equated lighter skin with beauty and desirability long before chattel slavery became the norm.

Early reports of European contact with indigenous people demonstrate that the Europeans had missionary ends in mind, but their means and motivations were questionable. During his first voyage Columbus wrote, "[The indigenous inhabitants] should be good servants and intelligent, for I observed that they quickly took in what was said to them, and I believe that they would easily be made Christians, as it appeared to me that they had no religion."[4] To Columbus and his followers, the people they encountered would make "good servants." Indigenous people were not considered intellectual or social equals but were valued based on their ability to do the will of Europeans.

Further, in the mind of Columbus and others, indigenous people did not have the sophistication to develop their own religious beliefs. Europeans failed to acknowledge the longstanding, well-developed religious beliefs and practices of the people they met. Instead, they viewed indigenous men and women as blank slates on which Christian missionaries could write the gospel. This paternalistic view of evangelism permeates American church history.

For the next century and a half, European colonists struggled to establish settlements in North America. They faced new climates, diseases, starvation, and a short supply of people. For a while, European hegemony over the land's original inhabitants was far from a foregone conclusion. For instance, historian Richard White refers to the "middle ground" between cultures when "whites could neither dictate to Indians nor ignore them."[5] Native Americans often resisted encroachment upon their lands through diplomacy and warfare. But vulnerability to European pathogens, frequent betrayal, and constant warfare decimated the indigenous American population. Slowly Europeans established towns and cities. They began raising crops and families. In turn, European countries demanded more raw materials from their colonies. To meet the growing European demands, the North American colonizers increasingly turned to slavery.

THE MIDDLE PASSAGE

Over the next 300 years, the transatlantic slave trade transported more than ten million Africans to the Americas in a forced migration of epic scale. About two million people perished on the voyage. The human cost in terms of suffering, indignity, and death caused by this commerce can never be fully comprehended, but the experience is often misunderstood or downplayed in the present day. The appalling nature of Christian cooperation with slavery cannot be understood apart from a description of bondage and its effects on Africans.

The process of enslavement began with the European desire for products that needed raw materials from the Americas. Ships would sail from England, France, Spain, Portugal, and other nations to the western coast of Africa. There, the Europeans would either barter with local African tribes for slaves captured in war—a common practice at the time—or kidnap their own slaves.[6]

Enslavers marched their captives sometimes hundreds of miles to the western coast of Africa. The slaves were tied together or had their necks clamped with wooden yokes. Many died of starvation or exhaustion. Some committed suicide along the way. Those who survived were taken to structures called "factories." These were fortress-like facilities designed to hold African slaves until they were loaded onto ships. Slave traders separated families and tribes so the Africans could not band together and rebel. Finally, sometimes after months of waiting, the slaves shuffled onto ships called "slavers" bound for the Americas.[7]

Though the process of dehumanization began at the moment of capture, it took on new dimensions on the ship. Slave traders often shackled Africans together to prevent them from jumping overboard or rebelling. African slaves endured a horrific journey, the so-called "middle passage," from their native land to South America, the Caribbean Islands, or North America. It normally took two or three months to cross the Atlantic, but for some the journey lasted up to six months.

Olaudah Equiano published an autobiography in 1789 called *The Interesting Narrative of the Life of Olaudah Equiano, or Gustavus Vassa* to record his life as a slave and eventually a free man. He was born around 1745 as part of the Igbo tribe in modern-day Nigeria, and slave traders kidnapped Equiano and his sister when he was about eleven years old.[8] Years later Equiano wrote about the traumatic experience of being packed into a slave ship as a piece of cargo. In one particularly stomach-churning recollection, Equiano described the heat, smell, and human waste that accompanied slaves as they languished below deck. "The stench of the hold while we were on the coast was so intolerably loathsome, that it was dangerous to remain there for any time." He continued, "This produced copious perspirations, from a variety of loathsome smells, and brought on a sickness among the slaves of which many died." Finally, he told of the tubs which held human excrement "into which the children often fell, and were almost suffocated."[9]

By the time he wrote his autobiography, Equiano had converted to Christianity. As he reflected on his life, he viewed his experiences through the lens of his faith and commented on the hypocrisy of slave traders who claimed to be Christian. Recollecting on the repeated rape of African women by slave traders aboard the ship, Equiano wrote that it was a "disgrace, not only of Christians, but of men. I have even known them to gratify their brutal passion with females not yet ten years old."[10]

On the kidnapping of unsuspecting Africans and their separation from family, Equiano asked, "O, ye nominal Christians! might not an African ask you, learned you this from your God, who says unto you, Do unto all men as you would men should do unto you?"[11] Black people immediately detected the hypocrisy of American-style slavery. They knew the inconsistencies of the faith from the rank odors, the chains, the blood, and the misery that accompanied their life of bondage. Instead of abandoning Christianity, though, black people went directly to teachings of Jesus and challenged white people to demonstrate integrity.

These depredations occurred before the slaves had even arrived in the Americas. The inhumanity of bondage began as soon as kidnappers snatched the Africans from their tribes, and most often the cruelty continued until the African's death, unless one happened to secure freedom.

John Newton, born in England in 1725, is best known for penning the hymn "Amazing Grace," and his life is remembered as a story of redemption. A lifelong sailor, Newton served as captain of a slave ship for a time. He marks March 10, 1748, as his Christian conversion. He did not stop his involvement in the transatlantic slave trade immediately, however. He continued slaving until he suffered a major stroke in 1754 and retired from the sea. After years of waiting and several attempts with different denominations, Newton was finally ordained as an Anglican priest in 1764 and became famous for his ministry at a church in Olney.

More than three decades after he retired from sailing, Newton wrote a pamphlet called *Thoughts upon the African Slave Trade*. He wrote it as both an encouragement for English politicians to abolish the slave trade and as a personal confession. "I hope it will always be a subject of humiliating reflection to me, that I was, once, an active instrument in a business at which my heart now shudders," he wrote.[12] Newton, a celebrated example today, stands out because he eventually repudiated slavery. If Newton had simply remained a slave trader, he would have been so typical that it is likely no one would remember his name.

Even after surviving the middle passage, Africans were only beginning to experience the horrors of slavery. Ships usually landed at a port in the Caribbean—Barbados or Antigua, for example. Then slave-ship captains did their best to sell their cargo as quickly as possible.

Sometimes buyers would purchase an entire ship's cargo. But they purchased enslaved people a few at a time. Slave captains would then sail from port to port looking for buyers. Sometimes the captains used the "scramble." With all the slaves corralled into one pen, potential buyers would rush into the pen, grabbing as many slaves as they could afford in a chaotic spectacle of greed and brutality.[13]

Upon purchase, the newly arrived Africans were "seasoned" to prepare them for their lives of bondage and labor in the Americas. Seasoning involved adapting to a different climate and new foods. It also involved teaching the Africans a new language, usually French, Spanish, or English. Africans were trained for their work, which was typically agricultural and involved plowing, hoeing, and weeding from sunup to sundown. This acculturation took a toll. As many as one-third of African slaves died within their first three years in the Americas.[14]

Britain abolished the slave trade in 1807 and outlawed slavery in Britain and its colonies in 1833. Much of the momentum for these changes came from Christians. For example, William Wilberforce was influenced by John Newton, who encouraged the young Parliamentarian to remain in his post and fight to end slavery.[15] Yet abolitionism did not arise from purely altruistic motives. The decline of slavery in Britain coincided with the rise of the Industrial Revolution. The factory became the urban farm that produced most British goods. The poet William Blake called factories "dark Satanic mills." Men, women, and children worked twelve-hour days in stifling heat tending whirring, steam-powered machines that could slice off a finger or crush a skull in the blink of a sleep-deprived eye. Although British slavery declined around this time, the rise in industrial productivity fed an astronomical demand for raw materials. The demand for cotton grew twentyfold in the decades after the turn of the nineteenth century.[16] North American slavery supplied the ravenous international appetite for cotton.

THE AFRICAN SLAVE TRADE IN NORTH AMERICA

In 1619, a Dutch trading ship landed off the coast of Virginia with "20. and odd Negroes."[17] The arrival of these enslaved women and men was a matter of economic convenience. The British colonists had not requested slaves, but the Dutch ship had stolen the Africans from a Portuguese slave trading ship called *São João Bautista*, or *Saint John the Baptist*, and were looking for a place to sell their "cargo." As historian Gregory O'Malley explains, "The arrival of African captives had less to do with planters' demand for enslaved laborers than with the privateers' desire for a market in which to vend stolen Africans."[18]

Prior to the arrival of Africans in the British Virginia colony, Europeans had been transporting enslaved Africans to the Americas for more than a hundred years. Haiti and Jamaica, as well as South American countries such as Brazil, used millions of Africans to work on farms producing rice, sugar, and coffee. In fact, these other regions received far more enslaved persons than North America ever did. An estimated ten to twelve million slaves were brought across the Atlantic, and the majority ended up in the Caribbean or South America.[19]

Enslavement was different in South America and the Caribbean than in North America. The labor-intensive crops and enormous plantations meant that Africans usually outnumbered Europeans. The Haitian Revolution broke out in 1791, and its success was due, in part, to the population discrepancy between enslaved Africans and European landowners.

The harsh working conditions on sugar plantations and deadly diseases resulted in a high mortality rate. Deaths outnumbered births, so it was more cost-effective for plantation owners to replace slaves rather than to invest in keeping them alive. This led to a gender imbalance as slaveowners preferred male slaves who they could literally work to death. North America, by contrast, developed more gender parity, so a growing population of the enslaved came through birth, often referred to as "natural increase." Slave women in North America had an average birthrate of 9.2 children, twice as many as those in Caribbean colonies.[20]

In North America, slavery developed differently but no less cruelly. At first, some Africans were treated as indentured servants—workers bound to an employer for a certain time, usually to pay off a debt. Indentured servants could marry, save money, and eventually work

themselves out of servitude. The women and men who arrived on the
Virginia coast in 1619 had names like Angelo and Pedro and were
likely Catholic. After a number of years, they may have gained their
liberty. As early as 1623, two Africans, Anthony and Isabella, married.
They had a son, William, who was baptized as an Anglican and likely
born free.[21]

By the mid-seventeenth century, some Africans lived as free people
and worked in a variety of professions. A few, like Anthony Johnson,
became wealthy enough to own land and buy enslaved Africans themselves. The life of an indentured servant was not a desirable one, but it
was not always permanent, nor was it limited to Africans. Indigenous
people and Europeans could become indentured servants too.

Although many Africans arrived as enslaved persons, colonists
sometimes permitted them certain rights, such as earning their own
money, purchasing their own and their family's freedom, and learning skilled trades. Edmund Morgan writes, "While racial feelings
undoubtedly affected the position of Negroes, there is more than a
little evidence that Virginians during these years were ready to think
of Negroes as members or potential members of the community on the
same terms as other men and to demand of them the same standards
of behavior."[22] As Morgan indicates, colonists may have initially seen
Africans in America as laborers just like any other and patterned their
economy and politics to allow for their full inclusion. American history
could have happened another way. Instead, racist attitudes and the
pursuit of wealth increasingly relegated black people to a position of
perpetual servitude and exploitation.

The practice of indentured servitude gradually gave way to slavery,
and Europeans preferred Africans as laborers over other Europeans or
the indigenous Americans. With the success of tobacco in the colonies and the increasing demand for the crop in Europe, agriculture
became big business. A larger appetite for cash crops meant planters
needed more labor. The indigenous population in America had been
decimated by war and disease. Additionally, indigenous people proved
to be difficult to control as enslaved workers because they often knew
the landscape better than their European masters and could escape or

count on help from their tribe. Africans, divorced from their homeland and potential allies, emerged as more vulnerable targets of enslavement.

The shift toward slavery over indentured servitude happened gradually over the last few decades of the seventeenth century. Conflicts such as Bacon's Rebellion (1676) had alerted the Virginia gentry to the ongoing threat of a disgruntled population of white indentured servants and African laborers. Much of the transition to slavery, though, had economic roots. In the early days of colonization, European and African mortality rates were both extremely high. The chance of living five years or more was about fifty-fifty, which made it more financially feasible to use indentured servants rather than enslaved persons, who had a higher up-front cost. As life expectancy increased, lifelong labor became a more lucrative investment. Tobacco, the most profitable crop in Virginia at the time, required less capital and less punishing labor than producing a commodity such as sugar, which was popular in the West Indies and parts of South America. Enslaved men and women thus lived longer making lifetime bondage even more attractive. A scarcity of labor also led to slavery. Fewer Europeans were moving to the colonies, and the indigenous population continued to decrease. Wealthy colonists looked to imported Africans as a steady supply of labor.[23]

As slavery became more institutionalized, more rules regulated its practice. By the mid-seventeenth century, colonies began developing "slave codes" to police African bondage. The codes determined that a child was born slave or free based solely on the mother's status. They mandated slavery for life with no hope of emancipation. The codes deprived the enslaved of legal rights, required permission for slaves to leave their master's property, forbade marriage between enslaved people, and prohibited them from carrying arms. The slave codes also defined enslaved Africans not as human beings but as chattel—private property on the same level as livestock.

As reliance on slave labor increased, sticky questions about Christianity, race, and bondage began to emerge. Slave-owning colonists and European missionaries often clashed over the issue of proselytizing. Christianity had inherent ideas of human equality imbedded in its teachings. If slaves converted to Christianity, would they not begin to demand their freedom and social equality? How could missionaries preach to the slaves when their owners feared the loss of their unpaid labor? Over time, Europeans compromised the message of Christianity to accommodate slavery while also, in their minds, satisfying the requirement to make disciples.

In *The Baptism of Early Modern Virginia*, historian Rebecca Anne Goetz explains how Europeans on the Atlantic coast of North America developed religious and racial categories in tandem. At first, colonists debated whether Africans were capable of becoming Christians. They adhered to a concept that Goetz calls "hereditary heathenism."[24] Just as parents passed down physical characteristics to their children, they also passed down their religion. Hereditary heathenism tethered race to religion. From their earliest days in North America, colonists employed religio-cultural categories to signify that European meant "Christian" and Native American or African meant "heathen." Over time, these categories simplified and hardened into racial designations.

Many Europeans initially held an optimistic view of their capacity to convert the indigenous peoples to Christianity. These Christians adhered to a "monogenesis" theory of humankind, meaning they believed that all people descended from Adam as described in Genesis. So according to European Christians, indigenous people had at least the potential to receive salvation, which meant colonists had a duty to teach the Scriptures to these so-called heathens.

The effort to convert indigenous people to Christianity was always tied to ideas of European colonization. Europeans evangelized non-Europeans with the intention not only of teaching them Christianity but also of conforming them to European cultural standards. One of the most well-known illustrations of how Europeans conflated religion and culture is in the marriage of John Rolfe and Metoaka (or Matoaka), better known as Pocahontas.

John Rolfe was an Englishman hoping to achieve fortune and notoriety in the new English colony of Virginia. He arrived in Jamestown in 1610 and eventually became a member of the Virginia General Assembly. He met an indigenous woman named Metoaka, the daughter of Chief Powhatan. Metoaka converted to Christianity in 1613 and received the "more Christian" name of Rebecca. She and Rolfe were married and had a child together. They only had a brief marriage, however. On a visit to England in 1617, she became ill and died abroad.

Although it lasted only briefly, Metoaka's marriage to Rolfe inspired hope in some English colonists. "For the English, Metoaka's marriage symbolized heathen submission to proper religion and to English gender norms," wrote Goetz.[25] The English colonists' goal was to evangelize and assimilate the indigenous peoples. Metoaka's conversion to Christianity, taking on a common English name, and bearing a son to an Englishman signified the possibility of making indigenous Americans into "respectable" English persons. Rolfe and Metoaka's marriage also meant that, according to English custom, their son would be born into Christianity. To the English colonists, hereditary heathenism could be interrupted by marrying into the "better" spiritual lineage of English Christians.

Of course, most indigenous people did not see it this way. European missionaries made few converts because converting to Christianity included European cultural assimilation and the loss of tribal identity.[26]

Europeans thought Africans, like indigenous peoples, could be "civilized" through cultural conformity and conversion to Christianity. European missionaries, such as the Franciscans and Dominicans, attempted to preach Christianity to the slaves. It must be noted, however, that Europeans did not introduce Christianity to Africans. Christianity had arrived in Africa through Egypt and Ethiopia in the third and fourth centuries. Christian luminaries like Augustine, Tertullian, and Athanasius helped develop Trinitarian theology and defended the deity of Christ long before Western Europeans presumed to "take" Christianity to Africans.[27] African people also had a rich history of practicing Islam and tribal religions, a history that Europeans disregarded in their evangelistic fervor.

Even though European missionaries sought to share Christianity with indigenous peoples and Africans, social, political, and economic equality was not part of their plan. Missionaries carefully crafted messages that maintained the social and economic status quo. They truncated the gospel message by failing to confront slavery, and in doing so they reinforced its grip on society.

In 1701, Anglican church leader Thomas Bray helped found the Society for the Propagation of the Gospel in Foreign Parts (SPG).[28] As the name suggests, the primary purpose of the SPG was to spread the Anglican version of Christianity, primarily in the English colonies. But SPG's motivations were more complex than that. While many officials had an interest in sharing the gospel with non-Europeans, they were not interested in sharing power or promoting equality. Instead, the SPG, like many European missionary endeavors in North America, preached a message that said Christianity could save one's soul but not break one's chains.

SPG's missionary Francis Le Jau illustrates their philosophy of evangelism well. The SPG sent him to South Carolina in 1706 where he stayed until his death in 1717. His journal entries from the time show his sincere desire to convert indigenous peoples and Africans. He even spoke out against British exploitation of the indigenous population.[29] However, his outrage had limits. To circumvent slave owners' opposition, Le Jau emphasized obedience instead of liberation among the slaves.

When Le Jau was able to persuade African slaves to adopt the Christian religion as their own, he confirmed their profession by baptizing them. The vows he made the slaves recite show how European missionaries maintained a strict separation between spiritual and physical freedom. "You declare in the presence of God and before this congregation that you do not ask for holy baptism out of any design to free yourself from the Duty and Obedience you owe to your master while you live, but merely for the good of your soul and to partake of the Grace and Blessings promised to the Members of the Church of Jesus Christ."[30]

Le Jau was more ardent than many European missionaries in his desire to convert indigenous peoples and Africans. He labored to convince slave-owning men that people of color were not mere beasts without souls. To make his case, he had to assuage fears that slaves would demand emancipation once they became Christian. So from the beginning of American colonization, Europeans crafted a Christianity that would allow them to spread the faith without confronting the exploitative economic system of slavery and the emerging social inequality based on color.

(DE)CONSTRUCTING RACE

This chapter began with the premise that race was constructed. It has shown how in the wet cement of early European colonial society the racial boundaries had not yet been traced. It took decades for patterns of unfree labor to harden into a form of slavery that treated human beings as chattel and dictated a person's station in life based on skin color. In European North America, Christianity became identified with the emerging concept of "whiteness" while people of color, including indigenous peoples and Africans, became identified with unbelief.

Christianity served as a force to help construct racial categories in the colonial period. A corrupt message that saw no contradiction between the brutalities of bondage and the good news of salvation became the norm. European missionaries tried to calm the slave owners' fears of rebellion by spreading a version of Christianity that emphasized spiritual deliverance, not immediate liberation. Instead of highlighting the dignity of all human beings, European missionaries told Africans that Christianity should make them more obedient and loyal to their earthly masters.

But if racism can be made, it can be unmade. Like a house with a crumbling foundation, it is more difficult to change an existing structure than to build a sound one from the beginning, but it is possible. "The fierce urgency of now," to borrow a phrase from Martin Luther King Jr., demands a recognition of the ways Christians, from before the founding of the United States, built racial categories into religion.[31] That knowledge must then be turned toward propagating a more authentically biblical message of human equality regardless of skin color.

CHAPTER
3

UNDERSTANDING LIBERTY IN THE AGE OF REVOLUTION AND REVIVAL

Indigenous American and African blood flowed through the veins of Crispus Attucks. But during the Boston Massacre of 1770, his blood spilled onto the streets along with four other men as part of the conflagration leading to the Revolutionary War. As well-known as Attucks is now, very little of his biography is certain. He was likely born in the early 1720s near Natick, Massachusetts, a "'praying town' of Christianized Indians."[1] He endured life as a slave, but in 1750 he escaped his master and made a living for himself as a sailor. Twenty years later he joined a crowd of Bostonians in a confrontation with a small contingent of British soldiers. The dispute turned violent, and a soldier shot and killed Attucks. He remained relatively obscure in American memory until the 1850s when the growing abolitionist movement appropriated his story.

However mythical his memory has become, Attucks is a fitting figure to associate with the beginnings of American independence. He took freedom into his own hands just like the colonists believed they were doing. He represented the racial mix of America and stands for indigenous men and women as much as black Americans. Moreover,

40

he died for a nation that failed to recognize his freedom because of his racial background. Attucks symbolizes that bitter combination of freedom and bondage, racism and patriotism, that characterized the Revolutionary era.

When colonists in North America fought and won the war for independence from Britain, they used the rhetoric of liberty and natural rights to argue for the righteousness of their cause. While white soldiers and political leaders were declaring their inalienable right to independence, they were also enslaving countless women, men, and children of African descent. And the American church participated in and defended the contradiction between freedom and slavery embedded in the constitution of its young nation. Revisiting early American history reveals the shocking forms of hypocrisy that helped shape our society.

THE DECLARATION AND WAR FOR INDEPENDENCE

English philosopher John Locke was raised by Puritan parents who instructed him in the Christian faith and taught him about the natural rights of humankind. He published an explanation of his political philosophy in a 1689 work entitled *Two Treatises of Government*. In it he wrote that natural law "teaches all mankind who will but consult it, that being all equal and independent, no one ought to harm another in his life, health, liberty or possessions; for men being all the workmanship of one omnipotent and infinitely wise Maker . . . they are his property."[2] Nearly a century later, Thomas Jefferson picked up on Locke's language and wrote about the "unalienable rights" of human beings when he penned the Declaration of Independence.

According to Locke's *Two Treatises of Government*, the government exists by the consent of the people. If the people determine that the laws of a commonwealth are contrary to their interests, then the consent they have given to political officials "must necessarily be forfeited, and the power devolve into the hands of those that gave it, who may place it anew where they shall think best for their safety and security."[3] Colonists in America would soon adopt this political philosophy to justify their rebellion against the British government.

After the British prevailed in the French and Indian War (1754–63), their territory in North America expanded greatly, and so did their war debt. Dissatisfied with lackluster support from the colonies during the war and desperate to recover financially, Britain levied new taxes and enacted new laws to consolidate power over the thirteen colonies. Some colonists, who had previously found little commonality with one another, started to unite around their resentment of British imperial policies.

In the years leading up to the Revolutionary War, the colonists began calling themselves Patriots. Laws such as the Stamp Act (1765) and the Townshend Acts (1767) consolidated colonial animosity toward imperial power and supported a sense of solidarity among the colonists. In 1774, a year after the British Parliament passed the Tea Act, Patriot leaders organized the Continental Congress to protest what they saw as oppressive imperial measures. The following year, the Battle of Lexington and Concord became the first skirmish of what became the American Revolution.

The Declaration of Independence, first drafted by a slaveholder named Thomas Jefferson, captured the spirit of revolution in its opening words. "We hold these truths to be self-evident, that all men are created equal, that they are endowed by their Creator with certain unalienable Rights, that among these are Life, Liberty and the pursuit of Happiness." Yet Jefferson, as with so many of his day, did not consider black people equal to white people. Few political leaders assumed the noble words of the declaration applied to the enslaved. A draft of the document denounced the transatlantic slave trade by accusing the British monarch of "violating its most sacred rights of life and liberty in the persons of a distant people . . . captivating & carrying them into slavery in another hemisphere or to incur miserable death in their transportation thither." The antislavery clause was excised from the final draft of the declaration due to the objections of delegates from Georgia and South Carolina as well as some northern states that benefited from slavery.[4]

One does not need to argue that the United States was founded as a "Christian nation" to see the obvious appeals to a higher power in the

Declaration of Independence. The document mentions "the Laws of Nature and of Nature's God," the rights bestowed on all people by the "Creator," and it appeals to the "Supreme Judge of the world" for the legitimacy of revolutionary cause. Whatever religion they practiced, the authors of the Declaration of Independence appealed to the idea of universal human liberty passed down from an all-powerful deity. Many Christians of the time would have understood this language as a reference to their God. But the "universal" rights referenced in the Declaration of Independence were not universally applied.

Revolution had its limits. Women, who had played a major role in supporting the Patriots during the war, did not gain significantly more political or civil rights as a result of independence. The indigenous Americans, whose populations had already been wracked by war and disease, found that colonial independence meant the loss of their own freedom.

When Africans in America heard white leaders proclaim natural rights and equality for all, naturally they applied those statements to their own situation. In a 1773 letter to the Massachusetts General Court, a committee of slaves wrote, "We cannot but expect your house will again take our deplorable case into serious consideration, and give us that ample relief which, as men, we have a natural right to."[5] The impulse toward liberty was so strong that Africans in the colonies took up arms to pursue it. Some fought for the British on the promise of freedom for their service against the rebellious colonists. Others fought for the Patriots, hoping victory would ensure abolition. In either case, the motivation was the same: freedom. Despite the vigorous efforts of African-descended people to apply revolutionary rhetoric to the problem of slavery, the institution endured long after the American Revolution had ended.

THE GREAT AWAKENING

The Great Awakening held both promise and contradiction when it came to the African population in the colonies. Prior to the revivals of the mid-1700s, few enslaved Africans converted to Christianity.

White enslavers feared that evangelizing would plant the troublesome seeds of liberation in the minds and hearts of their chattel. But Africans did not come to the American colonies devoid of spirituality. Many of them practiced the indigenous religions of tribes in West Africa, and a significant number were Muslim. Africans preferred their own forms of faith to that of their white enslavers.[6]

In the decades leading up to the American War for Independence, another revolution was taking place. The Great Awakening fundamentally altered the shape of Protestantism in the colonies and among African slaves. Influenced by the Enlightenment's emphasis on experience as the ground of knowledge, evangelists during the Great Awakening highlighted the necessity of a personal encounter with God and the role of emotion in the Christian faith. Historian Alan Gallay described it this way: "The driving goal of evangelical ministers was to spread the message of new birth while combating those who assumed that grace was achieved gradually and by good works."[7] In contrast to more staid forms of worship practiced by the Anglicans, Dutch Reformed, Congregationalist, and Presbyterian churches, the Great Awakening moved American Christians toward more informal and less structured forms of worship.

Revivalist preachers, especially Baptists and Methodists, tended toward dramatic and animated presentations in their sermons. Preachers "helped [their audience] to feel the weight of sin, to imagine the threats of Hell, and to accept Christ as their only Savior."[8] Preachers typically avoided complicated doctrinal matters and focused on the simple act of conversion. Black men and women, who were sprinkled among the crowds listening to revivalist preachers, began adopting Christian beliefs.

Enslaved Africans did not merely adopt Christianity, they made it their own. Aspects of the faith such as the notion of rebirth, baptism by immersion in water, and emotional expressiveness resembled African traditions.[9] For example, enslaved people in the South adapted a practice from West African known as the "ring shout." Worshipers got in a circle and rotated counterclockwise as they sang, danced, and chanted.

Although the proportion remained small, the Great Awakening

initiated the first significant number of conversions to Christianity among enslaved Africans in the colonies. Evangelical preachers, although European, pushed against the traditional customs of established denominations, including the segregation or exclusion of African people. Revivalists emphasized the spiritual equality of all people and preached to interracial crowds. They baptized anyone willing to accept Christ as their Savior. Black people even became ordained ministers and missionaries.

In 1785, Lemuel Haynes became the first black person ordained by any Christian fellowship in America.[10] Prior to his career in ministry, Haynes fought in the Revolutionary War. After his conversion, he sensed a call to ministry and became a Calvinistic preacher in the Northeast. He drew much of his theological convictions from the teachings of Jonathan Edwards and George Whitefield. A dedicated preacher, Haynes said, "Nothing is more conducive of divine glory and salutary to men than the preaching of the gospel. Unless these glad tidings are proclaimed, the incarnation of Christ is vain."[11] Likely biracial, Haynes nevertheless pastored an all-white church in Vermont.

Black people were attracted to revival preaching because it mirrored the familiar practices of West African religions. Full-throated singing, emotional expressiveness, and physical movement had cultural resonance with people of African descent. Christianity also held out the hope of freedom. Enslaved people connected spiritual salvation with earthly liberation. They believed that spiritual equality might lead their white slaveowners to see them as full human beings deserving of emancipation.

Affirmations of spiritual equality did not translate into social equality, however. Slaveowners still frowned upon Christianizing the enslaved. Black ministers usually were only allowed to preach to black people. The messages preached to black Christians leaned heavily toward messages on obedience and honoring one's earthly master. Only rarely would the enslaved be permitted to congregate on their own for fear that they would use the meetings to plot rebellion.

Restrictions on enslaved people congregating typically became more stringent after slave uprisings like the Stono Rebellion that occurred near Charleston in 1739. A native African and slave named Jemmy led about twenty enslaved men from Angola in a revolt against their white masters. Other enslaved people joined, and their numbers swelled to nearly fifty people. They broke into a store and stole guns and ammunition. They then killed the shopkeepers and about thirty more white people in an attempt to escape to Spanish Florida, where it was said escaped slaves could gain freedom and land. A white militia caught up with the group and killed about half the rebels. The rest fled and were captured and executed over the next month.

As a result of the Stono Rebellion, South Carolina passed the Negro Act of 1740. The act, which largely reiterated laws that had already been passed but not strictly enforced, prevented the enslaved from assembling in groups without white supervision, selling their own goods for profit, or learning to write. The Negro Act also purported to "restrain and prevent barbarity being exercised toward slaves" because "cruelty is . . . highly unbecoming those who profess themselves Christians."[12] As a result, the act mandated whippings on the back for recalcitrant slaves, but any slaveowner who cut out the tongue, put out the eye, castrated, or burned a slave would have to pay a fine. Because of laws like the Negro Act, it became increasingly difficult for enslaved people to gather.

GEORGE WHITEFIELD

More than any other two preachers, George Whitefield and Jonathan Edwards symbolized the spiritual revival that took place in the eighteenth century. Whitefield, an Anglican minister from England who was influenced by John Wesley, became what historian Harry Stout called "the first intercolonial religious celebrity."[13] He usually preached outside because the throngs who gathered to hear him were too large for any church building. Whitefield had been trained in theater and used his experience in drama to captivate his listeners. Most preachers at the time read highly doctrinal sermons from a manuscript. Whitefield's theatrical narrations appealed to the emotions in a way that established Christian leaders usually frowned upon. The dynamic preaching of revivalists during the Great Awakening broadened its appeal to include lower economic classes of whites and the enslaved.

Whitefield was more moderate on race than many of his white contemporaries. He excoriated enslavers for their physical abuse of slaves, calling them "monsters of barbarity." He expressed ambivalence about the practice of slavery itself, but he had no doubts about how masters should treat their laborers. "Unsure of 'whether it be lawful for Christians to buy slaves,' Whitefield was positive that 'it is sinful, when bought, to use them . . . as though they were Brutes.'"[14] The worst abuse, in Whitefield's view, was some enslavers refusal to allow the enslaved to be evangelized. He and others like his wealthy, slave-holding, Christian allies Hugh and Jonathan Bryan advocated for the rights of enslaved people to learn Christianity and to worship.

Over time Whitefield's moderation on slavery morphed into outright support. In 1732, Georgia became the last of the original thirteen colonies, and founders envisioned it as a Christian utopia where European inhabitants would have "freedom of conscience" when it came to religion. In line with this vision, James Oglethorpe, the colony's administrator, determined that Georgia would be a slave-free region. Oglethorpe and his supporters were not concerned with abolition, however. They simply wanted Georgia to be a settlement where poor Englishmen could labor without competition.[15]

On a trip to Georgia in 1738, Whitefield began planning for what would become the Bethesda Orphanage. Influenced by Methodism's focus on charity and caring for orphans as well as by a visit to a Lutheran orphanage in Germany, Whitefield found an ideal setting for a new venture in the small community of Savannah. In time, the evangelist raised enough money for some land near Savannah. He named the new orphanage Bethesda, or "House of Mercy." To this day, it operates under the name Bethesda Academy. Yet in the eighteenth century, the orphanage struggled to stay open. Due to mismanagement and its inability to generate much income, the fate of the orphanage was constantly in question.

Faced with the vicissitudes of starting a nonprofit organization and ensuring its financial viability, Whitefield looked to slavery to secure Bethesda's welfare. He turned to the wealthy allies he had gained during his revivals in South Carolina for support. With the help of his friends near Charleston, Whitefield purchased a 640-acre plantation and planned to use the profit from the crops produced there to support the work of the orphanage. Whitefield was virtually guaranteed a profit from his plantation activities because he did not plan to pay his laborers. "One negro has been given me," he wrote in a letter. "Some more I plan to purchase this week."[16]

Whitefield began petitioning the political leaders of Georgia, which had been founded as a free territory, to allow slavery. He suggested that allowing slavery could improve the financial fortunes of the land and claimed that economic ruin was the only alternative: "Georgia can never be a flourishing province unless negroes are employed [as slaves]."[17]

Historian Stephen J. Stein insists that financial concerns only partially explain Whitefield's advocacy of slavery. "The focus upon contrast and change in his ideas which has dominated discussion to date obscures a more significant feature of his thought, namely, his deep-seated fear of the blacks."[18] The economic impulse for slavery can never be separated from the racist ideas that typecast enslaved Africans as dangerous and brutish. Whitefield and countless other white Christians imbibed beliefs that encouraged fear and suspicion of African-descended people.

A few months after the Stono Rebellion in September 1739, Whitefield and a party of companions made their way through South Carolina. On a dark and moonless night, they stumbled across a group of enslaved black people. One of Whitefield's companions asked for directions to "the gentleman's house whither we were directed," but the group of blacks seemed not to know the person or the location of his home. "From these circumstances, one of my friends inferr'd, that these Negroes might be of those who lately had made an insurrection in the province, and were run away from their masters." After that, Whitefield's party quickened their pace fearfully "expecting to find Negroes in every place."[19] Virtually any gathering of black people—even when black Christians congregated for worship—was likely to elicit suspicion.

JONATHAN EDWARDS

As significant as George Whitefield was to American religious history, he was still British. America needed a homegrown pastor to celebrate as their own hero. Many Christians look to Jonathan Edwards, heralded as "America's Greatest Theologian." A Calvinist pastor in Northampton, Massachusetts, Edwards emphasized the need for a new birth and authentic conversion. Instead of focusing solely on the intellectual nature of religion, he spoke of a change in "affections"—redirecting passion away from oneself and toward God. Edwards defended the emotionalism of revivals against critics and argued that such expressions were evidence of personal experience with God. Known for works such as "Sinners in the Hands of an Angry God" and *Religious Affections*, Edwards's vaunted philosophical and theological acumen, however, did not lead him to reject race-based chattel slavery.

Born in 1703, Edwards displayed an insatiable curiosity and sharp intellect. At the age of eleven he penned a treatise on the spider's method of using air currents and web strands to move from place to place. In 1716 he enrolled in the Collegiate School of Connecticut, now known as Yale University, at just under thirteen years old. A year later, Edwards read John Locke and absorbed his teachings like a miser "gathering up handfuls of silver and gold, from some newly discovered treasure."[20] He also engaged with the works of Isaac Newton and saw the burgeoning field of empirical science as evidence of God's creative genius.

In 1729 Edwards took over the church in Northampton, Massachusetts, after his renowned grandfather, Solomon Stoddard, died. Revival broke out in 1733. "There was scarcely a single person in the town, either old or young, that was left unconcerned about the great things of the eternal world," reflected Edwards.[21] The revivals became the subject of ongoing controversy as more conservative preachers and theologians reviled the emotionalism of the events, and others defended the conversions and style of worship as authentic expressions of religion.

Although Edwards remains a significant figure in American religious history, his significance must also include the fact that he compromised Christian principles by enslaving human beings. By 1731, Edwards had purchased his first enslaved African, Venus, at an auction in Rhode Island. Throughout his lifetime he owned several other people, including Joseph, Lee, and a young boy named Titus. Edwards's slaveholding speaks for itself, but an unpublished manuscript provides the only written record of Edwards directly addressing his views on slavery.

Historian Kenneth Minkema unearthed Edwards's notes for a letter that appears to defend a slave-owning pastor from his critical parishioners.[22] The notes merely sketch an argument. Edwards did oppose the African slave trade for evangelistic reasons, noting that it would make Africans more resistant to the gospel. But he never objected to slavery in general. The theologian seemed to accept slavery, so long as masters treated their enslaved persons with dignity, on the basis of slavery's apparently tacit acceptance in the Bible. Edwards did not believe, as some Christians did, that enslaved Africans did not have souls or could not accept Christ. He advocated for evangelism among the enslaved and dreamed of a global flowering of faith.

Why did Jonathan Edwards support slavery? In part, the answer may have to do with his social status. Edwards represented an educated and elite class in New England society. Wealthy and influential people populated his congregation. Slave owning signified status. More deeply, though, the particular brand of evangelicalism developing in America during the Great Awakening made an antislavery stance unlikely for many. Mark Noll explains, "As a *revival* movement . . . evangelicalism transformed people within their inherited social setting, but worked only partial and selective transformation on the social settings themselves."[23] Evangelicalism focused on individual conversion and piety. Within this evangelical framework, one could adopt an evangelical expression of Christianity yet remain uncompelled to confront institutional injustice.

Ironically, Edwards's second son, Jonathan Edwards Jr., more fully grasped the revolutionary applications of his Christianity. A pastor himself, the younger Edwards had grown up around Mahican and Mohawk tribes and spoke their languages better than English as a boy.[24] Beginning in the 1770s, Edwards became an outspoken abolitionist. For instance, he wrote an article entitled "Some Observations upon the Slavery of Negroes" and in 1791 preached a sermon called "The Injustice and Impolicy of the Slave Trade." Edwards Jr.'s impact, however, would not come near to his father's, nor could the son's outspokenness about slavery drown out his father's conspicuous silence and support of the institution.

Edwards and Whitefield represent a supposedly moderate and widespread view of slavery. Both accepted the spiritual equality of black and white people. Both preached the message of salvation to all. Yet their concern for African slaves did not extend to advocating for physical emancipation. Like these two preachers, many other Christians did not see anything in the Bible that forbade slavery. In fact, the Scriptures seemed to accept slavery as an established reality. Instead, white Christians believed that the Bible merely regulated slavery in order to mitigate its most brutal abuses.

THE BAPTIST GENERAL COMMITTEE OF VIRGINIA

In 1793 the Baptist General Committee of Virginia had to decide whether it would accept slave owners as congregation members in good standing. Formed in 1782 to combat the privileged standing that the Anglican-Episcopal church had with the Virginia Assembly, the Baptist General Committee eventually issued a statement in 1785 opposing enslavement.[25] It posted an even stronger statement in 1790 when the outspoken white Baptist antislavery minister John Leland declared the institution of slavery to be not only against the law of God but also "inconsistent with a republican government."[26]

Backlash against the 1790 resolution was swift and fierce. In the Baptist tradition, each congregation must decide policies and stances independently, and no other congregation or body holds authoritative sway over another. As each congregation debated the Committee's resolution, sharp divisions emerged. Enslavers demanded rights to their "property" and promoted the idea that the Bible defended, or at least did not prohibit, slavery. In response, the Baptist General

Committee "again debated hereditary slavery and voted 'by a majority (after considering it a while) that the subject be dismissed from this committee, as believing it belongs to the legislative body.'"[27] Thus Baptists in Virginia declared slavery to be a civil issue outside of the scope of the church. Slave ownership became an accepted practice in most Baptist congregations, and whenever someone raised objections, leaders could demur and insist that the topic was an issue for the state, not the church. Black Christians, however, refused to leave the issues of slavery and racism outside the church doors.

THE FIRST HISTORICALLY BLACK CHRISTIAN DENOMINATION

Harsh though it may sound, the facts of history nevertheless bear out this truth: there would be no black church without racism in the white church.

The first congregations of black Christians in America often met in secrecy for fear of persecution. Enslaved people who converted to Christianity had to meet in "hush arbors"—secret places on farmlands, in the woods, or swamps where slaves gathered for worship. They usually met under cover of night after an exhausting day of manual labor. In a typical service, someone gave a word of exhortation and encouragement, which was accompanied by prayer and singing. The precariousness of their existence led Christian slaves to cry out to God with a passion and exuberance that has become characteristic of many black church traditions. The covert nature of the black church led some to call it the "invisible institution."

Black Christians did not always meet in secret. Sometimes they worshiped in the same congregations as white Christians, albeit under segregated seating. This was a pragmatic decision on the part of white believers. Controlling and monitoring slaves was easier if they were in the same building.

The divide between white and black Christians in America was not generally one of doctrine. Christians across the color line largely agreed on theological teachings such as the Trinity, the divinity of Jesus, and the importance of personal conversion. More often than not, the issue that divided Christians along racial lines related to the unequal treatment of African-descended people in white church contexts.

While black Christians left white churches and denominations en masse after the Civil War, the formation of African Methodist Episcopal Church (AME) stands as an early example of black Christians exercising agency to escape racism in the church and form their own more affirming fellowships.

One of the founders of the AME denomination, Richard Allen was born a slave in Philadelphia in 1760. He came of age during the American Revolution and was undoubtedly influenced by the message of liberty and independence circulated in pamphlets and speeches. Having been given permission by his white owner to attend church meetings, Allen converted to Methodism in 1777. He purchased his freedom in 1786 and began preaching in various Methodist churches.[28]

Allen received an invitation to become a regular preacher at St. George's, an interracial Methodist church in Philadelphia. Despite the racially mixed composition of the congregation, white Christians treated black worshipers as second class. Under Allen's preaching the number of black attendees increased dramatically. Racial tension increased as well. Allen tried to gain support to purchase a new church building to accommodate the growing number of black worshipers, but white leaders of St. George's insisted on segregated seating and relegated their darker-skinned brethren to certain sections of the sanctuary.

One Sunday in 1792, Richard Allen and fellow black minister Absalom Jones entered St. George's to worship. Unknowingly, they took seats reserved for white parishioners and thus violated the segregated seating arrangements. They knelt to pray but one of the church's white trustees soon interrupted them. Allen recounts the episode in his autobiography:

> We had not been long upon our knees before I heard considerable scuffling and low talking. I raised my head up and saw one of the trustees, H—M—, having hold of the Rev. Absalom

Jones, pulling him up off of his knees, and saying, "You must get up—you must not kneel here." Mr. Jones replied, "wait until prayer is over." Mr. H—M—said "no, you must get up now, or I will call for aid and I force you away." Mr. Jones said, "wait until prayer is over, and I will get up and trouble you no more."[29]

The white trustees insisted that Jones leave immediately. Another trustee came over to help pull up the black worshipers. The prayer ended, and Allen recalled, "We all went out of the church in a body, and they were no more plagued with us in the church."[30] Allen and his compatriots did not completely cut off contact with St. George's. They met with an elder from the church who discouraged them from raising money to build their own sanctuary and threatened them with church discipline.

But using his own money and plot of land he had previously purchased, Allen helped start the Bethel African Church in Philadelphia in 1794. Since so many black Methodists faced similar racial obstacles with their white coreligionists, Allen helped found the African Methodist Episcopal denomination in 1816 and became its first bishop.[31]

Black Christians have repeated their exodus from white churches throughout American history on both large and small scales. For instance, in 1833 Charles Colcock Jones, an early proponent of evangelizing the enslaved, preached to a slave congregation from the book of Philemon. When he said that the apostle Paul admonished slaves not to run away from their masters, "one half of my audience rose up and walked off with themselves." The remainder "looked anything but satisfied, either with the preacher or his doctrine."[32] Even when black people could not form their own congregations, they often refused to countenance any type of Christianity that sanctioned their enslavement.

A LIMITED REVOLUTION

Racial segregation in Christian churches occurred in the eighteenth century in large part because white believers did not oppose the enslavement of African persons. Instead, Christians sought to reform slavery and evangelize the enslaved. In the process, they learned to rationalize the continued existence of slavery. Many white Christians comforted themselves with the myth that slavery allowed them to more adequately care for the material and spiritual needs of enslaved Africans.

But the attempts of white Christians to reform slavery indicate that, at least in part, they realized its horrendous nature. Their guilt motivated them to try to soften its practice. They reasoned that even though slavery was bad for Africans, life for the enslaved would be far worse if not for the protective strictures of perpetual bondage. White clergymen like George Whitefield and Jonathan Edwards typify the contradiction of American Christianity. The two preachers attempted to treat the people they enslaved humanely, yet they still acquiesced to slavery, even practicing it themselves.

The American church compromised with racism in the eighteenth century by permitting slavery to continue. The Christian church grew in the 1730s and 1740s, but the racial hierarchy remained firmly entrenched in the church and society. In one of American history's clearest contradictions, not even Revolutionary ideals of independence and equality or the religious transformations brought on by the Great Awakening could deconstruct the foundations of the social pyramid. Instead, slavery and the meaning of race became more institutionalized as the country progressed through the opening decades of the nineteenth century.

CHAPTER
4

INSTITUTIONALIZING RACE IN THE ANTEBELLUM ERA

In 1809, St. Philip's became the first black Episcopal parish in New York City. The congregation grew steadily and became noted for attracting many of the city's leading black citizens.[1] However, the vitality of the church and the prestige of its members did not gain them equal standing with their white Episcopalian brethren. The church faced repeated rejection in its attempt to join the regional association of Episcopal churches, known as a diocese.

At the annual diocesan convention in 1846, the leaders of St. Philip's once again applied for admission, a status that would give them a voice in denominational matters and place them on equal footing with white churches. When the matter of the church's status came before the Committee on the Incorporation of Churches, someone objected. After considering the matter, the committee made its determination. They stated that "neither St. Philip's, nor any other colored congregation [will] be admitted into union with this Convention, so as to entitle them to representation therein." The committee explained its reasoning: "They are socially degraded, and are not regarded as proper associates for the class of person who attend our Convention." The committee members assured the convention that their objections had nothing to do with race. "We object not to the color of the skin, but we question their possession of those qualities which would render their intercourse with the members of a Church Convention useful."[2]

Neither a thriving congregation nor conducting worship according to established denominational practices nor properly applying for membership proved sufficient grounds to include a black congregation as equal members of the household of God. The story of St. Philip's was repeated throughout the antebellum period in varying ways and in different regions but with the same result—second-class citizenship for black Christians in the American church.

Despite the racism black Christians experienced, they did not abandon the faith. In fact, the decades before the Civil War served as an incubator for a newborn black American Christianity. Black Christians began developing distinctive practices that would come to characterize the historic black church tradition. Black Christianity in the United States grew alongside the explosive expansion of slavery and the hardening of racial boundaries in the United States. The faith of black Christians helped them endure and even inspired some believers to resist oppression.

At the outset of the nineteenth century, the United States could have become a worldwide beacon of diversity and equality. Fresh from the Revolutionary War, it could have adopted the noble ideals written in the Declaration of Independence. It could have crafted a truly inclusive Constitution. Instead, white supremacy became more defined as the nation and the church solidified their identities. This chapter outlines how early leaders embedded race into the foundation of both the fledgling American nation and the church.

SLAVERY'S CONSTITUTION

After the smoke of the Revolutionary War had dissipated in the winds of independence, the political leaders of the colonies set about forming a new nation. Their first order of business was to draft a document outlining how the government would function. Ratified in 1781, the Articles of Confederation were a weak initial attempt at a constitution. Fears of a strong central power and the desire for states to remain sovereign meant the federal government could not levy taxes or regulate commerce. Leaders quickly realized they would have to write a stronger piece of legislation, one capable of preserving the tenuous unity of the newly independent colonies. The result was the Constitutional Convention of 1787 which produced the US Constitution.

Although the Constitution outlines the duties and privileges of citizens and the scope and function of the government, who the Constitution applied to remained ambiguous. Without question, the Constitution had the rights of wealthy, white men in mind while other groups like indigenous peoples, women, and enslaved blacks held a lesser status. These other groups could not always count on the legal protections declared by the Constitution.

The US Constitution does not use the words *slave* or *slavery*, yet some scholars argue that it can be viewed as a proslavery document. "Of its eighty-four clauses, six are directly concerned with slaves and their owners. Five others had implications of slavery that were considered and debated by the delegates to the 1787 Constitutional Convention and the citizens of the states during ratification," writes David Waldstreicher.[3] For example, Article IV, Section 2 states, "No Person held to Service or Labour in one State, under the Laws thereof, escaping into another, shall . . . be discharged from such Service or Labour, but shall be delivered up on Claim of the Party to whom such Service or Labour may be due." This is known as the "Fugitive Slave Clause." Although the word *slave* is absent, this section clearly means that any enslaved person crossing state lines from a slave state to a free state had to be returned to his or her owner. From the beginning, the Constitution ensured that nowhere in America would be safe for an escaped slave.

Article 1, Section 2 of the US Constitution details how a state's population would be determined for tax and representational purposes in Congress. That number "shall be determined by adding to the whole Number of free Persons, including those bound to Service for a Term of Years and excluding Indians not taxed, three fifths of all other Persons." This clause is more popularly known as the Three-Fifths Compromise.

Keep in mind that the union of the diverse states was not a foregone conclusion. The South had a vested interest in protecting slavery (though the North benefitted as well), and some southern states refused to ratify the Constitution unless they had specific assurances protecting their right to possess human chattel. In matters of taxation, northern states wanted each state to be taxed according to its total population, including slaves, but the South did not want to be taxed for slaves. The reverse was true when it came to the matter of representation in Congress. Northern states did not want slaves to be counted, because that would give the South a numerical advantage over northern states. To avoid an impasse, the delegates compromised. Instead of acknowledging the full humanity and citizenship of black slaves, political leaders determined that each slave would count as three-fifths of a white citizen.

Southern states, particularly Georgia and South Carolina, threatened to reject any constitution that did not protect the practice of slavery. In what became known as the "dirty compromise," delegates agreed to include a clause that allowed for the continuation of the slave trade for another twenty years. Slavery was not open for debate again in the United States until 1808.

In 1808, Congress decided to cease the Atlantic slave trade, but the institution of slavery remained. In a preview of the growing divide between northern and southern states, Congress passed the Missouri Compromise of 1820. This agreement admitted Missouri as a slave state and Maine as a free state to preserve the balance of power between slave and free states. The Missouri Compromise effectively guaranteed that slavery would remain an American institution for the next several decades.

All of this demonstrates that early legislation in the United States protected, or at least did not dismantle, race-based chattel slavery. The nation's political leaders used black lives as bargaining chips to preserve the union of states and to gain leverage for other policy issues. Although the abolition movement started gaining momentum during this time, America made its peace with slavery for the next several decades.

What about the church? The American church made similar compromises at critical junctures to preserve the status of slaveholders and to justify the uniquely American manifestation of slavery. The tragedy of the church's compromise with slavery cannot be understood apart from a close examination of the day-to-day lives of slaves.

THE CHATTEL PRINCIPLE AND SLAVERY

If there is one concept that helps unlock the twisted logic of American slavery better than almost any other, it is the *chattel principle*. The chattel principle is the social alchemy that transformed a human being made in the image of God into a piece of property. African American minister and abolitionist James W. C. Pennington spoke of it this way: "The being of slavery, its soul and its body, lives and moves in the chattel principle, the property principle, the bill of sale principle: the cart whip, starvation, and nakedness are its inevitable consequences."[4]

In the book *Soul by Soul*, Walter Johnson looks at the slave market, the point of sale for human beings, the place that most tangibly illustrates the chattel principle and the way human beings were reduced to the personal property of slave owners. Johnson writes, "The entire economy of the antebellum South was constructed on the idea that the bodies of enslaved people had a measurable monetary value."[5] As property, enslaved people were valued for their physical aptitude and obedient attitudes. Prices increased based on height, skin color, perceived intelligence, and a reputation for following orders. Slaves could be used as collateral for loans and were often sold as part of the estate when an enslaver died.

Tragically, the economic value associated with an enslaved person was of more value than their family ties. According to Johnson, of the more than 600,000 interstate sales that occurred in the decades prior to the Civil War, 25 percent destroyed a first marriage, and 50 percent broke up a nuclear family. Oftentimes, children younger than thirteen years old were separated from their parents and sold, never to be reunited. "Under the chattel principle, every advance into enslaved society—every reliance on another, every child, friend, or lover, every social relation—held within it the threat of its own dissolution."[6]

Olaudah Equiano wrote about his separation from his sister as the most traumatic event of his enslavement. After their initial separation, Equiano and his sister experienced a brief, joyous moment of reunification. Upon meeting they "clung to each other in mutual embraces, unable to do anything but weep." Yet just as abruptly as they had been reunited, they were sold to different masters: "Scarcely had the fatal morning appeared, when she was again torn from me forever! I was now more miserable, if possible, than before."[7]

The suffering of black women was especially acute under the institution of slavery because women were valued both for their productive ability and their reproductive ability. In contrast to white women, who were viewed as delicate and in need of protection, black women were perceived as strong and durable. Even when they were pregnant, it was expected that they should work in the fields, often up until the very moment of birth. After delivery, women were allotted scant time for recovery and were soon forced back to work. Black women also bore the primary responsibility to care for their own families. Even as they had their own children to look after, many enslaved women were also responsible for raising the children of their enslavers.

Rape was an inevitable aspect of slave life for many black women, who had no social or legal power to resist the lascivious behavior of their white slaveowners. The mistresses of the plantation, from whom black women might have anticipated some empathy because of their shared gender, instead treated enslaved black women with contempt and jealousy.[8] Deprived of any recourse, black women had to resort to their own solutions to survive under harsh circumstances.

Harriet Jacobs, in her autobiography *Incidents in the Life of a Slave Girl*, relates the moral agony of choosing between being raped by her enslaver or a more willing but no less unequal sexual relationship with a free white man. Raised by a Christian grandmother who exhibited constant concern for Jacobs's safety and sexual virtue, the young slave girl agonized over her decision, unsure of how to respond to her sexual partners. For years she had done her best to avoid the lecherous tentacles of the man who had enslaved her, Doctor Flint. To her white female readers, she implored, "But, O, ye happy women, whose purity has been sheltered from childhood, who have been free to choose the objects of your affection, whose homes are protected by law. Do not judge the poor desolate slave girl too severely!"[9] In the end, Jacobs decided to partner with a free white man in the hopes that if they had children together, he would set them free. These were the types of impossible choices that characterized the life of black women under slavery.

Rather than defending the dignity of black people, American Christians at this time chose to turn a blind eye to the separation of families, the scarring of bodies, the starvation of stomachs, and the generational trauma of slavery. Some deliberately chose to shield themselves from the atrocities occurring in their own country, state, and community. Others witnessed slavery in action but chose not to confront it, preferring the political and financial advantages that came with human bondage instead of decrying the dehumanization they saw. Whether some Christians felt conflicted or remorseful about their support of slavery matters little. The practice continued, as did the suffering. While many Americans were complicit in the continuation of slavery, Christian support stands apart because the Bible clearly and frequently instructs believers in how they should treat others. In later chapters, we'll take a closer look at several Christian theological justifications for slavery. It was during this antebellum period that the American church truly made its uneasy peace with the enslavement of black people.

SLAVE RESISTANCE AND REBELLION

Black people in America recognized that the evil they suffered was imposed on them, not a result of their own actions. The enslaved recognized this injustice because they lived it every day. But they did not let the harm they endured hinder their hopes for a better future or extinguish their attempts at resistance. Enslaved blacks did not passively suffer abuse. Christianity, in fact, became a source of strength and survival, bringing hope to thousands of enslaved people. And they found other ways, both subtle and spectacular, to resist oppression.

Black resistance to enslavement took multiple forms. Some slaves deliberately broke tools to delay their work. Others would set fires or pretend to be sick. Denmark Vesey, for instance, faked epileptic seizures so effectively that the white man who bought him returned Vesey to the slave trader who sold him. Enslaved blacks feigned mental slowness to make their enslavers think they were less capable than they really were. They sometimes stole food or other items as compensation for their years of unpaid labor. Even learning to read was a form of resistance.

Of course, escape was also a form of resistance. But fleeing the plantation meant increased risk, punishment, and possibly death if recaptured. Plans had to be devised with the utmost secrecy. To hide their plans for running away, enslaved blacks embedded hidden messages into their songs. A well-known example is the song "Steal Away," which includes the line "Steal away home to Jesus." That double entendre could also serve as notification to indicate when slaves could escape or "steal away" from the plantation. Similarly, the song "Follow the Drinking Gourd" refers to a constellation in the night sky that slaves were supposed to follow to freedom. The words of the song pass along specific directions and give the time of day to execute the plan:

> When the sun comes up and the first quail calls
> Follow the drinking gourd.

A later couplet instructs the listener to follow the river and to look for dead tree branches arranged to point toward freedom in the north:

> The riverbank is a mighty good road
> The dead trees show you the way

The riskiest and most ambitious form of resistance was a slave rebellion. In Saint-Domingue, now known as Haiti, the black slaves of this Caribbean island accomplished the first successful slave revolution of the modern Atlantic world. From 1781 to 1804, enslaved blacks in France's richest colony rebelled against their enslavers, who were vastly outnumbered, and took the island from their European oppressors. News of the revolution spread across the globe and caused constant consternation for white colonizers. No specter cast a longer shadow in the minds of North American enslavers than the Haitian Revolution. Nightmares of a massive domestic rebellion of enslaved black people haunted the enslavers and those who relied on slave labor. Their fears were not unfounded.

From the moment the shackles clamped around the wrists or ankles of an enslaved black person, getting free became a dream and, for some, an obsession. Occasionally, those trapped in bondage organized and armed themselves in a campaign for liberation. In 1800, Gabriel, an enslaved man on the Prosser Plantation, attempted a revolution that might have involved up to a thousand other slaves. Gabriel stood over six feet tall, was a skilled blacksmith, and was one of the few enslaved people who could read and write. Inspired by the Haitian Revolution, he planned an uprising to take control of the armory in Richmond and hold Governor James Monroe as a hostage until their demands were met. But on the eve before the planned rebellion, a torrential thunderstorm struck the area and delayed the plans. A slave named Pharaoh reportedly divulged the plans to white men. Gabriel and his coconspirators' revolution was thwarted, and the would-be rebels were hanged.[10]

Denmark Vesey literally won the lottery when he became a freedman. Born into slavery and living in Charleston, South Carolina, with his slaveowner, Vesey won the city lottery and bought his freedom for $600. He could not, however, purchase freedom for his wife and children, a fact that served as a source of perpetual frustration for him. Vesey joined the new Emanuel African Methodist Episcopal Church, or "Mother Emanuel," in 1817 and became a leader in the congregation. Even in an all-black church, members faced constant monitoring from local whites, who feared that their preaching and teaching would lead to insubordination and insurrection. They were right to be concerned. Like Gabriel, Vesey knew how to read and drew inspiration from the success of the Haitian Revolution and from biblical passages on the exodus. In 1822, he planned a massive slave revolt, but again, a few timid enslaved persons gave away the plans to some white people, who began rounding up the ring-leaders. Vesey himself was captured and executed along with thirty-four others. As news of

Vesey's revolutionary plans spread, the white population of the city of Charleston burned the church, Emanuel AME, to the ground.

Less than ten years later, in February 1831, the moon eclipsed the sun, and an enslaved man named Nat Turner looked at the sky. Turner believed the eclipse to be a spiritual message. Turner was a deeply committed Christian, and in 1828, three years earlier, he wrote that God had revealed to him "by signs in the heavens that he would make known to me when I should commence the great work, and . . . I should arise and prepare myself and slay my enemies with their own weapons."[11] Turner planned what became one of the most infamous rebellions of enslaved people in American history. Unlike Gabriel and Denmark Vesey's aborted attempts, Nat Turner carried out his plans.

On the night of August 21, 1831, Turner and six of his followers entered the house of his slaveowner, Joseph Travis, and murdered the entire family in their sleep. Turner and his band moved on to other homes, killing whites along the way. At the end of two days, dozens of slaves had joined up with "Nat Turner's Rebellion." Around fifty-five white men, women, and children died by their hands. A hastily assembled militia dispersed Turner's forces, killing many of them. Ironically, the militia encountered the rebels while marching toward the county seat, a town named Jerusalem. Turner himself evaded capture until October 30, when he was seized, tried, and convicted. While he sat in prison, he dictated his story to his lawyer, Thomas Gray, in what became known as *The Confessions of Nat Turner*. On November 11, state authorities executed Nat Turner. In a final act of macabre dehumanization, Turner's body was given to scientists for study. According to lore, his decapitated skull circulated among many individuals for examination and entertainment.[12]

Nat Turner's rebellion sparked paranoia across the South. In fear and retaliation, white people killed more than 100 enslaved blacks suspected of participating in or sympathizing with the rebellion. The insurrection led to harsher laws governing slave mobility and limiting their ability to assemble. White Christians used this as an opportunity to advocate for slavery reform so that masters did not aggravate enslaved people to the point of violent rebellion, pointing to Turner as an example.

PATERNALISM AND PROSLAVERY CHRISTIANITY

The gospel of Jesus Christ planted the seeds of resistance and liberation in the minds and hearts of oppressed black people, driving white enslavers to repress and regulate the religion of the enslaved. White slave owners sought to erase African religion and cultural customs and endeavored to control the Christianity they dispensed to their involuntary laborers. Although groups of white Christians had insisted on evangelizing indigenous peoples and enslaved Africans, their efforts never produced a church defined by racial equality. Instead, paternalistic attitudes toward black people defined much of American Christianity.

White evangelists compromised the Bible's message of liberation to make Christianity compatible with slavery. They sought to allay the trepidation of enslavers by spiritualizing Christian equality—spiritual freedom did not change one's status as slave or free. To reinforce these ideas, white leaders tried to ensure that black Christians never had too much autonomy. Prior to the Civil War, black and white Christians commonly worshiped together in the same congregations. As Charles F. Irons wrote in *The Origins of Proslavery Christianity*, "Sunday morning only became the most segregated time of the week after the Civil War. Before emancipation, black and white evangelicals typically prayed, sang, and worshiped together."[13] Yet this interracial interaction did not come from the egalitarian aspirations of white Christians; rather, interracial congregations were an expression of paternalism and a means of controlling slave beliefs and preventing slave insurrection.

Under paternalistic Christianity, the slave plantation was seen as a household, with the male enslaver as the benevolent patriarch of both his family and his "pseudofamily" of enslaved black people. Theoretically, a Christian slave owner would care for his enslaved property as a father cares for his own children. But enslaved blacks could never truly be part of the white master's household, nor would they be considered full and equal human beings, let alone fellow Christians of equal status and dignity. George Fitzhugh, a lawyer from Virginia, clarified: "The negro race is inferior to the white race, and living in their midst, they would be far outstripped or outwitted in the chase of free competition. Gradual, but certain, extermination would be their fate."[14] Slaveholder paternalism viewed the enslaved as perpetual children incapable of adequately making their own decisions, dependent on white people for guidance and protection.

This paternalistic attitude led many white Christians to be remarkably openminded when it came to the activity of Black Christians—as long as the racial hierarchy remained unchanged. "So long as black evangelicals did not press for either civic privileges or equality within the biracial church, their white coreligionists were willing to open to them a relatively wide field of activity."[15] The American Colonization Society (ACS) vividly illustrates the paternalistic attitude of racially moderate white Christians. The organization, founded in 1816 by Presbyterian minister Robert Finley, sought to send freed black people in America back to Africa. Finley, like many other white Christians, believed that free black people could never effectively assimilate into American society. "Could they be sent to Africa, a three-fold benefit would arise," he suggested. "We should be cleared of them; we should send to Africa a population partially civilized and christianized for its benefits; our blacks themselves would be put in better condition."[16] Inherent in this plan for colonization was the assumption that blacks, as American citizens, would never meet the demands of democracy. Organizations like the ACS believed that exporting black Americans back to Africa would "civilize" a dark and barbaric continent through gradual cultural changes and Christian evangelism. As a pleasant byproduct of relocating black Americans to Africa, white Americans would also rid themselves of the endlessly troublesome racial issue. Notably absent from this proposed solution was an acknowledgment of the high mortality rates of people who moved to Africa. Nor did the prospect of making room for black people in America gain a serious hearing. Many misguided Christians viewed the work of the American Colonization Society as an act of benevolence, a way of "helping" free black people find a better life.

Even as they proposed ways of relocating black people back to Africa, some white Christians celebrated the flowering of interracial faith in the antebellum era. Much of this growth came from another wave of revivals that swept the nation. In the early decades of the nineteenth century, the Second Great Awakening added droves of new converts to the flock of American Christianity. The Cane Ridge Revival in Kentucky in 1801 attracted between 10,000 and 20,000 people and became known as "America's Pentecost." Territories at the western edge of the American expanse began to turn toward Christianity, fanning the hopes of evangelists for a nationwide Christian revival.

One of the theological legacies of the Second Great Awakening was postmillennialism, the view that Christ would return only after an extended era of peace and justice. Christians saw it as their duty to usher in this millennium and to prepare for Jesus's return by reforming society and tamping down its vices. As a result, dozens of new Christian-led social reform organizations sprang into being. These societies addressed issues related to poverty, orphan and widow care, alcoholism, and abolitionism. The loose organization of these societies became known as the "Benevolent Empire."

Yet despite energetic efforts at reform, slavery remained the most intractable issue of American life. A majority of white Christians refused to take a definitive stand against race-based chattel slavery, and this complicity plagued the church and created stark contradictions. Segregation and inequality defined most of American Christianity—even in an age of great revivals. For example, many black people attended the Cane Ridge Revival, but they were forced to meet in a separate area apart from the white worshipers.

One of the most well-known revivalist preachers of the day was Charles Grandison Finney. Finney led Oberlin College, which became the first institution of higher education to accept both women and black people. Finney was an outspoken abolitionist, but he was not a proponent of black equality. He advocated for emancipation, but he did not see the value of the "social" integration of the races. Though he excluded white slaveowners from membership in his congregations, he also relegated black worshipers to particular sections of the sanctuary. Black people could become members in his churches, but they could not vote or hold office.[17]

Finney's stance for abolition but against integration arose from his conviction that social reform would come through individual conversion, not institutional reform. Finney and many others like him believed that social change came about through evangelization. According to this logic, once a person believed in Christ as Savior and Lord, he or she would naturally work toward justice and change. "As saints supremely value the highest good of being, they will, and must, take a deep interest in whatever is promotive of that end. Hence, their spirit is necessarily that of the reformer."[18] This belief led to a fixation on individual conversion without a corresponding focus on transforming the racist policies and practices of institutions, a stance that has remained a constant feature of American evangelicalism and has furthered the American church's easy compromise with slavery and racism.

The antebellum period was a time of compromise and complicity. During this time, many Christians engaged in evangelism to enslaved and freed blacks. The black church grew, laying the foundation for a distinctive tradition that would stand at the center of the black freedom struggle for the next century. Even as slavery became further embedded in American culture, evangelical Christianity became more mainstream. Unwilling to confront the evil of this institution, some churches lost their prophetic voices, and those who did speak up were drowned out by the louder chorus of complicity. Competing understandings of freedom, equality, and belonging in both the country and the congregation would soon explode into Civil War.

CHAPTER 5

DEFENDING SLAVERY AT THE ONSET OF THE CIVIL WAR

The battles of the Civil War did not just happen in places like Shiloh and Gettysburg. The Bible itself became a battleground. With the onset of the Civil War, the nation faced not only a political and economic crisis but a theological one as well.[1]

As historian Mark Noll has written, no single individual characterized the conflict better than Abraham Lincoln.[2] When Lincoln was inaugurated for his second and very brief term as president in 1865, a Union victory was on the horizon. Robert E. Lee would formally surrender at Appomattox, Virginia, just a month later. Rather than gloat about his military success, Lincoln's address struck a somber and reflective tone: "Both [Union and Confederacy] read the same Bible and pray to the same God, and each invokes His aid against the other. . . . The prayers of both could not be answered. That of neither has been answered fully."[3] The president concisely summarized the theological tension that lay at the center of the conflict. Was God on the side of the Union or the Confederacy? Did the Bible sanction slavery or oppose it? Who were the righteous warriors in this conflagration? The war decisively ended slavery, but the fighting did not end. The bullets of competing biblical interpretations continued to ricochet across the country.

This chapter briefly recounts the events leading up to and including the Civil War, with an emphasis on the biblical and theological justifications Christians used to defend slavery and the Confederate cause. It unpacks the concept of sectionalism—the increasing tension between the North and South—over the issue of slavery. As the nation settled into its political identity, the differences between the slaveholding states of the South and the relatively free states of the North became more pronounced. Massive schisms along sectional lines in the major denominations—Methodists, Baptists, and Presbyterians—portended the national divide to come. Throughout the conflict, Christians of both the Union and Confederate forces believed that God was on their side.

TWO FACTS ABOUT THE CIVIL WAR

The Civil War remains the deadliest war the United States has ever waged. The latest estimates show that between 650,000 and 850,000 people died.[4] In the Battle of Gettysburg alone, 51,000 combatants perished. The war began just as technological innovations allowed for deadlier guns and cannons. Yet battle tactics still resembled those used in the Revolutionary War seventy years prior, and leaders adapted poorly to the threats the new weapons posed.

Disease claimed up to two-thirds of all who perished in the Civil War. Soldiers slept in tents stuffy with unventilated air. They endured cold, damp conditions on their journeys to the battle front. Unsophisticated medical techniques increased the likelihood of death. Dysentery was the most common cause of fatalities, but typhoid fever, pneumonia, small pox, and gangrene could decimate troops as surely as a hail of bullets.[5]

Two facts about the Civil War are especially pertinent to our examination of race and Christianity in America: that the Civil War was fought over slavery and that countless devout Christians fought and died to preserve it as an institution. The first fact, that the war was about slavery, was never in dispute during the conflict. The combatants knew what the stakes were. Even if there were additional disputed issues, such as the extent of federal versus state power, the future of slavery in America was paramount. Only after the war, when southerners and their sympathizers sought to give reasons for the Confederacy's defeat, was slavery's relevance to the war partially obscured.

The second fact, that many Christians supported slavery to the extent that they were willing to risk their lives to protect it, has not been fully considered in the American church, even though 150 years have passed since the war. Slavery has always been a profound contradiction at the heart of both the United States and the American church. The Civil War was the climactic, bloody reckoning of this contradiction. The nation, which emphasized liberty as a natural right, made repeated concessions to allow for slavery. The church, which prioritizes the love of God and love of neighbor, capitulated to the status quo by permitting the lifetime bondage of human persons based on skin color. A house divided against itself—with conflicting ideals at its foundation—cannot stand. The antebellum way of life had to fall, and the Civil War was the sledgehammer that knocked it down.

THE NATION'S BLOODIEST WAR AND ITS CAUSES

Amid the myriad streams that combined to break the dam of national political unity and usher in the Civil War, five events stand out: the Fugitive Slave Act of 1850, the Kansas-Nebraska Act of 1854, the Dred Scott decision of 1857, John Brown's raid in 1859, and the election of Abraham Lincoln in 1860.

In 1850, Congress passed the Fugitive Slave Act. Even though the Constitution stipulated that enslaved people who escaped to free territories remained in bondage and had to be returned to their masters, this was poorly enforced and often contested in northern states. At the time, California was petitioning to enter the Union as a free state, so legislators struck a compromise. To satisfy southerners, the law included harsher penalties for fugitive slaves. Under the Fugitive Slave Act, free people who failed to assist authorities in recapturing runaways could be fined up to $1,000. The Fugitive Slave Act also made it easier for enslavers to capture fugitive slaves; enslavers simply needed to supply an affidavit to a federal marshal for the capture and return of an individual. Since suspected fugitives had no rights in court, many legally free black people could now be captured and enslaved, often without recourse. The Fugitive Slave Act effectively protected and even expanded slavery nationwide. Black people were never completely safe from capture and enslavement, no matter where they were. Antislavery advocates expressed outrage that the federal government had compromised with southern slave owners.

Four years later, the Kansas-Nebraska Act of 1854 shattered the uneasy truce between slave states and free states. This act permitted the new territories of Kansas and Nebraska to decide for themselves whether to allow slavery. The act effectively nullified the Missouri Compromise of 1820, and soon Kansas became a battle ground between slavery and antislavery forces. Settlers on each side of the debate rushed into the territory in hopes of determining its fate concerning slavery. Proslavery politicians won the first election after the Kansas-Nebraska Act, but antislavery advocates accused them of fraud and unilaterally declared the results void. Armed groups attacked one another, and the territory became known as "Bloody Kansas" because of the casualties. The nation was on edge, and battle lines began to form.

Three years after the Kansas-Nebraska Act passed, the Supreme Court considered the case of a man named Dred Scott. Scott thought he had a good legal case when he sued for his freedom. Born into slavery in Virginia in 1795, Scott had labored for his master in the free state of Illinois and the free territory of Wisconsin. Scott sued when his mistress refused to let him buy his own freedom and that of his wife and daughter. He took the case all the way to the Supreme Court where the justices ruled seven to two against him. Writing the majority opinion, Judge Roger Taney stated that black people were of "an inferior order, and altogether unfit to associate with the white race." Taney went on to explain that the Constitution did not have black people in mind when it outlined the rights and duties of citizens. Instead, black people "had no rights which the white man was bound to respect."[6] This decision effectively closed courts to enslaved blacks. They could not sue for their freedom or pursue justice through the court system, and once again the American legal system had declared black people to be something less than fully human. The Dred Scott decision left no question in the minds of antislavery activists that the federal government, especially under the leadership of President James Buchanan, planned to extend and protect slavery across the growing nation.

Some abolitionists, frustrated by these events and the growing expansion of slavery, advocated extreme measures. John Brown, a white man who abhorred slavery, was a man of action. Brown had led raids during the "Bloody Kansas" days. He was convinced that slavery could only be overcome through violent means, and he was prepared to lead an insurgency against the government. Brown formed a small party of both black and white men, including his three sons, and they raided the federal armory at Harpers Ferry in what became West Virginia. Brown and his men successfully captured the armory, but within two days a force led by Robert E. Lee killed most of the men and captured Brown. The abolitionist was hanged a few weeks later. Brown's raid further escalated tensions between slavery and antislavery citizens, and it foreshadowed and fed the violent confrontation that would take place just over a year later.

In 1860, voters elected Abraham Lincoln, a Republican committed to limiting slavery's expansion, as president of the United States. This was the final event that pushed southerners to openly talk of secession and war, if necessary. Yet despite the anger of southern politicians, Lincoln was far from a racial egalitarian. He objected to the expansion of slavery, but he was not initially interested in abolishing it, nor did he advocate for civil or social equality for black people. During a series of political debates against Stephen Douglas in Illinois in 1858, Lincoln carefully explained, "I am not nor have I ever been in favor of bringing about in any way the social and political equality of the white and black races."[7] The president, later hailed as the "Great Emancipator," made it clear that abolitionists who opposed the institution of slavery could also be antiblack and even racist. At one point Lincoln invited five black leaders to the White House to discuss a colonization plan that would send freed black people to Liberia, Haiti, or Panama.[8]

As we have seen, colonization was an easy way for white people to skirt the issue of white supremacy. Rather than combatting racism, why not simply send people of other races far, far away?

If anyone today still doubts whether the Civil War was fought over the issue of slavery, they need only to read the declarations issued by the Confederate states upon their secession from the Union. With Lincoln's election in 1860, seven states quickly seceded from the Union with South Carolina leading the way. South Carolina's leaders clearly explained their reasons for withdrawing: "Those [non-slaveholding] States have assume[d] the right of deciding upon the propriety of our domestic institutions; and have denied the rights of property established in fifteen of the States and recognized by the Constitution." South Carolina and the other states that withdrew from the United States considered slavery a matter of personal property ownership, and citing Article IV, they saw slavery as an institution explicitly protected by the Constitution. Yet slavery was more than simply a legal issue; it was a moral and spiritual concern for the South as well. South Carolina's leaders lamented that northern states "denounced as sinful the institution of slavery."[9]

Mississippi was the second state to separate from the Union, and they made their position on slavery even more explicit. The legislators explained, "Our position is thoroughly identified with the institution of slavery—the greatest material interest of the world." Yet again, the chattel principle came into play as Mississippi's leaders used financial arguments to support slavery. In addition, they posited that the biology of black people uniquely suited them for slave labor because "none but the black race can bear exposure to the tropical sun."[10]

After the opening shots of the Civil War at Fort Sumter, South Carolina, in April 1861, four more states joined the Confederacy, and the schism was complete. Yet another split was happening as well—not between states but in the American church. Decades before the nation split into Union and Confederate sides, the dilemma of slavery had already frayed the unity of the American church. The three of the most influential denominations at the time—Methodists, Baptists, and Presbyterians—all divided and fought over whether Christians could own slaves and remain in good standing. Although each group split under slightly different circumstances, ultimately it was the issue of slavery that divided churches.

METHODISTS SPLIT OVER SLAVEHOLDING BISHOPS

In the mid-nineteenth century, the possession of slaves by a white man in the antebellum South was rather unremarkable. What made James Osgood Andrew stand out was the fact that he was a bishop in the Methodist Episcopal Church (MEC), a denomination that had opposed slavery since their founding in 1784. John Wesley, founder of the Methodist movement, found slavery appalling. "It cannot be, that either war, or contract, can give any man such a property in another as he has in sheep and oxen. Much less is it possible, that any child of man, should ever be born a slave," he said.[11] Although it was far from advocating for racial equality, this antislavery stance—along with Wesley's emphasis on revivalism, interracial camp meetings, a swift ordination process, and an appeal to the non-elite classes—initially attracted black Christians such as Richard Allen and Absalom Jones to the denomination.

Despite the Methodists' original opposition to slavery, as the denomination grew more socially conservative, views shifted, especially in the South. In southern states Methodist ministers became more comfortable with slavery and accommodated their preaching and practices to its presence. In 1808, the quadrennial General Conference determined that annual regional conferences could decide for themselves whether local Methodists could buy and sell black people. This led to an uneasy tension between Northern and Southern Methodists, a tension that continued to increase through the mid-nineteenth century with the surge of abolitionist sentiment among many Methodists.

James Andrew's status as both an enslaver of human beings and a bishop in the church became the focus of the 1844 General Conference. Split largely along sectional lines, the antislavery advocates held the ecclesiastical advantage, and in a 110–69 vote, they resolved to censure the bishop as long as he continued to hold slaves. Refusing to give up his church duties, Andrew and his allies split from the MEC to form the Methodist Episcopal Church, South (MECS), and they allowed their clergy to practice slavery.

BAPTISTS SPLIT OVER SLAVEHOLDING MISSIONARIES

A year after the Methodist schism, Baptists followed a similar course. Many religious organizations attempted to circumvent the conflict over slavery by claiming neutrality and letting local congregations decide the matter. Since the 1790s, the Baptist General Convention had taken this approach. These formal pronouncements, however, did little to conceal the growing sectional divide over slavery. Baptists in the South suspected that their denomination had a bias toward abolition, and they wanted to expose it. In 1844, the Georgia Baptist Convention put forth James E. Reeve as a missionary to the Home Mission Society. Like James Andrew of the Methodist church, Reeve enslaved black people.

Reeve's status as a slave owner forced members of the society's executive board to decide: either approve Reeve and tacitly endorse slaveholding for the entire denomination or reject him and demonstrate a bias toward an antislavery stance. Board members viewed the application as an attempt to purposely insert a divisive question into the denomination's work. So the committee tried to avoid the issue of slavery altogether. In considering Reeve's application, they wrote, "Resolved, That . . . it is not expedient to introduce the subjects of slavery or anti-slavery into our deliberations, nor to entertain applications to which they are introduced."[12] Instead of accepting or rejecting the slaveholding Reeve as a missionary, the executive board declined to deliberate at all.

Not to be deterred, other Baptists in the South, this time the Baptist General Convention of Alabama, submitted a resolution demanding that the national convention state plainly whether they viewed slaveholding as a sin. In their view, if Baptists thought enslaving people was truly a matter of ecclesiastic indifference, then they should not object to slaveholders working in foreign or domestic missions.

The Alabama Baptists demanded that their brethren acknowledge "the distinct, explicit avowal that slaveholders are eligible, and entitled, equally with non-slaveholders, to all the privileges and immunities of their several unions." Forced into making a definitive statement about slavery, the Home Mission Society responded with a clear rejection of any slaveholder to office: "If, however, anyone should offer himself as a Missionary, having slaves, and should insist on retaining them as his property, we could not appoint him." The mission board punctuated its statement by concluding, "One thing is certain, we can never be a party to any arrangement which would imply approbation of slavery."[13]

The battle lines between northern and southern Baptists had been drawn, and in May 1845, almost three hundred Baptist leaders representing nearly 400,000 churchgoers from southern states gathered in Augusta, Georgia, to form a new church association, one inclusive of slaveholders, called the Southern Baptist Convention (SBC). The convention's first president, William Bullein Johnson, explained the reason for the separation and the new convention. "These [northern] brethren, thus acted upon a sentiment they have failed to prove— That slavery is, in all circumstances sinful."[14] In light of this affront to the southern way of life and the assault on the institution of slavery, Southern Baptists viewed separation as their best option.

PRESBYTERIANS SPLIT OVER "CHRIST AND CAESAR"

A split among Presbyterians had already occurred in 1837, but it was primarily over the issues of revivalism and the question of adherence to a theological system outlined in the Westminster Confession of Faith. "New School" Presbyterians, following the thought of Puritans such as Jonathan Edwards, took a positive view of the religious experience of revivals. "Old School" adherents, such as Charles Hodge, preferred a less emotionally expressive and more traditional form of worship. Even though the conflict of the 1830s centered on a different set of theological issues, the slavery question lurked in the background. Tension continued to mount under the surface, and the Presbyterians split shortly after the start of the Civil War.

Following the story of one Presbyterian minister helps illuminate the Presbyterian denomination's divide. In 1809, Gardiner Spring had a young wife, a Yale education, and a promising legal career before him. In September, Spring entered College Chapel in New Haven and listened to a preacher from New York named John Mason. The title of Mason's sermon was "To the Poor the Gospel is Preached." As Spring listened, tears began to run down his face, and from that moment he committed himself to the ministry. After a year of seminary he gained ordination and became the senior minister of Brick Presbyterian Church in New York City. Contemporaries described his preaching as "vigorous, simple, and always interesting."[15]

Spring involved himself in the life of the church, but he was also involved in politics and the affairs of the state. As the Civil War approached, he aligned himself with the cause of abolition and the Union. After the start of the war, he presented a set of propositions at the 1861 General Assembly called the "Gardiner Spring Resolutions." The resolutions stated, "It is the duty of the ministry and churches under its care to do all in their power to promote and perpetuate the integrity of these United States, and to strengthen, uphold, and encourage the Federal Government."[16] Spring intended for his Presbyterian denomination to clearly align with the Union and the antislavery cause. His southern brethren did not view this favorably. They saw the resolutions as a direct attack.

The Gardiner Spring Resolutions called all Presbyterians to pledge their allegiance to the federal government and, by implication, to its stance on slavery. These were proposed as conditions of Presbyterian membership. According to one historian, "In the 1860s the issue centered on the question of Christ and Caesar, and whether or not the Church could require allegiance to any particular nation as a term of communion."[17] Given this ultimatum, Presbyterians in the South viewed separation as the only option available to them. They formed the Presbyterian Church in the Confederate States of America (PCCS), which later changed its name to the Presbyterian Church in the United States (PCUS). The forty-eight Presbyteries that separated from the Presbyterian Church of the United States of America (PCUSA) were all in southern states that advocated for each state's right to determine the legality of slavery.

As northern and southern denominations drifted apart and eventually split, they each hardened their stances toward slavery. Southern Christians devised increasingly complex theological arguments to argue for the existence of slavery, and in the process, southern Christians moved from viewing slavery as something permitted to something positive.

THE BIBLE AND SLAVERY

As soldiers in the Civil War waged battles with bullets and bayonets, Christian pastors and theologians fought with the words of the Bible. Southern white Christians, far from viewing slavery as wrong or sinful, generally affirmed that God sanctioned slavery in Scripture and that bondage under white authority was the natural state for people of African descent. To complicate matters, abolitionists and socially moderate Christians struggled to argue against what seemed evident to many people—the Bible never repudiates slavery. Indeed, many of the godliest people in the Bible enslaved others. So the Civil War also sparked a battle over the Bible.

It may be challenging for modern readers to grasp what was at stake for southern Christians when they considered slavery. Slavery was not just a civil issue; it was a religious one. Christians in the South believed the Bible approved of slavery since the Bible never clearly condemned slavery and even provided instructions for its regulation. Southern theologians challenged their abolitionist opponents to produce the chapter and verse where Jesus, or the Bible generally, condemned slavery. They gave extended treatises on the scriptural validity of slavery. Southern Methodist preacher J. W. Tucker said to Confederates in 1862, "Your cause is the cause of God, the cause of Christ, of humanity. It is a conflict of truth with error—-of Bible with northern infidelity—of pure Christianity with northern fanaticism."[18] Even as white southern Christians denounced northerners for making fidelity to the Union a requirement for fellowship, they made acceptance of race-based chattel slavery a requirement of biblical orthodoxy.

Robert Lewis Dabney, a southern Presbyterian minister and professor, originally opposed secession from the Union. Only after Virginia formally joined the Confederate cause in 1861 did Dabney change his position and become a powerful apologist for the South. During the war Dabney served as a chaplain for the Confederacy, and for a brief time, he was the adjutant, or "chief of staff," for General Stonewall Jackson. Even though illness forced Dabney out of the war, he and Jackson remained close friends. When Jackson died, his widow asked Dabney to write her husband's biography. As a Presbyterian minister, Dabney also marshaled his academic training to publish *A Defence of Virginia, [and through Her, of the South]* in 1867 shortly after the end of the Civil War. The release of this book *after* the war reveals that the formal end of military conflict did little to change the minds of southerners about slavery. Many remained committed to slavery as orthodox, biblical truth. In his book, Dabney explained in precise detail, quoting from the Old and New Testament and from economics and experience, why the North got it wrong and why the South's defense of slavery was justified.

Dabney not only believed that slavery was morally acceptable; he viewed it as a positive for the African: "Was it nothing, that this [black] race, morally inferior, should be brought into close relations to a nobler race?"[19] Dabney accepted the myth of the moral and intellectual inferiority of enslaved blacks, believing that if they were left to their own devices, they would only tend toward "lying, theft, drunkenness, laziness, [and] waste." In Dabney's theology, it was only through contact with the "nobler race" of white people in a master-slave relationship that there was hope of elevating the ethics of Africans.[20]

In addition, Dabney saw introducing Africans to Christianity as one of the most praiseworthy benefits of slavery for black people. Because black people were condemned to perish in their pagan beliefs, Dabney saw white Christian slaveowners as loving people standing between the enslaved and eternal damnation. "And above all, was it nothing that [black slaves] should be brought, by the relation of servitude, under the consciences and Christian zeal of a Christian people?"[21] In Dabney's mind, the gentle ministrations of the whip and the admonition of slaves to obey their masters had the positive effect of commending Christianity to black people. Had Dabney personally experienced the reality of enslavement, perhaps he would have been less confident about its salutary spiritual effects.

SLAVERY AND THE CURSE OF HAM

Genesis 9:18–29, sometimes referred to as the *curse of Ham*, is one of the most cryptic stories in the Old Testament. Subject to a multitude of interpretations, this passage has been widely deployed as the biblical basis for race-based chattel slavery. In the story, Noah gets drunk and falls asleep naked in his tent. His son Ham walks in on his sleeping father and sees his father naked. Ham leaves to tell his two brothers, Shem and Japheth, yet they respond differently. Instead of gazing upon their father's unclothed body, they quickly grab a blanket and walk backwards into his tent to cover him. When Noah wakes up and discovers what Ham has done, Noah curses Ham's son Canaan.

> Cursed be Canaan!
>> The lowest of slaves
>> will he be to his brothers. (Gen. 9:25)

Conversely, Noah blesses his other sons and consigns Canaan to serve them:

> Praise be to the LORD, the God of Shem!
>> May Canaan be the slave of Shem. (9:26)

Noah concludes with a final pronouncement: "May Canaan be the slave of Japheth" (9:27). Proslavery advocates used these verses to make a biblical case that black people—as descendants of Ham—belonged in a state of slavery.

For some, Ham's transgression provided an understanding of the origin of slavery and where it fit in the Bible's grand narrative. "It was in consequence of sin . . . that the first slave sentence of which we have any record was pronounced by Noah upon Canaan and his descendants," wrote Presbyterian minister George D. Armstrong.[22] Proslavery theologians taught that slavery had been a regrettable but necessary reality ever since Ham's transgression.

This passage from Genesis not only provided a basis for slavery's existence, but it was an indication for some that God decreed a specific race of people to be cursed and live their days in bondage. Alexander Stephens, vice president of the Confederate States of America, remarked in his well-known "Cornerstone Speech" that "the negro by nature, or by the curse against Canaan, is fitted for that condition which he occupies in our system."[23] And Dabney tentatively advanced a claim that many white Christians held as incontrovertible truth: "It may be that we should find little difficulty in tracing the lineage of the present Africans to Ham."[24] A racial genealogy underlies the racist interpretation of Canaan's curse. It assumed that the progeny of Shem became the Jewish people, the descendants of Japheth became white people, and these two were the rightful masters of those descended from Ham, the "degraded" black race. In one stroke of dubious demography, slavery became the right and proper place of Africans specifically and exclusively.

Abolitionists advanced several arguments to refute the curse of Ham as justification for the enslavement of black people. First, they pointed out that Noah pronounced the curse on Canaan, not Ham. Canaan's curse had been fulfilled, they said, when Israel conquered the Canaanite lands. Thus, there was no perpetual curse that still applied in the nineteenth century. Abolitionists also questioned whether black Africans were the genealogical descendants of Ham at all. And how could white people definitively trace their lineage to that of Shem or Japheth? One abolitionist challenged proslavery advocates by asking, "Where is the sentence [of Scripture] in which God ever appointed you, the Anglo-Saxon race [over another people], you, the mixture of all races under heaven, you, who can not tell whether the blood of S[h]em, Ham, or Japheth mingles in your veins"?[25]

But abolitionist claims were mostly met with skepticism because they advanced arguments based on the "spirit" rather than the "letter" of the law. Even when abolitionists made their case from the Bible, they were criticized because they were not able to cite a specific passage that explicitly condemned slavery. Instead, they had to argue from broader principles such as "love of neighbor" and the unity of humankind.[26] Southern theologians, by contrast, appealed to a "plain reading" of Scripture which they claimed clearly showed righteous and godly people who enslaved people with apparently no rebuke or accusation of sinfulness. Proslavery advocates grew confident in the Confederate cause because it seemed like the proslavery theological arguments respected the Bible's authority and employed a straightforward method of scriptural interpretation.

One of the best biblical cases against American slavery was not to deny that faithful people in the Bible enslaved others but to demonstrate how that form of slavery—the slavery of the ancient Near East—was far different from the slavery practiced in the eighteenth and nineteenth century in the American South. It was impossible to deny that some form of unpaid labor had characterized the economy of virtually every society for thousands of years. Yet enslaved people in these contexts had endured a different type of bondage. In most cases, they could legally marry and own property, and they worked for a specific term, not a lifetime. Slaves in other cultures were not born into servitude. They might offer their labor in order to pay off a debt, or they were captured in war. Slavery was not exclusively a matter of race or ethnicity in other cultures either. Of course, the point of this was not to suggest that slavery was a favorable way to live. Rather, this argument was used to demonstrate that southern theologians gave virtually no consideration to the unique form of slavery that existed in America.

So, unfortunately, the most potent biblical antislavery argument—demonstrating the differences between slavery in the ancient Near East and that of the American South—also took the most effort to understand. Attempting to list the differences between slavery as practiced in the Bible and race-based chattel slavery required an in-depth grasp of cultures thousands of years removed from the mid-1800s.

The argument required a rather sophisticated knowledge of the differences between Old Testament Israel and the New Testament people of God. For most Christians, even those sympathetic to the plight of black people, the southern proslavery advocates seemed to have a clearer and simpler biblical argument, one that did not require sources outside of Scripture or employ unfamiliar interpretations.

JAMES HENLEY THORNWELL AND "SPIRITUALITY OF THE CHURCH"

Many southern Christians admired James Henley Thornwell as their most adroit theologian. A respected teacher, a profound preacher, and a prolific writer, Thornwell distinguished himself as one of the most articulate proponents of a doctrine called the "spirituality of the church" in the years leading up to the Civil War.

Faced with growing pressure from their northern coreligionists to demonstrate allegiance to the Union and to the eradication of slavery within its borders, southern Christians rejected the call to take firm stances on the so-called "political" issue of slavery. In Thornwell's exposition of the spirituality of the church, he asserted that the church's one "Constitution" is the Bible, and the church has no jurisdiction over political or social matters. "The power of the Church, accordingly, is only ministerial and declarative."[27] According to Thornwell, the church can merely assert what the Bible teaches and must remain silent on that which the Bible is silent.

On the issue of slavery, the spirituality of the church meant that Christians could insist on the liberty of conscience to choose to practice or abstain from slaveholding since the Bible nowhere explicitly condemns it. Christians could morally regulate slavery and ensure that both enslavers and enslaved followed the commands of the Bible in their respective positions. What believers could not do was attempt to influence the government on slavery or other "political" matters. The church "has no commission to construct society afresh . . . to re-arrange the distribution of its classes, or to change the forms of its political constitutions."[28] Thornwell's vision of spirituality required the church, as an institution, to remain silent on the most critical social, political, and ethical question of the day.

The spirituality of the church reflected the ways segments of the American church set up dualities between physical and spiritual, moral and political, ecclesiastical and social. Just as the Virginia General Assembly legally separated baptism from emancipation in the 1660s and the Baptist General Convention separated the "political" issue of slavery from "church" issues in the 1790s, Christians during the Civil War made similar attempts to divide slavery's ethical implications from its political context.

The doctrine of the spirituality of the church has continued to influence the church in America, even to the present. Its adherents are diverse and often selective in how they apply the doctrine. The injunction against church involvement in policy issues was not upheld for the temperance movement, debates on evolution, attempts to keep prayer in schools, or discussions on how to overturn *Roe v. Wade*. Historically, the doctrine of the spirituality of the church tends to be most strenuously invoked when Christians speak out against white supremacy and racism.[29] Whenever issues like slavery and, later, segregation rose to the fore, the spirituality of the church doctrine conveniently reappeared.

This chapter did not cover many of the details of the nation's deadliest war. These events have been retold in countless articles, books, and documentaries. Disease decimated the young men on both sides who signed up or were drafted into the conflict. Battles claimed the lives of tens of thousands of Americans at a time. Women and children stepped in to fill the gap left by absent or deceased fathers, sons, and brothers. And amidst the chaos of the Civil War, the freedom of black people was left hanging in the balance. Despite the enduring racial prejudice on both the Union and Confederate sides, black soldiers joined the war and risked their lives for liberty.

It should give every citizen and Christian in America pause to consider how strongly ingrained the support for slavery in our country was. People believed in the superiority of the white race and the moral degradation of black people so strongly that they were willing to fight a war over it. This is not to suggest that the South had a monopoly on racism, but we cannot ignore that its leaders took the step of seceding from the United States in order to protect an economic system based on the enslavement of human beings. From then on, the Confederacy would always and irrevocably be associated with slavery. Pastors and theologians supported the Confederacy by providing theological ballast and biblical backing for the continuation of slavery. They prayed over the troops, penned treatises on the inferiority of black people, and divided denominations over the issue of enslavement. The Civil War paints a vivid picture of what inevitably happens when the American church is complicit in racism and willing to deny the teachings of Jesus to support an immoral, evil institution.

CHAPTER
6

RECONSTRUCTING WHITE SUPREMACY IN THE JIM CROW ERA

After the long night of enslavement and the chaos of the Civil War, African Americans turned their faces toward the warm dawn of freedom. For a brief, breathless moment it seemed as if the nation might finally live up to its guarantees of life, liberty, and the pursuit of happiness. But no sooner had the Confederates signaled surrender than the systematic machinations of white supremacists began to dismantle the hard-won opportunities of black Americans.

From 1865 to 1877, black citizens embraced their new roles as emancipated citizens. They ran for political office, opened businesses, started schools, and grasped at the American dream for the first time. This period witnessed one of the most vigorous seasons of opportunity for black people in the nation's history. But the end of the Civil War did not bring an end to the battle for black equality. White people in the North and the South sought to limit the civic and social equality of black people across the country. They devised political and economic schemes to push black people out of mainstream American life. To keep power, white Americans used terror as a tool through lynchings and rape, violently solidifying the place of people of color as second-class citizens.

Although the demise of legalized slavery could have led to full citizenship privileges for black people, white supremacists devised new and frighteningly effective ways to enforce the racial hierarchy. They romanticized the antebellum South as an age of earnest religion, honorable gentlemen, delicate southern belles, and happy blacks content in their bondage. They also constructed a new social order, what we refer to as Jim Crow—a system of formal laws and informal customs designed to reinforce the inferiority of black people in America.

This chapter details the events of those hopeful years of Reconstruction immediately following the Civil War, tracing the decline of black independence through the era known as "Redemption" and following the trajectory of the rising era of Jim Crow laws. Throughout this period many American Christians sought to take freedom away from black people, and they frequently invoked their faith to justify the injustice.

THE BRIGHT DAWN OF RECONSTRUCTION

No other period of American history held as much hope for black equality as the time of Reconstruction following the Civil War. For the first time in the nation's history, race-based chattel slavery was over, a thing of the past. Reconstruction could have been the start of a new America where black people enjoyed the full promises of liberty. Radical reforms could have led to the inclusion of other historically marginalized groups, including women, Native Americans, and the poor. While some significant reforms did happen, powerful forces conspired to re-create the former racial hierarchy in the postemancipation nation.

For around a decade after the Civil War, the newly freed black population energetically entered the civic life of the nation. In March 1865, President Lincoln established the Bureau of Refugees, Freedmen, and Abandoned Lands, typically known as the Freedmen's Bureau. Headed by General Oliver O. Howard, the bureau's capacious responsibilities included providing food and clothing to newly freed slaves, helping them locate family members who had been sold to other plantation owners, assisting the jobless in finding employment, setting up hospitals and schools (including higher education institutions such as Clark Atlanta and Howard University), and partnering with black people as they adjusted to life as free people. Chronically underfunded and understaffed, the Bureau suffered from corruption and ineffectual administration. Nevertheless, it signaled that at least some lawmakers believed the federal government had a duty to help the formerly enslaved and sought to offer some measure of restitution to address their centuries of persecution under slavery.[1]

This era saw a blossoming of black political participation. While many whites assumed that black people did not have the moral or mental capacity to participate in a democracy, black leaders quickly proved them wrong. Hiram Revels became the first black US Senator in the nation's history representing a state as notorious for racism as Mississippi, and P. B. S. Pinchback served for a brief time as the governor of Louisiana, the first black person ever to serve in the highest political office of a state. Fourteen black men served in the US House of Representatives at one time. During Reconstruction, 800 black men gained office in state legislatures, and at one point, black men became the majority in the South Carolina House. Countless other black men took on roles in government like postmasters, assessors, and customs officials.

Often led by black women, freed people aggressively pursued their education. Having been denied the right to literacy and other forms of systematic intellectual advancement, black people eagerly started public schools to learn their "letters and figures." One of the primary reasons black people showed so much enthusiasm about reading was because they were finally able to read the Bible for themselves. Literate black people no longer needed to rely on any white person's interpretation of Scripture; they could comprehend and apply God's Word on their own.

One of the heartbreaking but all-too-common activities many black people engaged in after emancipation was the search for friends and family members they had been separated from during slavery.

Because slaves were treated as property, white slaveowners would rupture black families by selling members off at any time for any reason. Husbands were torn from wives, children from parents, and siblings from one another. Many family members had no idea where their loved ones had been taken. After emancipation, thousands of freedmen and women embarked on a search for their families, often engaging in rudimentary detective work by posting an ad in the newspaper. One freedwoman looking for her father placed an ad that read: "INFORMATION WANTED: Of my father, Jerry Hodges, of Norfolk, Va. I was sold from him when a small girl, about 30 years ago. My mother's name was Phoebe, and she belonged to a man named Ashcroth." In the plea that follows she continued, "Should any of the family be living in the vicinity of Norfolk, they will please address EMMILENE HODGES, Leavenworth, Kans. Nb. Ministers please read in church."[2] Sometimes family members were able to find one another, but more often than not they were unsuccessful, never to meet again in this earthly life.

Formerly enslaved black people had a connection to the soil that few others did. They had toiled under the lash for generations, and the dirt from the land in the Delta and the "Black Belt" got under their fingernails and into their history. So it was only natural that after the Civil War, the men and women who had spent their lives working the land sought to own a piece of it. On January 16, 1865, Union General William T. Sherman handed down Special Field Order No. 15, which reserved a tract of land for black families 30 miles wide and 245 miles long along the east coast extending from Charleston, South Carolina, to Jacksonville, Florida. He promised each family a mule to help them work the land. Sherman's special order gave vitality to the dream of "40 acres and mule"—a hope for a redistribution of the land that would provide those formerly enslaved with a means of economic self-determination.[3] Yet the dream was short-lived. The blatantly racist President Andrew Johnson, who ascended to the presidency after Lincoln's assassination, ordered that the redistributed lands be returned to former enslavers, and many freed people went back to working the land under the sharecropping system.

RECONSTRUCTION ERA AMENDMENTS

Even after the calamitous events of the Civil War, many citizens and politicians maintained a moderate stance on race and civil rights. Unionists in the North tended to show more concern about the status of former white Confederates than for the status of freedpeople. Yet there were those who continued to fight ardently for the rights of black people in the post-Civil War era. They became known as "Radical Republicans."

White Radical Republicans such as Charles Sumner, Thaddeus Stevens, and James Ashley fought against the racist policies of President Andrew Johnson and his supporters. Johnson vetoed two bills—one intended to increase financial allocations to the Freedmen's Bureau and the other designed to guarantee black civil rights. The president claimed that using federal interventions to ensure black civil rights "violated 'all our experience as a people' and constituted a 'stride towards centralization, and the concentration of all legislative power in the national Government.'" Johnson also made claims that interceding for black people actually discriminated against white people. "The distinction of race and color is, by the bill, made to operate in favor of the colored and against the white race."[4] In opposing the use of government power to protect civil rights, Johnson voiced many themes that opponents of the political reforms that empower black people continue to invoke to this day.

Despite President Johnson's opposition and the timidity of many moderates, the Radical Republicans managed to pass three constitutional amendments that afforded black people unprecedented status in America. The Emancipation Proclamation issued by President Lincoln on January 1, 1863, only applied to a limited number of slaves. It freed enslaved persons in states that had seceded but not in the slaveholding border states that had sided with the Union. Even in the Confederate states, the proclamation did not apply to areas that had already succumbed to Union forces. Further, the effectiveness of the statement depended on the Union winning the war, which was not inevitable at the time.

To address this, the Thirteenth Amendment was passed, giving all black people in America their full freedom, decisively freeing all slaves: "Neither slavery nor involuntary servitude, except as a punishment for crime whereof the party shall have been duly convicted, shall exist within the United States, or any place subject to their jurisdiction," reads Section 1. The wording of one particular clause—"except as punishment for crime whereof the party shall have been duly convicted"— would later prove devastating to black people. For now, however, black people were free, at least in theory.

The Fourteenth Amendment followed, granting citizenship to "all persons born or naturalized in the United States." This did not apply to Native Americans who were still classified as "dependent" nations within a nation. Notwithstanding this failure to apply civil rights to all Americans, the Fourteenth Amendment effectively nullified the Three-Fifths Compromise of the Constitution and reversed the Dred Scott decision of 1857. After centuries of chattel slavery, the United States no longer legally considered black people as property.

Lastly, the Fifteenth Amendment granted black men the right to vote: "The right of citizens of the United States to vote shall not be denied or abridged by the United States or by any State on account of race, color, or previous condition of servitude." This amendment did not apply to women though, and racist whites devised numerous ways to suppress the black vote. It would take the Civil Rights Act of 1965 to reassert the right of all citizens to freely cast their votes.

THE MYTH OF THE LOST CAUSE

In the aftermath of military defeat, former Confederates searched for some way to make sense of their loss. They surveyed the devastation of the countryside around them, the disappearance of slavery, and the apparent demise of the southern way of life. Many southern eyes looked heavenward for an explanation of their loss and for a way to interpret the Civil War in cosmic and religious terms.

The "Lost Cause" is a narrative about southern society and the Confederate cause invented after the Civil War to make meaning of the devastating military defeat for southern white Americans. The Lost Cause mythologized the white, pre–Civil War South as a virtuous, patriotic group of tight-knit Christian communities. According to the Lost Cause narrative, the South wanted nothing more than to be left alone to preserve its idyllic civilization, but it was attacked by the aggressive, godless North, who swooped in to disrupt a stable society, calling for emancipation and inviting the intrusion of the federal government into small-town, rural life. Confederates reluctantly roused themselves to the battlefield not because of bloodlust or a nefarious desire to subjugate black people but because outsiders had threatened their way of life and because honor demanded a reaction. Even today, the Lost Cause mythology functions as an alternative history that frequently leads to public disputes over monuments, flags, and the memory surrounding the Civil War, the Confederacy, and slavery.

In the book *Baptized in Blood*, historian Charles Reagan Wilson details the religious character of Lost Cause mythology. More than just a story about the political fortunes of the South, southerners blended Civil War memory and Christian dogma together as a way of confirming their shared suffering and giving their losses divine significance. In an act of God's mysterious providence, former Confederates believed the Almighty had chastened them with the Civil War, allowing this bitter result to remind them of their first love and calling them to holiness.[5] The sense of holiness they were called to, though, did not include abolishing slavery or allowing black people their civil rights.

After the Civil War, the Lost Cause myth contributed to the cultural disenfranchisement of black people as they sought to participate as equals in a free society. While it is true that many southerners after the Civil War did not mourn the demise of slavery, others, including many clergy and religious leaders, did not change their mind on the biblical permissibility of slavery: "On the racial question, indeed, the southern historical explanation as embodied in the Lost Cause provided the model for segregation that the southern churches accepted."[6] White supremacy lurked behind the Lost Cause narrative and helped cement the practice of segregation in the church as the new normal.

Wilson points out that the Lost Cause functioned as a form of civil religion replete with saints, devils, liturgies, and symbolism. For advocates of the Lost Cause, no individual figured as prominently or garnered more respect than Robert E. Lee. Lee came to symbolize valor in battle and a manly Christianity that was equally chivalrous and courageous. A Confederate chaplain named R. Lin Cave lauded Lee's "reverence for all things holy." Another preacher of the time even went so far as to declare: "Lee was pure enough to have founded a religion."[7] In the Lost Cause myth, General Lee was the quintessential "crusading Christian Confederate."

In the aftermath of the war, southern women played a significant role in memorializing the losses and portraying them in a positive light. They engaged in fundraising, lobbying for, and erecting Confederate monuments and memorials. Founded in the 1890s, the United Daughters of the Confederacy viewed the raising of monuments as a core objective of their organization, and by all accounts, they and several other organizations proved successful. To date, North Carolina has over 140 Confederate monuments scattered in various public spaces. Texas has nearly 180 such pieces, and there are hundreds of others found in both northern and southern states. Tellingly, most of these monuments were erected several *decades* after the Civil War. There was a significant spike in monument construction from 1900 to the 1920s and a second explosion of Confederate flags and iconography from the 1950s to the 1960s.[8] These periods coincided with intense seasons of racial conflict in the Jim Crow era. Fitzhugh Brundage, a historian of lynching and the Jim Crow era, writes, "The installation of the 1,000-plus memorials across the US was the result of the orchestrated efforts of white Southerners and a few northerners with clear political objectives: They tended to be erected at times when the South was fighting to resist political rights for black citizens."[9] These monuments not only memorialized Confederate soldiers, but they also inscribed white supremacy into the landscape of public spaces across the North and the South.

In yet another sign of ongoing Christian complicity with racism, ceremonies like Confederate Memorial Day were often celebrated in Christian churches. Preachers eulogized Confederate heroes like

Jefferson Davis and invoked God's blessing on the "Old South." Organizations placed fundraising ads for Confederate memorials in denominational newspapers and magazines. The most prominent mouthpiece of the Lost Cause mythology after 1890 was *Confederate Veteran* magazine, which had its headquarters in the heavily Protestant city of Nashville where the Southern Methodist publishing house printed issues of the magazine.[10] In the South after the Civil War, the Christian-Confederate connection was visible in public spaces and in houses of worship.

WHITE SUPREMACISTS INITIATE "REDEMPTION"

The creation of the Lost Cause narrative furthered political battles to restore some semblance of the antebellum racial pyramid. Southerners had witnessed the destruction of their towns and the surrounding land as well as the abolition of the slavery-dependent lifestyle they had always known. If anything, the Civil War and the Reconstruction eras increased the animosity that some whites held toward black people. Supported by most whites in the South, several groups initiated a sustained and violent effort to reclaim the South from white northerners and freed black people. They saw their efforts as a divine mandate for the white man to take his rightful place atop the social hierarchy. They referred to this period as "redemption."

In biblical terms, redemption refers to God's plan to save people from their sins and make them into a holy nation. Christ achieved the redemption of his followers through his sacrificial death on the cross. He bought back, or redeemed, those who would believe in him by paying the price with his life. In many Christian traditions, redemption is a sacred theological principle that undergirds their hope of salvation. Yet in the hands of white supremacists, a social and political version of redemption justified the racial oppression and violence used to retain white power.

One of the primary goals of the "redeemers" after the Civil War was to prevent black people from voting. Black voters were an especially formidable power in southern states where black people formed a majority such as South Carolina and Mississippi. To circumvent the Fifteenth Amendment, white officials, often former Confederate soldiers and slaveowners, instituted restrictions on voters like the poll tax. The poll tax charged people money to vote, money that black people and even some poor whites did not have. They also enacted the "grandfather clause," which permitted people who could vote prior to 1867 and their descendants to vote. Of course, this excluded most black people. White voter registration officials also used "literacy tests" wherein potential voters had to read a portion of the state or national Constitution. Similarly, "understanding tests" asked black voters to answer obscure questions related to the Constitution. White "redeemers" selectively administered these tests to bar black voters from the democratic process.

White "redeemers" also introduced a deliberate and systematic reign of terror to prevent black people from voting, obtaining economic independence, and exercising their full humanity as citizens and human beings created in the image and likeness of God. This period of unrestrained abuse toward black people later led W. E. B. Du Bois to lament, "The slave went free; stood a brief moment in the sun; then moved back again toward slavery." White "redeemers" brought back the clouds of oppression to obscure the bright rays of freedom.

At every turn, southern Democrats blocked policies designed to enhance or defend black equality. In the 1868 presidential election, the first since the Civil War and the first since the death of Abraham Lincoln, famed Union general Ulysses S. Grant ran against Democrat Horatio Seymour, a northerner from New York and a supporter of the Union but a critic of Abraham Lincoln. Picking Francis Blair for his running mate, the two men ran on a platform supported by racism. One of their fliers proclaimed, "Our Motto: This is a white man's country; let white men rule." Sadly, this type of overt appeal to white racial resentment would remain a feature of American politics for most of the next century.

Several years later, the "Compromise of 1877" effectively ended federal Reconstruction. In a highly contested election, Democrats agreed to award the presidency to Rutherford B. Hayes on the condition that he withdraw support for Republican administrations and permit states to exercise "home rule" in the South. In 1877, Hayes ordered federal troops who were stationed in southern states back to their barracks. This meant that black citizens could no longer count on the government to enforce their civil rights, and they were left alone to face the terrorism of white supremacists in the South. One black man from Louisiana remarked, "The whole South—every state in the South—had got into the hands of the very men that held us as slaves."[11] One implication of this political compromise was that it effectively ensured that the battle for civil rights in America, even among Christians, would involve ongoing disputes over the role of the federal government in proactively ensuring the civil rights of marginalized people.

Conditions quickly degraded for black people in the South. In 1891, the Louisiana legislature codified segregation on trains, passing a law to force black people to ride in separate rail cars. The next year, in a challenge designed to reveal the absurdity of the rule, black citizens and lawmakers recruited Homer A. Plessy, who was one-eighth black (colloquially called an "octoroon") and could easily pass for white, to test the new law by riding in the "white" car. The railroad company had been alerted about Plessy's identity and promptly arrested him after he refused to move to the "colored car." Lawyers for Plessy argued that Louisiana's law violated the "equal protection under the law" clause of the Fourteenth Amendment.[12] Plessy's case against Judge John Howard Ferguson went all the way to the Supreme Court, and on May 18, 1896, the justices of the Supreme Court ruled that Plessy's rights had not been violated because it was a fallacy to believe that "the enforced separation of the two races stamps the colored race with a badge of inferiority."[13] The *Plessy v. Ferguson* decision legalized what soon became standard practice throughout the country for the next sixty years—the "separate but equal" doctrine. Had the nation's highest court ruled differently in this case, the color lines of the twentieth century might have been drawn much differently. In *Plessy v Ferguson* Americans had a choice—would they treat black people as full humans and fellow citizens? The court's decision meant they chose not to do so, and in the years that followed many white Christians upheld racial segregation and defended it as a biblical mandate.

CHRISTIANITY AND THE KKK

Though Nathan Bedford Forrest was nearly illiterate, he became one of the wealthiest planters and slave traders in the South by the start of the Civil War. When the conflict came, his wealth insulated him from serving in the Confederate Army, but ever-ready for a fight, he still chose to join as a private. His wealth earned him a quick promotion to Lieutenant Colonel where he quickly distinguished himself for bold military gambits and his accuracy with a gun. He recruited other southern white men with ads asking for soldiers who "want a heap of fun and to kill some Yankees." Forrest would eventually become infamous for his bloodlust as a Confederate commander.

Little was more offensive to a Confederate soldier during the Civil War than the sight of a black man in uniform. And on April 12, 1864, Nathan Bedford Forrest and his Confederate troops slaked their thirst for vengeance against the Union soldiers at Fort Pillow—about half of whom were black—by engaging in the utmost savagery. After a morning of heavy fire, the Union forces surrendered, and although Forrest later denied his part in what came next, it is clear that his Confederate soldiers commenced slaughtering their surrendered enemies. A letter from one of the witnesses later detailed the atrocities: "Words cannot describe the scene. The poor deluded negroes would run up to our men, fall on their knees and with uplifted hands scream for mercy but they were ordered on their feet and then shot down."[14] Nathan Bedford Forrest, the man who coordinated the butcher of black and white Union soldiers at Fort Pillow, went on to become the first Grand Wizard of the Ku Klux Klan.

The Ku Klux Klan (or KKK) has had three major iterations as an organization. The first came immediately after the Civil War. Six men in Pulaski, Tennessee, organized a "hilarious social" club to "have fun, make mischief, and play pranks on the public," calling themselves the Klan.[15] Within a few months the Klan turned violent, and their objective shifted to keeping whites in power by resisting Reconstruction efforts. In April 1871, the vigilante violence had become so unruly that Congress passed the Ku Klux Klan Act, fining or imprisoning anyone who "shall conspire together, or go in disguise upon the public highway or upon the premises of another for the purpose of . . . depriving any person or any class of persons of the equal protection of the laws."[16] Forrest sat for a Congressional hearing about his involvement with the KKK, and he apparently told a reporter, "I lied like a gentleman."[17]

The next movement of the Ku Klux Klan was in the early twentieth century. It did not focus on opposing Reconstruction, since Reconstruction had already failed. Instead, it fused Christianity, nationalism, and white supremacy into a toxic ideology of hate. In *The Gospel According to the Klan*, Kelly Baker argues that the Klan cannot be understood apart from its unique interpretation of Protestantism. The Klan of the early twentieth century "was not just an order to defend America but also a campaign to protect and celebrate Protestantism. It was a *religious* order."[18] Facing rising waves of European immigrants, many of them Catholic and Jewish, and the ongoing presence of free black people, the KKK crafted a vision of a white America and, more specifically, a white *Christian* America. Only native-born Protestant men, and a few women, were allowed to join. Many Klan members actively participated in their local churches, and some of the same men who conducted night rides on Saturday ascended to the pulpit to preach on Sunday.

The revival of the Ku Klux Klan in the early twentieth century was largely the effort of the son of a slave-owning Baptist preacher, a man named Thomas Dixon Jr. Like his father, the younger Dixon became an ordained Baptist preacher, but he found his true calling as a writer. Beginning in 1902, he penned a trio of books that romanticized the KKK—*The Leopard's Spots*, *The Clansman*, and *The Traitor*.

In 1915, filmmaker D.W. Griffith adapted Dixon's second book, a story about the founding of the Ku Klux Klan, into the nation's first blockbuster movie, a three-hour silent film called *The Birth of a Nation*. In this fanciful narrative, the Klan defends a noble South that faces invasion by northerners and arrogant black people who have the temerity to consider themselves equal to whites. One segment of the movie depicts a black Union soldier (actually a white actor in black face) pursuing a white woman into the woods to ravage her. Rather than succumbing to the brute's vile advances, she hurls herself off a cliff and dies. In the name of virtue and white power, the Klan assembles to kill the soldier and then embarks on a broader mission to "redeem" the South from outside agitators.

The Birth of a Nation was one of the first films shown in the White House, and President Woodrow Wilson enjoyed the movie so much that he allegedly remarked it was like "writing history with lightning!"[19] He held several showings for hundreds of guests in the White House. Woodrow Wilson's own racial views were rooted in his Southern Presbyterian upbringing. Wilson's father was a man named Joseph Ruggles Wilson, and he served as pastor of First Presbyterian Church in Augusta, Georgia. In 1861, Rev. Wilson hosted Southern Presbyterian ministers for the first meeting of what would become the Presbyterian Church of the Confederate States of America. Christian complicity with racism, as a generational trait, had now entered the White House in the person of Woodrow Wilson.[20]

The film proved so popular that it spurred a rebirth of the KKK. On Thanksgiving Day in 1915, a former Methodist circuit-rider assembled a group of white men to hold a ceremony. They ascended to the top of Stone Mountain, and in a ritual taken from Scotch-Irish lore, they burned a cross. They also constructed an altar of stone and placed on it an American flag and a Bible opened to Romans 12, a chapter that states, among other things, "be devoted to one another in love."

Religious themes permeated the ideology of the Klan and frequently appeared in its literature. Author Juan O. Sanchez explains that Klan members encapsulated their beliefs in the concept of "Klankraft—Klan activity in relation to its philosophies." According to the Grand Dragon of Oklahoma, Klankraft was "the sublime reverence for our Lord and Savior" coupled with "the maintenance of the supremacy of that race of men whose blood is not tainted with the colorful pigments of the universe."[21] The KKK interspersed Christianity with racism to create a nationalistic form of religion that excluded all but American-born, Protestant white men and women. To maintain their concept of a well-ordered society, the KKK utilized lynching, rape, and intimidation to keep undesirable people groups in their place.

The well-deserved disgust that is common today at the mention of the KKK can make it tempting for those in the twenty-first century to disregard them as an extreme group with marginal views that did not represent the majority of the American people and certainly not the Protestant church. But the KKK of the 1910s through the 1930s was far from marginal. Their views were quite popular with mainstream white citizens. As Kenneth Jackson, in his work *The Ku Klux Klan in the City, 1915–1930*, writes, "To examine the Ku Klux Klan is to examine ourselves."[22]

Far from being a regional group, the second Klan "was stronger in the North than in the South. It spread above the Mason-Dixon Line by adding Catholics, Jews, immigrants, and bootleggers to its list of enemies and pariahs, in part because African Americans were less numerous in the North."[23] Klaverns could be found in locales such as Indiana and Oregon. The Klan capitalized on white fears of just about anyone they defined as nonwhite, non-American, and non-Protestant. For example, Klan members successfully lobbied for the Immigration Act of 1924, also known as the Johnson-Reed Act, which limited immigration from select countries.

The second wave of the KKK proved immensely popular. Linda Gordon estimates that membership numbered between three and five million in the North alone.[24] Edward Young Clarke, one of the leaders of the public relations company that helped boost the Klan's membership said, "In all my years of experience in organization work, I have never seen anything equal to the clamor throughout the nation for the Klan."[25] Gordon also points to white Protestant complicity in the racism of the KKK: "It's estimated that 40,000 ministers were members of the Klan, and these people were sermonizing regularly, explicitly urging people to join the Klan."[26] The KKK's dedication to race and nation rose to the level of religious devotion because of its overt appeal to Christianity and the Bible. Many people believed that the KKK stood for the best of the "American way," and in their minds, that meant the Christian way as well.

THE RISE OF JIM CROW

The myth of the Lost Cause and the existence of the KKK bolstered the convictions of white people who still did not believe in the fundamental equality of black people. After emancipation, the white people in positions of power had to invent new ways to reinforce the racial hierarchy, and Jim Crow laws developed as a system of laws and customs to revive the older social order that slavery had enabled for much of US history.

The name "Jim Crow" comes from a minstrel character played by Thomas D. Rice in the 1830s and 1840s. Even though it is easy to characterize the worst forms of racism as an exclusively southern phenomenon, Rice actually hailed from Manhattan. Although he was not the first white actor to utilize "blackface," his career skyrocketed when he began painting his face black and playing the role of a likable trickster named Jim Crow. The plays portrayed stereotypes about black intelligence, sexual appetites, contentment under slavery, and obeisance to white people. In the years following the Civil War, as white people scrambled to recover a semblance of the racial order they once knew, they reached back to Rice's plays and saw them as an apt description of the social conditions of the late nineteenth century.

Jim Crow took the form of both legal policies and informal traditions designed to segregate and subjugate black people in American society. This system extended to all areas of the country, not just the former Confederate states. The North and West, for instance, had "sundown towns"—communities where black people had to be out before sundown or face violent repercussions. Some cities even posted signs that read, "Nigger, Don't Let the Sun Go Down on You in This Town." Towns such as Appleton, Wisconsin; Levittown on Long Island; and the Chicago suburb of Cicero, among hundreds of others, kept their communities intentionally all-white. Larger cities, including New York and Tulsa, could not entirely exclude racial minorities, but they conducted periodic "purges" of black neighborhoods to intimidate residents into moving out or staying confined to certain parts of the city.[27] Other Jim Crow laws and customs mandated that black and white baseball teams could not play on the same field, black and white people had to be buried in separate cemeteries, white students could not have textbooks that originally had been assigned to black students, and prison inmates had to be divided by race.

The sexual dimensions of Jim Crow deserve special attention. During this era, the prohibition against interracial sexual relations and marriage became one the most inviolable of social conventions in America. Under Jim Crow, the myth of the Lost Cause positioned white women as the epitome of purity and vulnerability, and by contrast, black men came to symbolize raw lust and bestiality. According to the racist myths about sexuality, brutish black men always prowled around for delicate white women on whom they could unleash their unholy appetites. In a stark demonstration of the hypocrisy and illogical nature of racism, Jim Crow advocates almost never mentioned the long-standing and more common pattern of powerful white men raping vulnerable black women.

On September 3, 1944, Recy Taylor was on her way home from late-night worship at Rock Hill Holiness Church in Abbeville, Alabama. Historian Danielle McGuire wrote that Taylor had been walking with two other churchgoers when a green sedan filled with seven young white men pulled to a stop on the road. Holding her hostage at the point of a shotgun, they accused Taylor, who had been with her companions at the church all that day, of stabbing a white man earlier that night. They ordered her into the back of the car and drove her to a secluded pecan grove. "Get them rags off," ordered the white ringleader. He and his companions took of their pants, and six of them raped her. Afterward, they left her on a dark highway, and she walked home alone. As word of the atrocity spread, the NAACP dispatched an investigator named Rosa Parks, who would launch what the black newspaper the *Chicago Defender* called "the strongest campaign for equal justice to be seen in a decade."[28]

Unfortunately, crimes such as the one Recy Taylor suffered had been an all-too-common feature of American life, beginning from the earliest days of slavery. In the Jim Crow era, rape persisted as a sexualized form of racial terror. Women were targeted for reasons as varied as retribution for perceived offenses to drunken fits of lasciviousness. As civil rights activist Fannie Lou Hamer would later explain, "A black woman's body was never hers alone."[29]

One of the implications of the Christian attempt to justify slavery by positing the inferiority of black people was the belief that black and white people should not have sexual relations or risk having mixed-race children. In the minds of Christian segregationists, racial mixing would dilute the purity of the white race and result in the "mongrelization" of white people. Southern lawmaker and notorious segregationist Theodore Bilbo wrote a book entitled *Take Your Choice: Separation or Mongrelization*. Among a litany of pseudoscientific reasons he listed for keeping the races separate, he also invoked the will of God: "Nothing could be more foreign to the ideals of the Christian religion than miscegenation and amalgamation. There is absolutely no foundation for advocating the mixing of the blood of the races as a part of our religious doctrines."[30]

Jim Crow proved devastating for black people. White racial terrorism during Jim Crow resulted in horrific atrocities like the development of the convict-lease system, reproducing what is often called "slavery by another name." The Civil War led to the elimination of America's most traditional form of forced labor—slavery—but the Thirteenth Amendment allowed for an exception. Those who were "duly convicted" of a crime could be forced to labor as part of their punishment. After the Civil War and emancipation, convict-leasing developed as a "legal" way for corporations to gain cheap labor and for state and county governments to get money. The process of convict-leasing began by entrapping black people, usually men but occasionally women, for minor offenses such as vagrancy, gambling, or riding a freight car without a ticket, and then saddling them with jail time and court fees. If the person could not pay the fee, as was often the case, they could have their sentence increased. A company, or even an independent employer, would then contract with a prison for inmate labor, putting them to work in mines, factories, or fields. In return the company would pay the local government entity a certain fee per worker. The workers themselves, as prison inmates, were never paid for their labor. They worked in appalling conditions that bred disease and violence. Many died and were dumped into unmarked graves.

The convict-lease system made black inmates "slaves in all but name."[31] Together with sharecropping, convict-leasing provided a way for white supremacists to methodically corral black people into the most menial jobs, depriving them of opportunities for economic advancement, and stripping them of their voting rights. Most notoriously, any perceived infraction of the Jim Crow codes could earn a black person "death by tree"—lynching.

LYNCHING

Jim Crow could not have worked as effectively as it did without the frequent and detestable practice of lynching. Laws alone were not enough to reify white supremacy; what bred terror was the combination of legal segregation coupled with the random and capricious acts of violence toward black people. Anyone black—man, woman, or child—could become the next lynching victim at the slightest offense, real or imaginary. Often, the murder followed a spurious accusation of sexual assault. Other misdeeds were more quotidian. For instance, white people lynched Elizabeth Lawrence for telling white children not to throw rocks at black children. Such voyeuristic and violent deaths represent the heinous apotheosis of American racism.

The exact details of the conflict leading up to the lynching of Luther and Mary Holbert in February 1904 are not clear, but we know it was about love. According to historian Chris Myers Asch, Luther Holbert, a black worker on the James Eastland plantation in Sunflower County, Mississippi, had been living with Mary, who was the wife (or ex-wife) of another worker, Albert Carr. Holbert and Carr had a dispute over the romance, and the plantation owner, Eastland, intervened. Carr and Eastland went to the Holbert's cabin armed with guns. Only the results, not the details, of the encounter are known.

But at the end of the altercation at the cabin, both Eastland and Carr lay dead at the hands of Luther Holbert.[32]

Jim Crow "justice" was quick and certain for any black man who killed a white man. Fearing for their lives, Luther and Mary Holbert went on the run. The alleged crime ignited the white population. Hundreds of white men, led by James Eastland's brother Woods Caperton Eastland, pursued the Holberts with bloodhounds guiding them to their prey. Mary disguised herself as a man, and they hid in the swamp. Three days later, the Holberts were captured. What happened next is a horror of inhumanity.

The lynching didn't happen immediately. It was planned for the next day, a Sunday afternoon after church so a larger crowd could gather. The murderers strategically chose their location for maximum intimidation of the black populace. It was to take place on the property of a black church in Doddsville, Mississippi. The black church has historically been the locus of religious and communal life for black people, so performing a lynching on church grounds would send a message to all black people in the area that no place was safe from white power and hatred.

More than a thousand people showed up to gawk at the lynching of Luther and Mary Holbert. The lynchers tied up the Holberts and commenced with "the most fiendish tortures."[33] First, the white murderers cut off each of the fingers and toes of their victims and gave them out as souvenirs. Then they beat the bodies of Luther and Mary so mercilessly that one of Luther Holbert's eyes dangled from its socket. Then followed the most heinous abuse. The *Vicksburg Evening Post* reported, "The most excruciating form of punishment consisted in the use of a large corkscrew in the hands of some of the mob. This instrument was bored into the flesh of the man and woman, in the arms, legs, and body, and then pulled out, the spirals tearing out big pieces of raw quivering flesh every time it was withdrawn."[34] Finally, the Holberts, who were still alive, were taken to a pyre. The white men cruelly forced two black men under threat of death to drag the Holberts to the fires. They burned Mary first, so Luther could see his beloved killed. Then they burned him.

Sadly, this was not an isolated incident. In 1918, Walter White of the NAACP, writing about a recent spate of lynchings in Georgia, warned readers of his article that "the method by which Mrs. Mary Turner was put to death was so revolting and the details are so horrifying that it is with reluctance that the account is given."[35] Mary Turner had been vocally protesting the lynching of her husband, and her cries for justice made her a target for a white racist lynch mob. When they caught up to her, they tied her ankles and hung her upside down from a small oak tree. Turner was eight months pregnant at the time, but that fact elicited no mercy from the mob, who applied gasoline and oil to her pregnant body. They struck a match and lit it, burning off her clothes. Then, while she was still alive, one man took a knife commonly used for killing hogs and cut open her womb. The child fell from Turner's midsection, and according to White, "The infant, prematurely born, gave two feeble cries and then its head was crushed by a member of the mob with his heel."[36] In the aftermath of this event, five hundred black people fled the community.

The tragic and infuriating lynchings of the Holberts and Mary Turner are just two examples among thousands. Lynchings usually took place because of a perceived crime—the killing of a white person in self-defense, calls for justice by the spouse of a lynching victim, or even for something less. Antilynching crusader Ida B. Wells found that many lynchings were over economic disputes. In 1892, white supremacists in Memphis lynched one of Wells's close friends, Thomas Moss, and two of his companions for no other reason than the fact that they ran a prosperous grocery store.[37] Imagined sexual predation on the part of black men toward white women was frequently an excuse too. But whatever the cause, the violence and exhibition of brutality were all too common features of the racial tyranny of lynching.

Few of the white people who participated in the lynching of black citizens ever faced legal consequences. Woods Eastland, who led the mob that lynched the Holberts, did face charges in the murders, but his acquittal was a foregone conclusion. After the all-white jury found him innocent, Eastland hosted a party on his plantation to celebrate. Lynch mobs would sometimes target black preachers with their violent attacks. Clergy often had the most education and influence in the black community and were more likely to be engaged in politics, either as advocates of specific candidates and policies or as elected officials themselves. This made black church leaders natural targets of white supremacist brutality. One such minister singled out for silencing by the Ku Klux Klan was Henry McNeal Tuner, a well-known and sometimes controversial bishop in the African Methodist Episcopal (AME) church. Born in 1834, Turner led a remarkable life as the first chaplain for "colored troops" during the Civil War, as a state legislator in Georgia, and as a bishop in the AME church during a period of unprecedented denominational growth.[38]

Turner's political activism and theology helped position the black church as a staunch opponent of racism and an advocate for the dignity of black people. According to a biographer, "For anyone wanting to know about forerunners of the modern civil rights and black power movements, Turner will be of great interest."[39] In one incident in 1869, the KKK warned, in a letter addressed to the "Radical H. M. Turner," that "your course of conduct is being closely watched by the owls of the night; do not be surprised if you should be aroused from slumber ere long by a boo hoo, boo hoo." Not to be intimidated, Turner responded with a public reply in the newspaper that said he attempted to live "square with God and man." Turner said, if that made him a radical, "I thank God for it." Turner concluded with a word of defiance: "If this Ku Klux don't like it, let him bring on his owls, and [see] if I don't send them to pandemonium faster than lightning ever crossed the heavens."[40]

Many white Christians failed to unequivocally condemn lynching and other acts of racial terror. Doing so poisoned the American legal system and made Christian churches complicit in racism for generations. While some Christians spoke out and denounced these lynchings (just as some Christians called for abolition), the majority stance of the American church was avoidance, turning a blind eye to the practice. It's not that members of every white church participated in lynching, but the practice could not have endured without the relative silence, if not outright support, of one of the most significant institutions in America—the Christian church.

Black Christians struggled to make sense of lynching from within their Christian faith. Writing many decades later, James Cone penned *The Cross and the Lynching Tree* as a theological reflection on racial terrorism. "Both Jesus and blacks were 'strange fruit,'" he wrote. "Theologically speaking, Jesus was the 'first lynchee,' who foreshadowed all the lynched black bodies on American soil."[41] Cone goes on to explain, "The cross helped me to deal with the brutal legacy of the lynching tree, and the lynching tree helped me to understand the tragic meaning of the cross."[42] Cone showed that black people could better understand Christ's suffering by recalling their own sorrow as it related to the lynching tree. At the same time, the cross provided comfort because black people could know for certain that in his life and death, Christ identified with the oppressed.

The decades after the Civil War proved that racism never goes away, it just adapts. Although the Union had won the military victory, the ideology of the Confederate South battled on. Attorney Bryan Stevenson put it this way: "The North won the Civil War, but the South won the narrative war."[43]

Some white Christians used their faith to support the fiction of the Lost Cause narrative and notions of a romanticized white Protestant South. Others bent Christianity to support the Ku Klux Klan and its racial terrorism designed to reinforce white power. The American church's complicity with racism contributed to a context that continued to discriminate against black people even after the deadly lessons of the Civil War. As the next chapter will show, this racist atmosphere and Christian complicity therein did not reside only in the South but permeated the entire country.

CHAPTER
7

REMEMBERING THE COMPLICITY IN THE NORTH

Ida B. Wells, the antilynching activist who always had her senses attuned to matters of racial justice, had a complaint with the organizers of the World's Columbian Exposition. Held in Chicago in 1893, the fair commemorated the 400th anniversary of Columbus's encounter with North America, and it sought to showcase the country's innovation. The massive event spanned 600 acres, featured the world's first Ferris wheel, and attracted twenty-seven million visitors. At the heart of the fair stood the White City, a cluster of white buildings in the neoclassical style that glowed at night from the illumination of electrical lights.[1]

Even at this amazing fair, white supremacy reigned. Black visitors had a special day set aside just for them called "Colored American Day" when organizers promised to serve 2,000 free watermelons.[2] Black people participated in the fair in many ways, but most controversial was an exhibit featuring sixty-nine Fon, black African people colonized by the French. Onlookers gawked at these human beings, and one journalist remarked on their "barbaric ugliness."[3] Ida B. Wells, who had moved to Chicago from Memphis in 1893, strongly opposed the underrepresentation and misrepresentation of black people at the fair, and Wells, along with others such as Frederick Douglass, wrote a protest pamphlet entitled "The Reason Why the Colored American Is Not in the World's Columbian Exposition." In a portion written by Douglass, he aimed to "explain the grounds of the prejudice, hate and contempt in which [black people] are still held. . . . So when it is asked why we are excluded from the World's Columbian Exposition, the answer is Slavery."[4] Douglass, himself a former slave, understood better than most that racist ideas of black inferiority not only persisted but permeated the country, including urban areas of the North.

The racism Wells and Douglass objected to at the World's Fair happened not in Charleston, Birmingham, Memphis, or some other southern city, but in Chicago, Illinois. Popular imagination has cast the South as racially backward while the North, although not perfect, has been characterized as more open-minded and accepting, a land of tolerance and freedom for black people. This notion harmfully depicts racism as primarily a southern problem while exonerating white people in the North of racism. In reality, the struggle for black freedom took place everywhere throughout the country, not just in the South.[5]

This chapter takes a closer look at the racial dynamics of areas outside the South, especially in urban areas of the Midwest, California, and the East Coast. The illustrations derive mainly from the Jim Crow era, but some examples from the civil rights era and beyond are included to further emphasize the national scope of racism. Racism played out differently across different regions but stretched from coast to coast and border to border. As the following examples will show, the church's complicity with racism was not just a southern problem but an American one.

CATHOLICS AND PENTECOSTALS WRESTLE WITH RACISM

Most of the stories included in this book speak about the racism of Protestant Christians, but some American Roman Catholics outside of the South demonstrated complicity in racism too. Although Catholics had maintained a presence in North America since the sixteenth century, waves of immigration in the early 1800s—mostly German and

Irish at first but then others from southern and eastern Europe—resulted in large populations of Roman Catholics in the urban North and on the East Coast. Recent immigrants soon adapted to America's biracial system of social segregation and subsumed their ethnic heritage under the label of whiteness.[6] Catholic schools generally excluded black people or included them only on a segregated basis.

Augustus Tolton was born a slave in Missouri in 1854 and fled to the free state of Illinois during the Civil War. Having been baptized Catholic in Missouri, Augustus was enrolled by his mother at the school associated with St. Peter Parish in the small town of Quincy. Although young Augustus sensed a call to the priesthood at the age of sixteen, no Catholic seminary in the country would accept a black student. With the help of some benefactors, Augustus worked for ten years to save enough money to attend seminary in Rome. Augustus literally had to cross an ocean and travel to another continent to escape the racism that prevented him from becoming a priest in America. His persistence paid off, and in 1886, he became the first person of known African descent to become a Roman Catholic priest in the United States.[7] The cardinal who ordained him reportedly told Augustus, "If America has never seen a black priest, it has to see one now."[8] Tolton went on to pastor St. Monica's Parish, which became a thriving congregation of black Catholics on the south side of Chicago.

Pentecostals faced their own issues with racial compromise. William J. Seymour, born in Louisiana in 1870, suffered from blindness in one eye. In his midtwenties Seymour moved to Indianapolis for work and contracted small pox, which partially took away his sight. His lack of vision in one eye did not stop him from receiving what he believed were divine visions from God. He pursued an ardent religious life, and after he moved to Cincinnati in 1900, he became acquainted with the holiness doctrines that taught a person could be completely rid of sinfulness through the power of the Holy Spirit. It was his encounter with the white minister Charles Fox Parham that set him on a trajectory that would impact Christianity nationwide and beyond.[9]

After moving to Houston, Texas, in 1903, Seymour joined a small holiness church, and the pastor there put him in touch with

Parham. The Pentecostal evangelist had recently started a school, and he encouraged Seymour to attend. Texas law at that time prohibited interracial schools, so Seymour had to sit in the hallway to listen to lectures while his white classmates sat in desks inside the room. Three years later in 1906, a holiness church in Los Angeles invited Seymour to preach for them, but they rejected his teachings on speaking in tongues and locked him out of the church. Undeterred, Seymour prayed and fasted for a month while he stayed as a guest in the home of Richard Asberry on Bonnie Brae Street. Seymour began preaching again, this time at the house. The crowds that gathered to hear him preach soon overwhelmed the small residence, so the evangelist began searching for a suitable venue for the worship services. He found the perfect site at an abandoned African Methodist Episcopal church on Azusa Street.[10]

After Seymour began services at the church on Azusa Street, hundreds of seekers crammed into the forty-by-sixty-foot structure to earnestly pray for the gifts of the Holy Spirit. Seymour and his fellow Pentecostals believed that the Holy Spirit gifted believers with the ability to speak in tongues, divinely heal illnesses, and obtain the blessing of entire sanctification, that is, utter freedom from sin. Spontaneity marked the gatherings. No order of worship regimented the time. People got up and preached as the Spirit guided them. Many shouted, danced, or fell into holy trances. The phenomenon attracted people from a wide variety of racial backgrounds: "Blacks, whites, Chinese, and even Jews attended side by side to hear Seymour preach. Eventually what began as a local revival in a local black church became of interest to people all over the nation, regardless of race."[11] One participant marveled, "The 'color line' was washed away in the blood."[12] But this exceptional moment of interracial Christian unity would be short-lived.

As the revival spread from Azusa Street in Los Angeles to various locations in the South, some segments of the Pentecostal movement began to split along racial lines. The Church of God denomination initially promoted integrated gatherings. Eventually, at the request of a black minister and his supporters who desired more autonomy, the denomination permitted a separate black General Assembly so long as it was overseen by a white man. Even Charles Parham, Seymour's erstwhile mentor, began to sharply criticize Seymour and the Azusa Street revival. He disdained the meetings "because of their 'disgusting' similarity to 'Southern darkey camp meetings.'"[13] By the time leaders had gathered to form the Pentecostal Fellowship of North America in 1948, not a single predominantly black Pentecostal denomination was invited to join. Although poor whites and blacks continued to mingle in more rural areas, the nationwide Pentecostal movement had become divided by race. Yet again, the church had demonstrated its complicity in racism, and the racial splits between certain Pentecostal denominations remained significant enough that the division required a very public moment of reconciliation called the "Memphis Miracle" in 1994.[14]

THE SOCIAL GOSPEL, FUNDAMENTALISM, AND RACISM

Concerned about the Industrial Revolution's tendency to concentrate wealth in the hands of a few and the growing problem of urban poverty, some Christians proclaimed it their duty to ameliorate the conditions that led to such large-scale poverty and suffering. In 1896, Walter Rauschenbusch graduated from Rochester Theological Seminary and accepted a pastorate in the New York City neighborhood known as Hell's Kitchen. Stunned by the overcrowding, inhumane working conditions, pitiful wages, and chronic health issues local residents endured, "Rauschenbusch realized that in order to serve the spiritual needs of his congregation he had to address the whole of their lives."[15] He deployed his Christian faith to challenge the structures that dehumanized his neighbors and in 1907 wrote *Christianity and the Social Crisis*. The book stirred many Christians to become actively engaged in politics and reform in their communities in a theological tradition known as the "social gospel."

In contrast to the social activism proposed in *Christianity and the Social Crisis*, a set of articles published between 1910 and 1915 called *The Fundamentals: A Testimony to the Truth* "repudiated the Protestant modernist movement" and "warned against getting too caught up in politics."[16] One chapter written by a professor at Princeton Theological Seminary criticized the social gospel: "To those who are crying for equality and opportunity and improved material conditions," he admonished, "the Church repeats the divine message, 'Ye must be born again.'"[17] His statements both echo and foreshadow the sentiments of many theologically conservative Christians, who insisted that converting individuals to Christianity was the only biblical way to transform society. Fundamentalists dissuaded other Christians from certain forms of political involvement and encouraged them instead to focus on personal holiness and evangelism.[18]

Historian Mary Beth Swetnam Mathews points out that Fundamentalists harbored a race-laced understanding of theology. When publishers distributed volumes of *The Fundamentals* to pastors and other church leaders, they neglected to place black ministers on the list of recipients. Instead, white Christians who adhered to fundamentalism coded their movement as white. When they explicated their beliefs, "white fundamentalists relied on racial interpretations that marginalized [African Americans]." These contenders for the faith "constructed their racial notions on the twin pillars of black inferiority and white paternalism, pillars that were common beliefs among whites in general."[19]

For their part, black Christians in the 1920s and 1930s did not fit neatly into either fundamentalist or social-gospel categories. Some advocates of the social gospel treated the Bible as a human book and subjected it to modern critical literary theories. In the view of some black Christians, this theological method seemed to substitute "old-time religion" for a new and unfamiliar kind of faith. Fundamentalism, while more recognizable in its emphasis on the Bible as the inerrant Word of God, fell short in failing to include a focus on racial progress. Black Christians might take a more traditional or a more progressive stance, depending on the issue. While they often exhibited conservatism in areas such as biblical interpretation, dancing, and prohibition, they also applied their religious beliefs to questions regarding the spiritual, political, and social equality of black people.[20]

The ongoing conflicts that social gospelers, fundamentalists, and black Christians faced over matters of race, as well as over the challenging conditions of urban environments, formed part of a broader picture of racism that pervaded areas beyond the South during the first two decades of the twentieth century. The decades that followed would only further exacerbate these racial tensions.

THE GREAT MIGRATION AND THE GREAT DEPRESSION

When Woodrow Wilson ran for his second term as president in 1916, his campaign slogan was "He Kept Us Out of War." At the time, the United States did not consider the ongoing conflict in Europe to be a problem that required American intervention. Wilson initially took a neutral stance, but escalating acts of aggression committed by the Germans toward the United States convinced Wilson to present Congress with a resolution of war in April 1917. During Wilson's resolution speech, he pledged to "make the world safe for democracy."[21]

As with every war America has fought, black soldiers participated despite racial discrimination within the military ranks. More than 350,000 black people served in the US armed forces during World War I, but they remained largely confined to menial jobs. Only about 42,000 black soldiers saw battle, and even then, white leaders questioned their valor and capability. Still, black soldiers often distinguished themselves. France awarded their highest medal, the Croix de Guerre, to the all-black 369th, 371st, and 372nd regiments for their fierceness on the front lines.[22] But no amount of courage abroad could eliminate antiblack racism at home.

Armed with a stronger conviction to fight for their civil rights, returning black soldiers refused to defer to Jim Crow laws and inspired other black people to do the same. W. E. B. Du Bois captured the spirit of their resistance in an essay titled "Returning Soldiers." He declared, "We return fighting. Make way for democracy! We saved it in France, and by the great Jehovah, we will save it in the United States of America, or know the reason why."[23] With a firmer sense of their own civil rights, many black activists began engaging in armed self-defense and open resistance to racism.

Just a few months after the United States entered World War I, a "race riot" broke out in East St. Louis, Illinois, which sits across the Mississippi River from St. Louis, Missouri. The riot began when a local aluminum plant brought in black strikebreakers to replace white workers who refused to work. In response, a group of white men drove through a black neighborhood of East St. Louis firing their guns. When two white plainclothes police officers drove through the neighborhood a short time later, they were shot and killed by residents, who did not recognize them as cops.[24]

The white mobs that descended on the city afterward did not have a specific target for their vengeance. Any black person would do. One family—a husband, wife, teenage son, and thirteen-year-old daughter—were visiting East St. Louis for the day when a mob unhooked their streetcar from the power lines. They pulled the family off and assaulted them with bricks. The woman was knocked unconscious, and she awoke in an ambulance lying next to her murdered husband and son. Her daughter had been kept safe from the mob by a sympathetic white store owner who hid her until the danger had passed. Official reports put the death toll at thirty-nine black men, women, and children as well as nine white people. The unofficial count, the one that included the people who had died in fires or were thrown into the river, reached over a hundred.[25]

The unrest in East St. Louis was a precursor to what became known as the Red Summer. In 1919, more than twenty-five cities across the nation, usually large urban areas outside of the South, descended into bloody racial conflict. A few of the more well-known riots occurred in Chicago, Washington DC, and Houston. Dr. George Edmund Haynes wrote a report on the causes and impact of Red Summer, and he concluded that much of the violence occurred because of "the persistence of unpunished lynching" that gave whites permission to seek retribution through mob action. Individuals in these groups fed each other's racial hatred so that "a trivial incident can precipitate a riot."[26] The presence of racial hatred in these areas outside the South demonstrated that the violence of white supremacy was not confined to former Confederate states.

Despite the pervasive racism that corrupted communities nation-wide, it still seemed better for many black folks to live anywhere other than the Jim Crow South. This led to a mass movement of black people from the South to cities in the North, Midwest, and East and West coasts, which has been referred to as the Great Migration. It would not be wrong to cast these migrating blacks as refugees fleeing the racial terror of the South. Some major cities saw their black populations more than double between 1920 and 1930. Chicago's black population grew from 109,500 to 234,000, New York City from 152,000 to 328,000, and Detroit from 41,000 to 120,066.[27] These rapid and massive changes were not without problems. The influx of southern black people changed white perceptions of the city and increased interracial tensions.

Around this time, Marcus Mosiah Garvey began bringing his international perspective to bear on the global issue of black disenfranchisement. Garvey grew up in Jamaica and then spent time in Costa Rica. He traveled broadly and went to school in England. Eventually, he became an advocate for Pan-Africanism, a view that emphasized the unity of all African-descended people throughout the world. Garvey started the Universal Negro Improvement Association (UNIA) and established his base of operations in Harlem. Though it had a brief and dynamic life as an organization, UNIA became the largest black organization in the nation. Garvey and UNIA started a newspaper, developed the Black Star shipping line, held international conferences, and became a touchpoint for nearly any black person interested in racial pride and uplift.[28] Garvey's UNIA coincided with the rise of the black population in urban areas like New York City and capitalized on a renewed sense of opportunity and assertiveness felt by many black people in the 1910s and 1920s.

Following on the heels of the Great Migration, the Great Depression further exacerbated interracial tensions when it began in 1929, leading to skyrocketing unemployment. This led to fierce competition for jobs between poor ethnic whites and the newly settled urban blacks. The depression quickly overwhelmed Christian churches and nonprofit organizations, and in the midst of the worst economic disaster in the nation's history, many charitable institutions ran out of money and resources to help the downtrodden. Poor people could not offer much help to other poor people. "Their churches and charities were broke. It was time for a higher power to intervene. They looked to God, and then they looked to Roosevelt."[29]

Franklin Delano Roosevelt was elected to the presidency in the 1932 election, and he held office until his death in 1945, just three months into his fourth term. During his time as president, he initiated the New Deal and instituted massive reforms that shifted the relationship between the federal government and everyday citizens. Prior to the 1930s, citizens viewed the role of the federal government as limited to protecting the rights of the people by providing checks on the government's ability to interfere with the practice of religion, assembly, and speech. The New Deal reforms ushered in a "rights revolution—that is, the extension of citizenship to include positive rights."[30] The government became involved in proactively securing and protecting the rights of its citizens, not simply restraining action that might impinge on individual liberties. Although FDR did not pass all the legislation he desired, some of the lasting results of the New Deal include Social Security, the Federal Deposit Insurance Corporation (FDIC), the Securities and Exchange Commission (SEC), and the end of Prohibition.

Liberal Christians generally supported the New Deal and, more specifically, the efforts on the part of the federal government to assist the poor and to grant workers the right to organize against corporations to secure better conditions. The Catholic Church weighed in on labor issues with its *Quadragesimo Anno*, an encyclical issued by Pope Pius XI in 1931 that warned of the dangers of unrestricted capitalism and declared that the function of the state was to protect everyone's rights, but that "chief consideration ought to be given to the weak and the poor."[31] The Federal Council of Churches updated its teachings in 1932 to explicitly promote "the right of employees alike to organize for collective bargaining and social action."[32] But not all Christians were as excited: "Fundamentalists were building vast institutional and associational networks within which Christian mission was reduced almost entirely to winning converts."[33] Many conservative Christians were not enthused about the growing influence of the federal government and its attempts to impose regulations on public institutions and private enterprises.

In 1937, Pepperdine College opened its doors in South Central Los Angeles. The founder and funder of the college, George Pepperdine, was a devout Christian and a millionaire who had gained his fortune in auto parts. Pepperdine applied his business acumen to starting the school, and from his initial concept early in 1937, he formed a small startup team that managed to open the school later that fall after just six months of preparation. The college's urban location promised to be an ideal setting to apply the college's "Head, Heart, and Hands" philosophy of intellectual development, spiritual growth, and training in practical trades.[34]

Pepperdine's efforts to start the college stemmed from his sincere desire to instill in young people both a practical education and a vibrant Christian faith. The Scopes trial of 1925—concerning the teaching of evolution in public schools—had convinced many conservative white Christians that public education promised only to inculcate their children with liberal social values and teach concepts that ran contrary to their interpretation of the Bible. Pepperdine stated that he "had seen young people go off to college with strong Christian faith and after four years of training under the guidance of cynical and materialistic professors, return home unsure of their spiritual nature . . . and faith in God." By contrast, his college would be subject to "conservative, fundamental Christian supervision."[35]

Unfortunately, this form of Christian education also included complicity in racism. For the first ten years of its existence, Pepperdine admitted black students but did not permit them to live on campus. Perhaps even more subtly, the free market became a form of economic gospel truth for Pepperdine. Spurred by the open-market business philosophy of its founder and a growing number of Christian entrepreneurs, the school taught its students to distrust unionism and federal intervention, specifically in the form of welfare programs geared toward the poor.[36] Schools such as Pepperdine indoctrinated a new generation of white Christians with ideas that would lend educational and ideological support to an individualistic approach to race relations and that would lead to an aversion to government initiatives designed to promote and protect civil rights.

FDR's New Deal had problems as well. Like many churches, the politicians who promoted reforms to the political economy conformed to the contours of Jim Crow. Ira Katznelson argues that the interventions of the New Deal in the 1930s and 1940s "excluded, or differentially treated, the vast majority of African Americans."[37] Due to the resistance of high-level southern politicians seeking to insulate the racial hierarchy in their communities from federal interference, Roosevelt and his administration compromised with racists to pass racially discriminatory laws. For example, while avoiding explicitly race-based language, Social Security provisions excluded most base-level agricultural and domestic workers—the vast majority of whom were black women and men.[38] This exclusion was not accidental; it was by design.

COMPLICITY WITH RACISM IN THE POST WORLD WAR II ERA NORTH

When Japanese forces bombed Pearl Harbor on December 7, 1941, America roared back, entering World War II. Yet the Roosevelt administration sought to exploit black people as soldiers while simultaneously maintaining racial segregation, effectively forging two separate but unequal militaries. Despite issuing Executive Order 8802—banning racial discrimination in the federal defense industry—earlier in 1941, FDR and his military leaders were unable or unwilling to dismantle racism in the everyday practices of the armed forces. Most black troops had white commanders at the senior levels. As with the first World War, black soldiers often remained in menial labor roles, and aside from a few notable exceptions such as the Tuskegee Airmen, they did not have access to advanced training. Most of the training camps for soldiers were in the South, and military life reflected the segregation of the surrounding community.[39]

Racial discrimination did not end after World War II. Laws designed to benefit returning soldiers often did not apply to black veterans. The Servicemen's Readjustment Act, better known as the GI Bill, included substantial aid designed to help military veterans reintegrate into civilian life. This welfare program assisted GIs in purchasing homes, paying tuition for college, and gaining health coverage. The GI Bill helped usher in a period of extended and rapid economic prosperity in America, but the privileges extended almost exclusively to white men. The Veteran's Administration, created to disburse benefits to returning soldiers, denied mortgages to black soldiers and funneled these veterans into lower-level training and education rather than into four-year colleges.[40]

In the postwar era, residential segregation became a major battle front in the black freedom struggle both in the South and beyond. Few decisions are more personal than choosing where to live. Proximity to good schools, extended family, grocery stores, workplace, and local amenities, among other factors, play into where one decides to reside. Owning a home in the neighborhood one chooses has often been seen as a decision based on hard work, individual effort, and free choice. Consequently, patterns of racial segregation appear to be the innocuous and unavoidable coincidence of individual preference, devoid of any major racist component. Views like these belie the deliberate and intentional nature of residential segregation. Through a series of rules and customs, government employees and real estate agents have actively engineered neighborhoods and communities to maintain racial segregation.

Current residential segregation has roots going back at least to the Great Depression. The financial debacle at the end of the 1920s led to a housing crisis because many homeowners could no longer pay their mortgages. Banks foreclosed on homes, and the rate of home ownership plummeted. In 1933 the federal government created the Home Owners' Loan Corporation (HOLC) to purchase the homes of people who were at imminent risk of defaulting, issuing new loans under new terms. To manage the risk associated with purchasing homes and offering loans, the HOLC investigated the surrounding neighborhood and other potential properties to determine if they were likely to retain or increase in value. The racial demographics of the neighborhood were often a key factor in assessing property values. "The HOLC created color-coded maps of every metropolitan area in the nation, with the safest neighborhoods colored green and the riskiest colored red."[41] Neighborhoods with any black people, even if the residents had stable middle-class incomes, were coded red, and lenders were unlikely to give loans in these areas. This practice became known as redlining. The HOLC policy was a form of government-sponsored racism. Today, even though many people think of segregation as something that occurred primarily in the South, the truth is that redlining affected countless neighborhoods in metropolitan areas across the country—St. Louis, San Francisco, Chicago, Cincinnati, and New York City, just to name a few.

Redlining practices persisted into the 1950s and 1960s, making residential desegregation one of the main fronts for civil rights activism in the North. In Detroit, Black Christians and their allies knew their white neighbors, even fellow Christians, were committed to maintaining this residential segregation, so an alliance of religious leaders—Catholic, Protestant, and Jewish—came together in 1962 to form the Religion and Race Conference. Their primary goal was "to assist middle-class blacks to move into the larger community." Members of the conference wanted to pose a "challenge to conscience" to compel white residents to embrace integration. A similar organization, the Greater Detroit Committee for Fair Housing Practices, focused on white churches. They handed out "Covenant Cards" that white Christians could sign as a demonstration of their commitment to residential desegregation.[42]

In addition to federal redlining policies, realtors and neighborhood associations used private measures to enforce residential segregation. For much of the twentieth century, "restrictive covenants" provided a legal, race-based mechanism to exclude black people from purchasing homes in white communities. "Private but legally enforceable restrictive covenants . . . forbade the use or sale of a property to anyone but whites."[43] These restrictive covenants, which also dictated details such as what color residents could paint their houses, effectively kept black people out of communities, especially new growth suburbs, for decades. Even after the 1948 Supreme Court ruling in *Shelley v. Kraemer* forbidding these racial covenants, real estate brokers simply dropped explicitly race-based language but still effectively excluded minorities from buying homes in white areas.

In the 1940s and 1950s, business and popular opinion readily recognized Levitt & Sons as the most well-known and prolific real estate company in the nation. The company had pioneered a way to mass-produce single family detached homes in a twenty-seven-step process based on the industrial assembly line model. Levitt & Sons built homes at a rapid clip to match the postwar demand for housing. They purchased large parcels of land and built houses close together in an almost uniform architectural style and size. These clusters of homes became known as "Levittowns" and formed the earliest pattern for the modern suburban subdivision.[44]

Unfortunately, Levittowns repeated the patterns of residential racial segregation that existed in other communities. In a nod to social pressures, federal policies, and the pursuit of profit, Levitt & Sons maintained a policy of racial restrictions. The company's president, William Levitt, defended his racist policies by proclaiming his innocence in serving the needs of his customers: "That is their [white customers'] attitude, not ours." He went on to emphasize that the commercial nature of the business precluded their ability to promote racial integration: "As a company our position is simply this: 'We can solve a housing problem, or we can try to solve a racial problem. But we cannot combine the two.'"[45] In this way, private businesses participated in forming the racially segregated housing patterns that have permeated municipal areas in every region of the United States, not just the South.

To maintain residential segregation, white homeowners would sometimes resort to forms of violence as brutal and terror-inducing as any found in the South. Like many other people living in Detroit, Easby Wilson, a black factory worker, found employment in the auto industry. Yet unlike many others, he kept his job during a recession in the mid-1950s and saved enough money for his wife and five-year-old son to purchase a home in a comfortable neighborhood. A white community on the northeast side of the city offered sidewalks, tree-lined streets, and ready access to the plant where Wilson worked. When he began looking for a home there, his real estate agent assured him that racism would not be an issue. However, once Wilson had closed on the home, the troubles began.[46]

Even before the Wilsons moved in, a vandal "broke into the house, turned on all the faucets, blocked the kitchen sink, flooded the basement, and spattered black paint on the walls and floors." That was just the start of a five-month-long assault on the Wilsons in retribution for their presence in an all-white northern neighborhood. Soon after they moved in, a crowd of more than four hundred white protestors held picket signs and chanted to protest their new black neighbors. Harassers frequently threw rocks and bricks at the home. An elderly white lady was found pouring salt on the lawn of the Wilsons' property. Police posted a car outside of the Wilsons' home on a twenty-four-hour basis, but even that did not help. Easby Wilson and his wife finally decided to move when their son started waking up in the middle of the night with "nervous attacks." A psychologist told them that their son, Raymond, "risked 'becoming afflicted with a permanent mental injury'" if they stayed and endured more assaults.[47]

The Wilsons' saga illustrates a wider trend of resisting desegregation in the North. For example, over the next several years, white residents in Detroit initiated more than two hundred instances of opposition to black integration, including "harassment, mass demonstrations, picketing, effigy burning, window breaking, arson, vandalism, and physical attacks."[48] Detroit illustrates a pattern that played out across the country. Although many white residents stayed and attempted to keep their downtown neighborhoods racially homogenous, many others decided to relocate to the suburbs. This phenomenon would become known as white flight—"a massive migration of whites to the suburbs"—and it certainly had many "nonracial" causes as well. White residents might have moved away from a neighborhood for issues related to "crime, schools, services, and property values."[49] But the presence of other factors in white flight does not preclude race from being an important consideration. The complex mix of issues—which include race—is a part of the way racism has adapted to changing social conditions in the United States. Subsequent chapters will take a closer look at how class and race concerns combined to make white flight not simply a spatial transformation but a political one as well.

In some cases, real estate brokers accelerated this white flight through a practice known as "blockbusting." Salespeople used racial fears for financial profit: "Through blockbusting, brokers intentionally stoked fears of racial integration and declining property values in order to push white homeowners to sell at a loss."[50] Brokers would warn white residents of an impending "invasion" of black home buyers. Whites, who feared losing property value and who harbored stereotypes about black people, would sell at a lower price to the broker. The brokers would then sell the properties at inflated rates to black people desperate for homes and comfortable neighborhoods. Blockbusting is an example of how some agents leveraged racism for their personal advantage.

The American church once again proved complicit in this racism by cooperating with residential segregation. In examining the white flight, Mark Mulder argues that churches actively participated in the racial relocation of whites from the city to other locales. "In many cases, churches not only failed to inhibit white flight but actually became co-conspirators and accomplices in the action."[51] Mulder examined seven Dutch Reformed churches in the Englewood and Roseland neighborhoods of Chicago. Over the course of the 1960s and 1970s, as neighborhood demographics changed, these churches relocated to suburbs where there was a higher population of white people. Certain evangelical theological positions may have made it easier to leave demographically transitioning neighborhoods rather than adapting to a new environment. For example, Mulder explains that congregational church governments meant that churches often owned their own building and had few outside checks on how they made decisions. "This manifestation of congregational church polity allowed for an easier departure of whites from central cities. . . . [These congregations] eventually found it much easier and attractive to leave the core city."[52] Rather than stay and adapt to a new community reality or assist in integrating the neighborhood, many white churches chose to depart the city instead.

Residential segregation only lent fuel to another dimension of the northern struggle for civil rights. During the civil rights movement, activists from the Coordinating Council of Community Organizations (CCCO) called on Martin Luther King Jr. for help. In a 1965 speech, King said, "We stand at the gate of a new understanding of the dimensions and depth of the struggle with racial injustice in this country; dimensions not limited by geographic boundaries or adequately addressed by civil rights laws."[53] King well understood the national scope of racism and the inadequacy of changed laws alone in eradicating antiblack discrimination. After studying several cities, King's Southern Christian Leadership Conference (SCLC) finally settled on Chicago as the site to advance their northern civil rights campaign.[54]

King announced his participation in the Chicago Freedom Movement in January 1966. The civil rights campaign encompassed residential desegregation as well as transportation, employment, and education issues. To effectively lead the movement, King decided that he needed to live in the same conditions as the people he intended to serve, so he and his family took up residence in the West Side neighborhood of North Lawndale nicknamed "Slumdale" by the local residents. Even though the landlords scurried to fix up the apartment in advance of the civil rights leader's presence, King's wife, Coretta, recalled, "The smell of urine was overpowering."[55] In August of that year, King led a march of 5,000 protesters in Marquette Park. The opposition from white racists was fierce. With police in riot gear waiting in the wings, counterprotesters waved Confederate flags and held signs saying, "The Only Way to End Niggers Is to Exterminate."[56] As King threaded his way through the throng, someone from the crowd threw a rock, striking him behind the ear. King's knees folded, and he sank to the ground, dazed. Resolute and determined, King stood back up and continued marching. That evening King told reporters, "I have never seen such hate. Not in Mississippi or Alabama. This is a terrible thing."[57]

Although the SCLC and local Chicago activists secured some

concessions from Mayor Daley and his administration, by 1967 it was clear that conditions for black people had not improved. King's foray into the North to continue the black freedom struggle illustrates the national scope of the civil rights movement and the pervasive problem of racism across the country—not just its ongoing presence in the South. The intractable problems of segregation and inequality contributed to a more self-confident assertion of "black power" that would later come to define the movement, especially after King's assassination in 1968.

EVERY REGION HAS RACISM

In the book *Up South*, Matthew Countryman writes, "Racism was never just a southern problem."[58] Racism stretched far beyond the states of the former Confederacy, affecting every region of the country. Though it would be far simpler to relegate racism to a single region such as the South as the historic site of slavery and the Confederacy, this is simply not possible. The South has often been used as the foil for the rest of America. People in other parts of the country could always look below the Mason-Dixon Line and say, "Those are the real racists." Yet the very conspicuousness of white supremacy in the South has made it easier for racism in other parts of the country to exist in open obscurity. Christians of the North have often been characterized as abolitionists, integrationists, and open-minded citizens who want all people to have a chance at equality. Christians of the South, on the other hand, have been portrayed as uniformly racist, segregationist, and antidemocratic. The truth is far more complicated.

In reality, most of the black people who left the South encountered similar patterns of race-based discrimination wherever they went. Although they may not have faced the same closed system of white supremacy that permeated the South, they still contended with segregation and put up with daily assaults on their dignity, and the church contributed to this. Compromised Christianity transcends regions. Bigotry obeys no boundaries. This is why Christians in every part of America have a moral and spiritual obligation to fight against the church's complicity with racism.

COMPROMISING WITH RACISM DURING THE CIVIL RIGHTS MOVEMENT

Fourteen-year-old Emmett Till did not live in Mississippi, but he would die there. Emmett begged his mother, Mamie Till Mobley, to let him go down south so he could visit his cousins and get a break from the confines of city life in his hometown of Chicago. Mrs. Mobley relented, and Till headed to a small rural town in the heart of the "Closed Society." On a hot August day in 1955, he and a few other black children went to Bryant's Grocery in Money, Mississippi, to hang out. The precise details of what happened next are not clear. It seems likely that Till had crossed an invisible line of Jim Crow propriety by flirting with or whistling at the white shopkeeper, Carolyn Bryant.[1] In any event, the perceived slight enraged Bryant's husband and his brother-in-law enough to drive to the house where Till was staying. They planned to grab the boy and teach him a lesson. Emmett would never be seen alive again.

Till's mutilated body—an ear sliced with a knife or shears, his femur broken, an eye missing, a cracked skull, and a bullet hole above his ear—turned up in a river a few days later. In a fateful and brave decision, Till's mother decided to have an open casket funeral so that the world could see what the hatred of white racists had done to her boy. The shocking pictures of Emmett's body showed up in *Jet* magazine and other media outlets and led to a national outcry.[2]

A few months later, Rosa Parks still had the lynching of Emmett Till on her mind when a white bus driver demanded she get up from her seat to allow a white person to sit there.[3] Although many people remember Parks as a meek little old lady, she had long been a fierce civil rights activist. Parks helped advocate for the wrongly accused Scottsboro Boys. She helped defend Recy Taylor, a black woman who had been gang-raped by a group of white men, and helped bring the despicable crime to light. Just a couple of months prior to the incident on the bus, Parks had attended the famed Highlander Folk School to learn more about civil rights organizing and nonviolent direction action techniques. Parks's refusal to move from her seat on the bus fit into a long history of her own defiance of Jim Crow and was just one prominent example of the vital role women have played in the black freedom struggle. Parks's actions helped spark a boycott that would catapult a young minister named Martin Luther King Jr. to national renown.[4]

Just twenty-six years old at the time, King had been recommended as an able young preacher who could mobilize the black middle class and church community. King considered himself first and foremost a preacher. He wanted to attend to his first pastorate at Dexter Avenue Baptist Church and pay attention to his wife and newborn daughter, Yolanda, not even one month old yet. At a vote to choose officers for the newly created Montgomery Improvement Association, Rufus Lewis nominated King for the presidency. Still hesitant, King said, "Well, if you think I can render some service, I will."[5] Thus started the public career of one of America's most well-known activists.

Examining the civil rights movement through the actions of Martin Luther King Jr. and another behemoth in American religious history—Billy Graham—provides two vastly different perspectives of the civil rights movement. King and Graham each had large grassroots followings and reached countless people in the United States and beyond through their speeches, sermons, and writings. Both show up frequently in the examples below because their views, while not universal, represent two approaches to religion and justice—moderation and activism.

This chapter focuses on the Christian moderates—mostly white and evangelical but also some black churches and ministers—who played it safe, refusing to get involved in the civil rights movement. These people of faith may not have given their full support to the most extreme racists, but neither did they oppose racists outright or openly disagree with racist objectives. While the civil rights movement has a well-earned reputation as a faith-based movement led by Christian pastors and lay people, our collective memory of the proportion of Christians involved may be somewhat skewed. In reality, precious few Christians publicly aligned themselves with the struggle for black freedom in the 1950s and 1960s. Those who did participate faced backlash from their families, friends, and fellow Christians. At a key moment in the life of our nation, one that called for moral courage, the American church responded to much of the civil rights movement with passivity, indifference, or even outright opposition.

BROWN V. BOARD AND "A CHRISTIAN VIEW OF SEGREGATION"

Nine-year-old Linda Brown likely had no idea that she would be part of a group of black families who would overturn the nearly sixty-year old *Plessy v Ferguson* decision and the nation's legal commitment to segregation in public facilities. In 1951, Brown's father simply did not want his little girl to have to cross railroad yards and a busy street to get to a school that offered a substandard education compared to the white schools in Topeka, Kansas.[6] Sumner Elementary school stood much closer to the Brown home and offered better facilities, better-trained teachers, and more funding for its programs. It also happened to be all-white. When the school's officials refused to let Brown's daughter Linda attend there, he joined with four other cases in the now-famous court decision *Brown vs. The Board of Education of Topeka.*

In explaining the unanimous decision of the Supreme Court,

Chief Justice Earl Warren wrote, "We conclude that in the field of public education the doctrine of 'separate but equal' has no place. Separate educational facilities are inherently unequal."[7] Warren was merely making explicit what was quite evident, that black and white facilities—whether schools, hospitals, or housing—were definitely not equal. The ideology that had led to segregation had never provided for the equitable distribution of resources. The *Brown v. Board* decision removed the legal keystone that had propped up racial divisions in public spaces, and in doing so it outraged segregationists.

The Supreme Court decision in *Brown v. Board* struck the South like a bolt of lightning. The reaction was swift and fiery. It came from all segments of southern society, including many white southern churches. Some preachers quoted the Bible to battle against the decision. In 1954, clergymen in the conservative and mostly southern Presbyterian Church in the United States (PCUS) gathered for their regular regional meeting of churches, and this assembly of pastors heard a message from G. T. Gillespie, the president emeritus of a Christian school, Belhaven College, in Jackson, Mississippi. In a carefully argued speech to the pastors in attendance, Gillespie outlined a "Christian View of Segregation." His argument reveals some of the specific ways Christians compromised with racism during the civil rights era.

Although Gillespie utilized various biblical passages to argue for segregation, he acknowledged, "The Bible contains no clear mandate for or against segregation as between the white and negro races." Segregationists like Gillespie resorted to so-called "natural law" arguments to bolster their case for racial segregation. In a section titled "Segregation Is One of Nature's Universal Laws," he stated, "There are many varieties of the bird family, but under natural conditions, so far as known, bluebirds never mate with redbirds, doves never mate with blackbirds, nor mockingbirds with jays."[8] This analogy invokes the specter of interracial sex to frighten segregationists about the possibility of black men sleeping with white women. It also refers to color—the white dove and the blackbird, the redbird and the bluebird—as an allusion to the racial issue at hand.

Then Gillespie's speech turned from "natural law" arguments to examine Scripture from which he contended he could still make "valid inferences" about segregation. Leviticus admonished the Israelites not to mix "diverse things" like wool and linen as well as different strains of cattle and seeds. Reasoning from this injunction, Gillespie figured that "the same principle would apply with even greater force with respect to human relations."[9] In other words, if different fabrics, animals, and plants could not mix in the Old Testament, it was best for black and white peoples not to mix either. Gillespie also referred to warnings against intermarriage between the Israelites and non-Jewish tribes as a reason to prohibit interracial relationships and integration.

Other ministers such as Carey L. Daniel, pastor of First Baptist Church in West Dallas, followed Gillespie's example. In a sermon later adapted into a pamphlet entitled "God the Original Segregationist," Daniel went so far as to make a direct comparison between desegregation and the schemes of the devil himself. Conversely, Daniel labeled Jesus the "Original Segregationist."[10] Though he could find no statements from Jesus supporting segregation, he argued that the Savior had never repealed the laws of segregation supposedly espoused in the Old Testament.[11]

Not all Protestant Christians were openly supportive of segregation, of course. Many were racial moderates, seeking to find a middle way between the various positions. One of the best-known and most respected evangelical leaders of the time, the Reverend Billy Graham, was a racial moderate when it came to segregation. To his credit, Graham went much further than many white evangelicals in an effort to desegregate his religious gatherings. At a crusade in California in 1953, Graham personally took down ropes segregating black and white seating in the audience. "Either these ropes stay down, or you can go on and have the revival without me," he said.[12]

Yet Graham, like many white evangelicals, held back from actively pushing for black civil rights. After the Supreme Court handed down the *Brown v. Board* decision, Graham deliberately avoided scheduling crusades in the South for a period to avoid getting embroiled in the more heated conflicts about desegregation. Shortly after *Brown*, Graham stated, "I believe the heart of the problem of race is in loving our neighbor."[13] While few Christians would object that racism is a failure to love one's neighbor, Graham did not carry that statement any further into the realm of institutional racism. Like many evangelicals, Graham believed race relations would gradually improve—one conversion and one friendship at a time. He viewed racial conflict as a local issue and a social matter. Furthermore, Graham was quite vocal in his denunciations of communism, something many conservatives also associated with the civil rights movement, and this association effectively dissuaded him and others from supporting the activists who protested racism.[14] Ultimately, Graham made it clear that his primary goal was evangelism. He took measured steps to desegregate his crusades and encourage Christians to obey the *Brown v. Board* decision, but he assiduously avoided any countercultural stances that would have alienated his largely white audience and his supporters.

Of course, other ministers of the gospel spoke prophetically against segregation, and we should applaud their stand. But their numbers should not be overestimated, and the backlash they faced for their bold action should not be overlooked. During the civil rights movement, activists who courageously risked their well-being for black freedom were few and far between, but Christian moderates who were complicit with the status quo of institutional racism were numerous.

THE CHRISTIAN MODERATE AND THE "LETTER FROM A BIRMINGHAM JAIL"

The year 1963 had been an especially eventful year for the civil rights movement, especially for Martin Luther King Jr. and the city of Birmingham, Alabama. A slew of bombings—including over fifty in a white neighborhood that was slowly integrating and was nicknamed "Dynamite Hill"—earned Birmingham the moniker "Bombingham."[15] Earlier that year, King had helped lead a boycott of downtown businesses in protest of segregation. On April 12, Good Friday, he was arrested and put into jail where he penned his renowned "Letter from a Birmingham Jail." Then in the late summer of that year, 200,000 marchers converged on Washington DC for the "March on

Washington for Jobs and Freedom" where King delivered his most famous speech, "I Have a Dream." The Sixteenth Street Baptist Church bombing happened just over two weeks later.

Martin Luther King Jr. knew that there would be a price to pay for his decision to support the black civil rights campaign in Birmingham in 1963. He did not take this decision lightly. King and his compatriots knew that to take on the city of Birmingham meant taking on their public safety commissioner, Eugene "Bull" Connor. King and the executive leadership team of the SCLC spent two days at a retreat to consider the implications of a campaign in the city. Bull Connor had a reputation. During Connor's tenure over the local law enforcement, several racially motivated bombings remained "unsolved." There was such a substantial risk of physical harm and even death that King reportedly said to his fellow leaders, "I have to tell you that in my judgment, some of the people sitting here today will not come back alive from this campaign. And I want you to think about it."[16] At the same time, a grassroots campaign of civil rights activism was gaining momentum in Birmingham. But it needed a boost, something only King and the SCLC could offer, if it hoped to secure lasting victory.

As expected, police soon arrested and jailed King. While he was incarcerated, eight white clergymen wrote a letter to King and his supporters advising them to depart and let the community handle race relations for itself. Today, much of the attention focuses on King's letter, but the message King received from white, moderate Christians also deserves attention. Their message provides a stark illustration of how much of the American church responded to King and the civil rights movement.

In a missive, which was published in the local newspaper, the ministers criticize both the protests and the involvement of non-Birmingham residents. "We are now confronted by a series of demonstrations by some of our Negro citizens directed and led in part by outsiders. We recognize the natural impatience of people who feel that their hopes are slow in being realized. But we are convinced that these demonstrations are unwise and untimely."[17] In their estimation, King did not know the contours of the local situation, and they believed his presence, along with the protests he led, threatened to undo the encouraging progress Birmingham had seen in recent months.

This group of mostly Christian, white moderates—which included Baptists, Methodists, a Presbyterian, and a Jewish Rabbi—contended that civil rights remedies should be pursued through litigation instead of through boycotts and marches: "When rights are consistently denied, a cause should be pressed in the courts and in negotiations among local leaders, and not in the streets."[18] While they recognized King's rhetoric of nonviolence, they still believed that his tactics would actually undermine democracy and increase the likelihood of bloodshed.

What comes through in the letter, more than anything else, is their reasonableness. They acknowledge the "natural impatience" of black people whose civil rights have been denied. They affirmed that "hatred and violence have no sanction in our religious and political traditions."[19] They even allowed that black people had recourse to pursue remedies for certain issues in the courts. What then could be objectionable about a group of religious community leaders uniting to encourage restraint and patience in pursuing civil rights for black people?

But it is the very reasonableness of the letter that reveals the underlying problem of complicity with racism. This letter from white Christian moderates illustrates the broader failure of the white church, a failure to recognize the daily indignity of American racism and the urgency the situation demanded. These clergymen likely had good intentions, but they did not realize that the talking and negotiating for which they advocated had been attempted and had yielded little to no progress. They denounced the violence that direct action would *supposedly* incite, but they did relatively little about the countless lynchings, church bombings, and beatings black people across the nation suffered at the hands of segregationists. They were overly cautious when the circumstances demanded a measure of outrage and courageous confrontation. In general, this approach exemplifies how many Christian moderates during the civil rights movement responded, promoting a gradual approach to resolving racial issues and minimizing the suffering and hardship of the marginalized, who had been waiting centuries for justice.

Martin Luther King Jr.'s "Letter from a Birmingham Jail" has since proven to be one of the greatest works of Christian political theology ever produced by an American. His eloquent and rich response conveys the philosophical and spiritual issues at stake in the civil rights movement. King recognized the need for Christians to be allies, working together in the black freedom struggle, while acknowledging that most of the white church had chosen the path of complicity over advocacy.

Even though King's "Letter from a Birmingham Jail" was a direct response to white Christians, we should acknowledge that not all Christian moderates were white. Rev. Joseph H. Jackson was the pastor of Olivet Baptist Church in Chicago and president of the National Baptist Convention. He was even known by some as the "Negro Pope."[20] His authoritarian style and influence over the largest black Baptist body in the nation made him either a valuable ally or a formidable opponent. Martin Luther King Jr. had known Jackson since King was ten years old because Jackson had been a frequent houseguest of King's father, "Daddy King," in Atlanta. But when the younger King became active in the civil rights movement and gained a reputation as the most prominent black minister, Jackson chose to strongly oppose the movement and King in particular. He labeled King a "hoodlum" and "powder-keg philosopher." Jackson deplored the direct-action campaigns of civil rights activists, and Jackson's opposition to the movement's tactics ultimately led King and 2,000 others to leave the denomination and form the Progressive National Baptist Convention (PNBC) in 1961.[21]

But King was not alone in advocating for a more direct and active approach to securing civil rights for black Americans. Fannie Lou Hamer, a Mississippi sharecropper turned national civil rights icon, also advocated for direct action—and for good reasons. Born to sharecropping parents as the youngest of twenty children, Hamer grew up in the Mississippi Delta and experienced some of America's worst poverty. In 1963, police officers arrested her and other black civil rights workers as they returned to Mississippi on a bus. The officers took the activists to a rural jail and proceeded to mercilessly beat them. Hamer's abuse only served to fuel her conviction to secure racial equality and economic justice. Given all she endured, she had little patience for anyone too complacent to get involved in the black freedom struggle. Hamer frequently criticized "chicken-eatin' preachers" who were more concerned about comfort and "selling out for the big Cadillacs" than sacrificing for the sake of justice.[22]

It is far more difficult to trace the actions of Christian moderates when compared to the more bombastic resisters in the movement. Their actions were at times supportive of black civil rights, while at other times they stood against the movement. But what we must not ignore is that while segregationist politicians spewed forth words of "interposition and nullification,"[23] while magazines published editorials calling civil rights activists Communists, and while juries acquitted violent racists of criminal acts, none of this would have been possible without the complicity of Christian moderates.

THE CIVIL RIGHTS ACT OF 1964

On July 2, 1964, Martin Luther King Jr. stood directly behind President Lyndon B. Johnson at the White House, beaming with satisfaction. King and a mixed-race crowd of observers looked on as the commander-in-chief signed into law the most sweeping piece of civil rights legislation since the nineteenth century. The act Johnson signed created the Equal Employment Opportunity Commission (EEOC), which authorized the federal government to enforce desegregation and prevented other types of discrimination based on religion and sex.

The passing of the Civil Rights Act only happened in the wake of some of the most tumultuous events in modern American history. In 1961, the Freedom Riders tested law enforcement's commitment to desegregation among interstate travelers, and the interracial group of riders ended up bloody and imprisoned. In 1962, a mob of white segregationists rioted in protest of the University of Mississippi admitting its first black student, James Meredith, which left a French journalist dead. In June 1963, an assassin murdered NAACP Field Secretary Medgar Evers outside of his home in Jackson, Mississippi. In August 1963, the March for Jobs and Freedom in Washington DC brought hundreds of thousands of people to the nation's capital in support of racial justice. In September of that year, the Sixteenth Street Baptist Church bombing stole the lives of four young black girls. And in November 1963, an assassin shot and killed President John F. Kennedy as he rode in a motorcade in Dallas.[24]

Martin Luther King Jr. and his Southern Christian Leadership Conference stood at the center of the prominent events of the civil rights movement in the early 1960s. King understood the price this piece of legislation had cost him and his fellow activists. After Congress approved the Civil Rights Act, King asserted that the law would "bring practical relief to the Negro in the South, and will give the Negro in the North a psychological boost that he sorely needs."[25] To King and his allies in the struggle, the Civil Rights Act and similar legislation represented significant steps toward his dream of racial equality. King recognized the necessity of changing the laws to ensure the rights of all citizens, and he did not shy away from direct action that caused constructive conflict in his efforts to bring about change.

By contrast, when we look at Billy Graham and the moderate Christians he represented, we see they took a more subdued stance toward the Civil Rights Act. Graham helped start and was intimately involved with the publication of *Christianity Today*, the de facto voice of white evangelicalism. The magazine refused to endorse the act, largely because it was not in keeping with the magazine's evangelical belief that social change came best through personal conversion. A black journalist reflecting on Graham's position on legislation like the Civil Rights Act remarked that Graham did not "walk with protestors or call for open housing or desegregated churches" because "he's too busy praying."[26] While Graham did not denounce the civil rights legislation, he did not put forth much effort to commend it either.

The responses of King and Graham to the Civil Rights Act, and their participation or lack thereof in achieving its passage, illustrates the gulf between the approaches taken by Christian activists and

Christian moderates. Throughout the civil rights movement, a small cadre of Christians courageously defied the status quo at the risk of their freedom, livelihoods, and even their very lives. Christian moderates may not have objected to the broader principles of racial equality, but they offered tepid support and at times outright skepticism.

URBAN UPRISINGS AND "LAW AND ORDER"

Martin Luther King Jr. once said, "I think we've got to see that a riot is the language of the unheard."[27] By contrast, in a sermon entitled "Rioting or Righteousness," Billy Graham stated, "There is no doubt that the rioting, looting, and crime in America have reached a point of anarchy."[28] Each of these Christian leaders was responding to a recent string of urban uprisings involving black inner-city residents and their conflicts with the police. Throughout the 1960s, civil unrest bubbled over into rioting across the nation in places such as Harlem, Philadelphia, Omaha, and Newark. The differing responses of King and Graham to these riots further shows how Christian activists interpreted the civil rights movement differently from Christian moderates. The story of Ronald Frye illustrates the difference.

Ronald Frye wanted to celebrate. He had just been discharged from his service with the Air Force on August 11, 1965. Frye and his older brother Marquette went out for drinks. Later that night they got into a car to drive home. Just a few blocks from their house in the Watts neighborhood of Los Angeles, police officers pulled the younger Frye over for weaving in and out of the lane. Frye, who was black, got into an extended verbal altercation with the white police officers, and as the argument continued crowds of neighbors gathered. Soon their mother, Rena Frye, heard about the commotion and walked over to where her sons and the police were clashing. Mrs. Frye berated her boys for drinking even as she tried to defend them from getting arrested. The tumult turned physical as more officers arrived, and they arrested all three Fryes as the crowd taunted and jeered at the police. Rumors of police brutality swirled throughout the growing crowd, and groups began throwing rocks at the dozens of officers who had gathered to quell the chaos. Then the crowd turned to other property, breaking windows, stealing goods, and roving the streets.[29]

The following six days of urban uprisings in the Watts neighborhood of Los Angeles resulted in 34 deaths, over 1,000 injuries, $34 million in damages, and nearly 4,000 arrests.[30] The violence, damage, and vocal opposition to calls for civility contrasted with the peaceful marches and freedom songs of the civil rights movement in the South. Christians, like the rest of America, watched the events unfold with a mixture of curiosity and confusion.

When Billy Graham learned of the unrest in Watts, he flew to the site to personally survey the scene. Graham strapped on a bulletproof vest and boarded a helicopter to hover above the devastation and destruction. Graham was appalled. He saw in Watts the unraveling of the fabric of the nation. "It cannot be overlooked that this kind of disturbance is being used by those whose ultimate end is to overthrow the American government." He called it a "dress rehearsal for a revolution." Graham said that the nation needed "tough laws" to crack down on such flagrant disregard for authority.[31] This "law-and-order" rhetoric resonated with white evangelicals as well, and it led many to be critical of civil rights activists in general. These Christians were not denying that blacks were discriminated against or that conditions in the inner city were troublesome. But they believed the solution to the problem was to trust the system. Christian moderates insisted on obeying the law, working through the courts, and patiently waiting for transformation.

King and other activists took a different view. King understood that the chaos of Watts did not emerge from a single incident. While not excusing the violence or the indiscriminate lawlessness, he also knew that the black residents of Watts had witnessed the nearly all-white police force repeatedly brutalizing their neighbors. The people living in this South Central Los Angeles neighborhood felt trapped by the forces of poverty, incarceration, failing schools, and racism. Though activists had been working for change over the course of many years, the cries of the people went largely unheard. As an alternative to gradual change through the system, which was frequently ineffective and ignored, they used the riots to call attention to their plight. In contrast to moderates like Graham who emphasized respect for existing laws and a crackdown on the "radicals" as the solution to urban uprisings, King saw a different remedy: "Social justice and progress are the absolute guarantors of riot prevention. There is no other answer."[32]

Many Christian moderates failed to incorporate the larger context of the years of systemic racism into their understanding of the civil rights movement. The failure on the part of these moderate Christians and the broader citizenry of the nation to respond to the evils of segregation and inequality experienced in black communities would, in subsequent years, help spur another expression of the black freedom struggle, the Black Power Movement.

BLACK POWER MOVEMENT AND BLACK ALTERNATIVES TO CHRISTIANITY

Stokely Carmichael of the Student Nonviolent Coordinating Committee (SNCC) did not invent the phrase "black power," but he certainly helped popularize it. In 1962, James Meredith became the first black person to integrate the University of Mississippi. Four years later, Meredith initiated his solo "March Against Fear," but on the second day of his nonviolent walk from Memphis to Jackson, Mississippi, a gunman shot him. Meredith survived, and the incident mobilized activists across the country including the twenty-four-year-old Carmichael. After Carmichael was released from yet another stint in jail for protesting, he ascended a makeshift stage erected on the back of a pickup truck and said, "This is the twenty-seventh time I have been arrested. I ain't going to jail no more." Then, at the urging of his associate Willie Ricks, Carmichael unleashed a fateful phrase: "We been saying freedom for six years and we ain't got nothin'. What we got to start saying now is Black Power. We want Black Power! We want Black Power!"[33]

The phrase "black power" resonated with black people all across the United States. It echoed Marcus Garvey's exhortations of black pride and black self-sufficiency. The history of calls for black independence and racial defiance is a long one. The Nation of Islam (NOI) began in Detroit in the 1930s and became an alternative to Christianity for many black people who had become disillusioned with the Christian religion's seeming impotence in the face of potent American prejudice. The movement gained several prominent adherents during the 1960s. Malcolm X served as its charismatic spokesman, and his penetrating insights about the racial conditions of black people and the corresponding racism of white people both enraged and enthused his listeners.

One of the most well-known Nation of Islam converts was the bombastic boxer Muhammad Ali. Born as Cassius Clay in Louisville, Kentucky, in 1942, Clay became a world champion heavyweight known for his braggadocio as well as his activism. In 1966, Ali refused to submit to the draft and fight in Vietnam, citing his religious beliefs for doing so. By this time Clay had changed his name to Muhammad Ali and had converted to the Nation of Islam. In a letter to his wife just a couple of years after his conversion, Ali explained in more detail why he had embraced "the Nation." As a teenager, a NOI member had given him one of their newspapers, and inside was a cartoon depicting a white slave owner whipping an enslaved black man while also telling him to pray to Christ. As one biographer explains, "The cartoon awakened [Ali], and he realized that he hadn't chosen Christianity. He hadn't chosen the name Cassius Clay. So why did he have to keep those vestiges of slavery?"[34] A century had passed since the Civil War, and it was the height of the civil rights movement, yet Ali and many other black people still saw Christianity as the religion of the enslavers, the belief system of those who oppressed black people.

THE EVERYDAY RACISM OF AMERICAN CHRISTIANS

Up to this point, the discussions about the civil rights movement of the 1950s and 1960s have revolved around a few famous individuals and organizations—Martin Luther King Jr., Rosa Parks, Billy Graham, the NAACP, SNCC, and others—but this should not prevent our examination of everyday Christians, those who never made headlines or marched for or against black enfranchisement. These women and men filled the pews in their churches on Sunday morning, prayed before family dinners, and did their best to work hard and provide for their loved ones. Some collaborated with the vocal and visible individuals who enforced racial segregation in their communities. Sadly, millions of everyday Christians saw no contradiction between their faith and the racism they practiced in subtle yet ubiquitous ways.

In a book on the development of modern conservatism titled *White Flight*, historian Kevin Kruse details how many Christians actively opposed residential desegregation in their Atlanta neighborhoods. In the mid-1950s, Christians in Kirkwood, Georgia—a neighborhood in the city that was "Too Busy to Hate"—declared the boundaries of their racial tolerance to be their own backyards. In a survey that asked, "Do you attend church in this neighborhood?" seventy percent of respondents said yes, indicating a clear Christian, or at least church-going, majority.[35] Pastors and other church leaders actively urged their members not to sell their homes to black people. "'If everyone simply refuses to sell to colored,' the pastors assured residents, 'then every-thing will be fine.'" They pleaded with church members: "Please help us 'Keep Kirkwood White' and preserve our Churches and homes."[36] When these efforts failed, and one or two black families moved into the neighborhood, many of the white residents moved out. Churches shut their doors or fled to the all-white suburbs.[37] Today, even more than fifty years later, many of these communities remain almost as racially segregated now as they were then.[38]

Schools also became a battleground for Christians committed to segregation. Some Christian parents, faced with the unconscionable prospect of little white girls attending school with little black boys and eventually growing up, falling in love, and having brown babies, started "segregation academies." Because these were private schools, these institutions did not have to abide by the *Brown v Board* mandate for racial integration, which only applied to public schools. A 1972 report entitled "It's Never Over in the South" found that many of these newly formed schools used the word "Christian" or "Church" in their name. The report went on to state that "individual Protestant churches in most cities have participated and often led the private school movement during desegregation."[39]

In the book *Blood Done Signed My Name*, an autobiographical narrative of a lynching in his hometown, historian Timothy Tyson speaks of his experience growing up as a preacher's kid in segregated Sanford, North Carolina. His father, Vernon Tyson, was a relatively progressive Methodist pastor who intentionally sought to work for racial justice and integration. Rev. Tyson's Christian convictions about race earned him frequent trouble with his congregation and the local townspeople. Inspired by MLK's leadership and the sacrifices of the activists in the Birmingham campaign of 1963, the elder Tyson wrote a letter to the editor of the local newspaper. Echoing themes from "Letter from a Birmingham Jail," Tyson enlisted churches in the task of racial reformation. "Our churches ought to open their doors to every person for whom Jesus Christ died and thus become the headlights of our community rather than the tail-lights." In response, the newspaper editor chided the pastor that leaders who went "too far, too fast" ended up without anyone to lead and possibly without a pulpit too.[40]

In another instance, Rev. Tyson opened a house where the Methodist Youth Fellowship could meet. The "hippies" with long hair and guitars soon showed up, and a few of them even had black friends who accompanied them. When word got out that young white girls might be associating with young black boys, the preacher recalled, "some of my members came in and asked me to keep the blacks out."[41] On multiple occasions, Rev. Tyson had to decide whether to preach the word or pursue popularity. The younger Tyson recalls a time when his father invited a well-known black preacher, Dr. Samuel Proctor, to preach for his congregation. Upon hearing of the invitation, fifty of Tyson's church members called a "protest meeting" to compel the minister to rescind the invitation. Tyson even received several death threats. In the end, though, Dr. Proctor came to preach and won over a great many of the congregation.[42]

Vernon Tyson's experience is just one example of one person in one town. But it reminds us of the countless preachers and lay Christians who worked to promote racial integration, even as they faced reprisals from other white Christians. Many a well-meaning minister has been held hostage by the racial prejudices of the congregation. Preachers who desired to hasten the day of racial equality often face speed bumps and road blocks put in place by the racial prejudices of their parishioners.

The barriers to overcoming racism are not easily removed. Even the material culture of the postwar and civil rights era surreptitiously supported an ongoing racial caste within the American church. Edward J. Blum and Paul Harvey, in their book *The Color of Christ*, demonstrate how images of Jesus created or printed during this time betray the racial assumptions of the culture. One of the most famous images of Jesus ever promulgated is called "Head of Christ" by Warner Sallman. According to the authors, by the 1990s this image had been printed over 500 million times and had "achieved global iconic status."[43]

You can probably picture it now. "This new Jesus had smooth white skin, long flowing brown hair, a full beard, and blue eyes."[44] Sallman painted the image in 1940, but it has enjoyed a decades-long international influence. This image of a white Jesus even became ubiquitous among black Christians. In fact, the bombing at Sixteenth Street Baptist Church, the one that killed those four girls and blew out the face of Jesus, destroyed a stained-glass window picturing a white Jesus. This picture, and hundreds of others like it, subtly reinforced the idea that Jesus Christ was a European-looking white man, and many added to that the assumption that he was a free-market, capitalist-supporting American as well. One Lutheran from Chicago distributed wallet-sized pictures of Sallman's Christ so that "card-carrying Christians" could oppose "card-carrying Communists."[45]

Importantly, it was everyday Christians, including many "mothers and fathers, Sunday School Teachers and new Christian entrepreneurs" who made this image of a white Jesus famous. Depicting Jesus as a white American man hampered the cause of the civil rights movement because, as Blum and Harvey explain, "fashioning Jesus into a particular and visualized body made it impossible for any universal savior to rise above the conflicts."[46] Warner Sallman's famous but contrived image of Jesus served to reinforce among Christians the status quo of the American racial hierarchy. Certainly, some black ministers pushed back against this Eurocentric image of Christ. On Easter Sunday in 1967, Rev. Albert Cleage Jr. consecrated the Shrine of the Black

Madonna, formerly Central Congregational Church, and revealed a seven-foot-tall painting of Mary and the baby Christ, both depicted as black people.[47] And needless to say, his alternate depiction of Jesus proved to be quite controversial.

EVANGELICAL RESPONSES TO MARTIN LUTHER KING JR.

Although Martin Luther King Jr. remains the face of the mid-twentieth-century civil rights movement, our present-day social memory of him obscures much of his life. In a seminal essay on the civil rights movement, Jacquelyn Dowd Hall wrote that King has been "endlessly reproduced and selectively quoted, his speeches retain their majesty yet lose their political bite."[48] For many Christian evangelicals, he has become the "quotable King," whose entire message has been reduced to his dream when his children would "not be judged by the color of their skin but by the content of their character." Some of the more "radical" elements of King's message—which included democratic socialism, ending the war in Vietnam, nuclear de-escalation, a Poor People's Campaign to force the federal government to address systemic poverty, and support of a sanitation workers' strike in Memphis when he was killed—have largely been omitted from popular American memory. Along with the unpopular elements of King's and the civil rights movement's platform, people have also forgotten how strongly many moderate Christians opposed him.

Back in 1961, King spoke at the Southern Baptist Theological Seminary, the flagship school of the largest Protestant denomination in the United States. Although he was there at the invitation of a professor, powerful Southern Baptists opposed his visit. As historian Taylor Branch wrote in his biography of King, "Within the church, this simple invitation was a racial and theological heresy, such that churches across the South rescinded their regular donations to the seminary."[49]

King saw an indissoluble link between the Christian faith and the responsibility to change unjust laws and policies. But his emphasis on the social dimensions of Christianity, especially regarding race relations, angered many white evangelicals in his day. Some Christians opposed King's activism because they considered race relations a purely social issue, not a spiritual one. They tended to believe that the government should not force people of different races to integrate. As shown above, some even thought that segregation was a biblical requirement.

Again, Billy Graham represents the moderate position well. After his death in February 2018, news outlets and admirers across the country unearthed pictures of Billy Graham smiling alongside Martin Luther King Jr. Christian commentators made much of Graham's gestures toward supporting black civil rights, such as the time when he personally removed the ropes dividing white and black attendees of an evangelistic crusade he held in 1953—a year before the *Brown v. Board* ruling. In 1957, Billy Graham even invited King to give the opening prayer at one of his rallies, an invitation that King accepted. Yet a few years later, as the civil rights movement continued and King became an even better-known figure, Graham advised King and his allies to "put on the brakes." Like the white moderates King wrote about in his letter from jail, Graham never relented from the belief that "the evangelist is not primarily a social reformer, a temperance lecturer or a moralizer. He is simply a *keryx*, a proclaimer of the good news."[50] Though it is evident that Graham did more than many during his time, he held back from making bold public proclamations of solidarity with black citizens and from demonstrating alongside activists during the March on Selma, a move he later said he regretted.[51]

For decades, Billy Graham claimed membership at First Baptist Church of Dallas. Even though Graham officially resided in North Carolina, he made frequent trips to Texas and had great respect for the church's pastor, W. A. Criswell. At the time, First Baptist had the largest congregation of any Southern Baptist Convention church. Criswell was a magnetic preacher, but like Graham, he had a dim view of the civil rights movement and of activists like Martin Luther King Jr. When officials invited Criswell to preach at an evangelism conference for the South Carolina Baptist Convention in 1956, he railed against government enforced integration. Criswell stated that desegregation is "a denial of all that we believe in." He went on to say that *Brown v Board* was "foolishness" and an "idiocy," and he called anyone who advocated for racial integration "a bunch of infidels, dying from the neck up."[52] Notably, Criswell did moderate some of his stances and statements later in life, but not before thousands of Christians in his own congregation and tens of thousands more of his followers nationwide had absorbed his views of civil rights and activists like King.

One final example offers a particularly distasteful illustration of how a moderate Christian during this time viewed Martin Luther King Jr. Writer Edward Gilbreath relates the experience of a black college student at a predominantly white Christian school in the late 1960s, who received the offer of a spot on the basketball team through the persistent efforts of an admissions director. The student, Dolphus Weary, a black rural Mississippian, agreed to attend Los Angeles Baptist College, which is now known as the Master's University. Weary was one of the first two black students at the school, and at first it was a positive experience. He earned good grades and helped lead the basketball team to a 19–5 record that season.

On April 4, 1968, a white classmate ran up to Weary and asked whether he had heard the news about Dr. King. When Weary turned on the radio to get an update, he was "devastated" to hear that King had been shot. As he sat in his room he could hear his white peers down the hall, laughing. Then came the awful news that King was dead. As soon as commentators reported this news, the young black man "could hear white voices down the hall let out a cheer." Reflecting back on this experience, Weary said, "Laughing at Dr. King's death was just like laughing at me—or at the millions of other blacks for whom King labored."[53] Remarkably, Weary did not let the hate of others consume him. He has spent his life working for racial reconciliation in his home state, Mississippi.

The Bible says, "A prophet has no honor in his own country" (John 4:44). We might extend it: A prophet (or truth-teller) has no honor in his or her own *time.* A couple of decades after his death, white evangelicals finally came to recognize King's contribution to American democracy and biblical justice. During his lifetime and at the height of the civil rights movement, a large segment of the American church derided King and other activists and even resisted the efforts of the civil rights movement. Certainly, changing attitudes can be viewed as a form of progress, but it is also helpful to remember that such positive perspectives on the movement have not always been popular.

As with other periods in America's sordid racial history, the Christian church of the mid-twentieth century often served to reinforce racism rather than oppose it. The *Brown v Board of Education* decision by the Supreme Court offered a clear sign to segregationists that the federal government could no longer be trusted and that the "southern way of life" was once again under assault. In response to government efforts to desegregate, moderate Christians, organized to oppose racial integration of neighborhoods, started segregation academies to keep their white children separate from black kids in schools, and continued to approve of church leaders who espoused prejudiced remarks and actions. While not all moderate Christians were racists or feared integration, enough went along with the Jim Crow consensus for those like Martin Luther King Jr. to abandon the hope that they would find many allies among their white brothers and sisters in Christ in their struggle for black freedom. Instead, the American church largely chose to compromise with racism through passive complicity, rejecting yet another opportunity to come alongside black people in the nation's "Second Reconstruction."

ORGANIZING THE RELIGIOUS RIGHT AT THE END OF THE TWENTIETH CENTURY

Lee Atwater once said he had two great aims in life: "To manage a presidential campaign and to be chairman of my party." He achieved both goals before the age of forty.[1] A strategist for George H. W. Bush's presidential campaign, Atwater became one of the youngest chairs of the Republican National Convention the following year. In his early thirties Atwater had begun working in the Reagan White House as an adviser. He earned that position for his shrewd insights into the electorate and his sometimes brutal advertising tactics.[2]

Before his untimely death from a brain tumor in 1991, Atwater had laid bare the racially coded appeals used by some Republicans to recruit voters: "You start out in 1954 by saying, 'Nigger, nigger, nigger.' By 1968 you can't say 'nigger'—that hurts you, backfires. So you say stuff like, uh, forced busing, states' rights, and all that stuff, and you're getting so abstract." He said all of this in an interview recorded in 1981.[3] "Now, you're talking about cutting taxes, and all these things you're talking about are totally economic things and a byproduct of them is, blacks get hurt worse than whites," he continued. "'We want to cut this,' is much more abstract than even the busing thing, uh, and a hell of a lot more abstract than 'Nigger, nigger.'"[4]

Atwater articulated what has become known as "color-blind conservatism." By excising explicitly racial terms like "black," "white," or "nigger" from their language, practitioners can claim they "don't see color." As a result, people can hold positions on social and political issues that disproportionately and adversely harm racial and ethnic minorities, but they can still proclaim their own racial innocence. As Atwater articulated, it is clear that the switch from racial language to supposedly color-blind discourse was once a conscious and deliberate choice. Today, it has become second nature—and the unconscious practice of many American Christians.

This chapter traces the rise of the "Religious Right," a politically conservative movement organized to resist the liberal turn in national sociopolitical life and to return America to "traditional" values. From the late 1960s through the 1980s, conservative Christians coalesced into a political force that every major Republican politician had to court if they hoped to have lasting success. But there was also a cost to this influence; it meant that American evangelicalism became virtually synonymous with the GOP and whiteness. While neither Democrats nor Republicans adequately addressed the multitude of issues that continued to plague black communities, people of color increasingly felt disregarded and even, at times, degraded by political conservatives. Politics became a proxy for racial conflict, and because of the Religious Right, that conflict translated into divisions in the church.

EVANGELICALS AND POLITICS IN THE LATE TWENTIETH CENTURY

Evangelicalism in America exploded during the 1970s and 1980s. The "Jesus Movement" inspired a generation of college-age Christians to devote their lives to religion. President Jimmy Carter described himself as a "born again" Christian and taught Bible study at his church. Newly formed evangelical megachurches, like Rick Warren's Saddleback Church in Orange County, started cropping up. Hal Lindsay's book

The Late Great Planet Earth, based on a literal interpretation of biblical end-times prophecies, sold twenty-eight million copies.[5] Evangelicals had so captured national attention that *Newsweek* magazine dubbed 1976 "The Year of the Evangelical."

The term *evangelical* has been used for centuries, but its definition is something of a moving target. Historian David Bebbington's definition serves as a good starting point. According to "Bebbington's quadrilateral," evangelicals accept and promote four principles: *conversionism*, an emphasis on a personal decision to follow Jesus Christ; *biblicism*, an understanding of the Bible that interprets miracles as true and Scripture as divinely inspired; *crucicentrism*, a focus on the crucifixion of Christ as a sacrifice for his followers; and *activism*, an engaged faith whose adherents seek to work out their faith through evangelism and advocacy.[6]

In late twentieth century America, *evangelicalism* took on a decidedly more political tone. In their article on the reinvention of evangelicalism in American history, scholars Hannah Butler and Kristin Du Mez conclude that "it seems reasonable to assume that when Americans self-identify as evangelicals today, many are identifying with the movement as it has taken shape in recent decades—a conservative politicized movement—and not with a static conception rooted in a centuries-old history."[7] This swift and energetic mobilization of evangelical voters that began in the 1970s has been labeled as the "rise of the Religious Right."[8] A 1976 article in the *New York Times* declared that the evangelical movement had "become the major religious force in America, both in numbers and in political impact."[9] Evangelicals had become a political movement, and the nation was starting to pay attention to them. But even then, Christian complicity with racism remained a factor influencing the American church.

An honest assessment of racism should acknowledge that racism never fully goes away; it just adapts to changing times and contexts. This is evident when we trace the development of the relationship between race and politics after the civil rights era. The civil rights movement certainly made a difference; there was a monumental shift in the rights afforded to black Americans. In 1964, President Johnson signed the Civil Rights Act into the law. The next year, the Voting Rights Act passed, and in 1968 the Fair Housing Act became law. Legalized segregation in the form of Jim Crow was now officially banned. Given these shifts, one might be tempted to declare that systemic or legal racism in America had ended, and that aside from a few backwards thinking people—the *real* racists—the progress of the civil rights movement indicated that the nation had largely overcome its racist past. Such an optimistic assessment would be wrong.

Though it was necessary to enact civil rights legislation, you cannot erase four hundred years of race-based oppression by passing a few laws. From the earliest years of slavery in the 1600s, through the legal end of Jim Crow in 1954, and in the numerous and varied ways in which racism is still enacted in law and culture today, the United States has had more than 300 years of race-based discrimination. A few short decades of legal freedom have not corrected the damage done by centuries of racism.

In previous eras, racism among Christian believers was much easier to detect and identify. Professing believers openly used racial slurs, participated in beatings and lynchings, fought wars to preserve slavery, or used the Bible to argue for the inherent inferiority of black people. And those who did not openly resist these actions—those who remained silent—were complicit in their acceptance. Since the 1970s, Christian complicity in racism has become more difficult to discern. It is hidden, but that does not mean it no longer exists. As we look more closely at the realm of politics, we see that Christian complicity with racism remains, even as it has taken on subtler forms. Again, we must remember: racism never goes away; it adapts.

Much of the discussion in this chapter focuses on white, theologically conservative Christians and the Republican party. This focus should not be taken to imply that Democrats don't have their own problems with racism. The point here is not to advocate for one political party over and against another, as most Christians would agree (at least in principle) that there is no single "Christian" party with which all believers should align. Nevertheless, the historical reality is that theologically conservative people of faith have not traditionally organized to support Democratic candidates, but as seen in the election of Ronald Reagan, they intentionally organized to help elect Republican candidates.[10]

This emphasis on the Republican Party should not be construed as tacit support for the Democratic Party or as an indictment of every single Republican voter or official. It should also be recognized that the politically active coalition known as the Christian Right included far more than just evangelicals. Many fundamentalists, Pentecostals, and Catholics joined with Protestant evangelicals in uniting over political issues such as anticommunism and opposition to abortion. Their combined electoral force became a coveted vote for Republican politicians to pursue.[11]

THE RISE OF LAW-AND-ORDER POLITICS

Richard Nixon and Billy Graham had been friends for a long time. According to one of Graham's biographers, William Martin, the two cemented their friendship in the 1950s. United by anticommunist sentiments, associating with many of the same evangelical leaders, and both nearly the same age, "Dick" and Billy became buddies. "Anytime you have a few days this winter," Graham wrote in a letter to Nixon, who was vice president at the time, "we can take a swim or play a game of golf in Florida or, better still, in Hawaii."[12] For his part, Nixon reciprocated. When it came time for Nixon to decide whether to run for president the second time, he invited Billy Graham down to Florida for a few days to help him think through the decision. Even though Graham was fighting a bout of pneumonia, he made the trip. They went for long walks on the beach, watched football games, studied the Bible, and talked politics. Graham advised Nixon that if he didn't run, then he would always wonder whether he would have won.[13] Nixon, of course, decided to enter the presidential race and won the election with 68 percent of the evangelical vote. When he ran for reelection four years later, he boosted his share of the evangelical vote to 84 percent.[14] Part of Nixon's appeal to white evangelical voters depended on his commitment to the racially loaded stance of law-and-order politics.

The words *black power* proved controversial for black and white people alike. Their increased use coincided with highly visible urban uprisings in cities such as Watts, Newark, Detroit, and Chicago. The destruction of property coupled with an attitude of black pride and independence concerned and frightened many observers. The rising protests against the Vietnam War along with the push for women's rights and gay rights gave some Americans a sense that the country was teetering on the brink of collapse. Politicians, including Nixon, began delivering a message of "law and order" to convey to voters their commitment to social stability.

"Who is responsible for the breakdown of law and order in this country?" queried Nixon in a 1966 article for *U.S. News & World Report*. His answer: the seeds of anarchy had been "nurtured by scores of respected Americans: public officials, educators, clergymen, and civil rights leaders as well."[15] One of Nixon's campaign ads depicted scenes of riots and demonstrations. The narrator's voice articulated what the pictures were meant to convey. "I pledge to you, we shall have order in the United States." A caption read, "This time . . . vote like your whole world depended on it."[16] In effect, Nixon was pointing to the civil rights movement and its nonviolent direct action, not as the endeavor to secure long-denied justice to black Americans but as the tarmac to tyranny and disregard for the law.

Law-and-order rhetoric fueled an increasingly aggressive criminal justice establishment. Today, the United States has just 5 percent of the world's population but 25 percent of its incarcerated persons. While the reasons for this are many, some of the seeds were planted under Nixon's administration when the federal government began issuing harsher sentences for criminal offenders, supporting the deployment of undercover police squads in cities, and providing incentives for the construction of prisons. The result was "a significant expansion in America's carceral state."[17]

Some historians and political analysts have called Nixon's approach the "Southern Strategy."[18] The Southern Strategy exploited racial backlash against the civil rights movement, as well as an emerging sense of white, middle-class suburban identity, to mobilize disaffected white voters in support of the Republican Party. Richard M. Nixon and his advisers adopted this Southern Strategy as they reached out to the "great silent majority of Americans," a demographic that increasingly included evangelicals.[19] The conservative approach to politics in the 1970s and in the decades that followed began to court voters with white racial resentment and to downplay the concerns of black communities. In 2010, the chairman of the Republican Nation Convention, Michael Steele, who is black, admitted this: "For the last 40 plus years we had a 'Southern Strategy' that alienated many minority voters by focusing on the white male vote in the South."[20] Politically conservative elected officials aimed to recruit not only white male voters in the South but white evangelicals as well.

Yet the idea of the Southern Strategy, however accurate it may be in some ways, furthers the erroneous idea that political conservatives resided mainly in the South. While there were many conservatives in the South, a new coalition of Republican voters had formed in cities and suburbs across the western United States, many of whom identified as white and evangelical. In the 1969 book *The Emerging Republican Majority*, Kevin Phillips, who coined the term *Sunbelt*, articulated an ethos designed to appeal to this emerging group that was "fiscally and socially conservative enough to win the confidence of the new moneyed suburbanite, but also racially conservative enough to attract [George] Wallace's voters."[21] These Sunbelt voters lived in places like Dallas, Phoenix, and Orange County, California. Indeed, rather than being confined to a particular region of the country, the Sunbelt ideology was a suburban value system.[22] These were men and women who believed in free-market capitalism, meritocratic individualism, local control of communities, and the idea that America had been founded as a "Christian Nation." Historian Darren Dochuk argues that these Sunbelt citizens blended their evangelical religion into their political outlook as well, as Sunbelt evangelicalism "melded traditionalism into an uncentered, unbounded religious culture of entrepreneurialism, experimentation, and engagement—in short, a Sunbelt Creed."[23]

Given this Sunbelt Creed, it should not surprise us to learn that Billy Graham first came to national prominence not in his home state of North Caroline or anywhere else in the "Bible Belt" but during a crusade in Los Angeles in 1949. The preacher's message resonated with LA audiences so much that even though planners scheduled it to last three weeks, they extended it to a full eight weeks. Thousands of Californians, most of them white and conservative, converted to Graham's evangelical version of Christianity, and over the next several decades nurtured their faith in the milieu of conservative Sunbelt politics. Twenty years later, parts of California have become something of a haven for conservative evangelicals. At the start of another crusade in Southern California in 1969, Graham said to an audience of fifty-thousand faithful, "I feel more at home here than any place I've ever been."[24]

While Martin Luther King Jr. was proclaiming, "I have a dream!" on the steps of the capitol in Washington, grassroots conservatives were working on their dream from kitchen tables in California. A white suburban homemaker may not fit the typical image of an activist, but that is the best way to describe Estrid Kielsmeier. Historian Lisa McGirr writes about a day in early 1964 when Kielsmeier set her kitchen table with coffee cups and chairs and prepared for a gathering of her friends and neighbors. This would not be a simple social visit, however, but a political action meeting.[25] Next to the coffee cups, Kielsmeier laid a stack of petitions to nominate Barry Goldwater as the Republican candidate for president. As people trickled in throughout the day to sign the petition, Kielsmeier and her fellow "kitchen table activists" amazingly gathered the requisite 30,000 signatures before noon on the first day of their drive. The rise of the Religious Right was predominately a grassroots movement with origins among these "suburban warriors" of the 1960s who "set in place the ideas, strategies, and politics that would pave the road to national power."[26]

That national power was on full display when Billy Graham officially endorsed Nixon for president in the reelection campaign of 1972. Graham had been in close contact with presidents since Truman, but this was the first time he had endorsed one. The well-respected preacher and evangelist not only lent his support but actively encouraged the president to court the evangelical vote. "I have been pointing out to you in a number of conversations that we have had that there is an emerging evangelical strength in this country that is going to have a strong bearing on social and political matters probably for a generation to come," Graham said to Nixon. Graham believed that evangelicals would be the critical constituency to "promoting the president's vision of 'law and order.'"[27]

At this point, readers of this book may be searching for the proverbial "smoking gun"—explicit evidence that connects the American church with overt cooperation with racism. But racism, since it is socially constructed, adapts when society changes. By the late 1960s, politicians at the national level had moved on from explicitly racist rhetoric (George Wallace's prosegregationist platform in the 1968 presidential election being an obvious exception), but the absence of that language did not mean that racism no longer affected politics. In place of obviously racist policies, law-and-order rhetoric "had become a surrogate expression for concern about the civil rights movement."[28] One of Nixon's closest advisers, H. R. Haldeman, said, "[Nixon] emphasized that you have to face the fact that the whole problem is really the blacks. The key is to devise a system that recognizes this while not appearing to."[29] At the time, several black evangelicals publicly criticized the Nixon administration, and many Christians of color likely recognized the rhetoric, even if it was subtler this time. To wit, only 4 percent of black Protestants voted for Nixon in his first presidential victory.[30]

Should this be taken to mean that the more than eight out of ten evangelical voters who pulled the lever for Nixon were racist? It is possible that white evangelicals were not concerned with matters of race when they voted. But even a color-blind ideology is problematic since it "depended upon the establishment of structural mechanisms of exclusion that did not require individual racism by suburban beneficiaries."[31] Since the late 1960s, the American church's complicity in racism has been less obvious, but it has not required as much effort to maintain. Nowadays, all the American church needs to do in terms of compromise is cooperate with already established and racially unequal social systems.

RACIAL INTEGRATION AND THE TRUE
ORIGINS OF THE RELIGIOUS RIGHT

When most people think about the Religious Right, the matter of abortion comes to mind. Like no other issue, the rejection of legalized abortion has come to define the Religious Right. Repealing *Roe v. Wade* stands as a perennial high-priority issue for conservative Christian voters, so much so that today it is hard to imagine a time when that was not the case. But in the early 1970s, abortion was not the primary issue that catalyzed the Religious Right, as it would in later years. Initially, the Christian response to *Roe v. Wade* was mixed.[32] Instead, conservative voters coalesced around the issue of racial integration in schools.

Perhaps some will be surprised to learn that abortion has not always been the defining issue for evangelicals. In 1971, the Southern Baptist Convention, the nation's largest Protestant denomination, passed a resolution on abortion that called upon Southern Baptists "to work for legislation that will allow the possibility of abortion under such conditions as rape, incest, clear evidence of severe fetal deformity, and carefully ascertained evidence of the likelihood of damage to the emotional, mental, and physical health of the mother."[33] No less than W. A. Criswell, pastor of the largest SBC congregation, stated after the *Roe v. Wade* decision that "I have always felt that it was only after a child was born and had life separate from its mother . . . that it became an individual person." He further explained, "It has always, therefore, seemed to me that what is best for the mother and for the future should be allowed."[34] A poll in 1970 discovered that 70 percent of Southern Baptist pastors "supported abortion to protect the mental or physical health of the mother, 64 percent supported abortion in cases of fetal deformity and 71 percent in cases of rape."[35] Like the Southern Baptists, many other conservative Christians were not uniformly against abortion in the early 1970s.

Instead, the impetus that galvanized the Religious Right came from an unexpected source, the Internal Revenue Service (IRS). Historian Randall Balmer explains that conservative power brokers originally came together as a political force to combat what they perceived as an attack by the IRS and the federal government on Protestant Christian schools.[36] Three black families in Mississippi sued the Treasury Department, headed by David Kennedy, to disallow tax-exempt status for three new "segregation academies" in the county. The plaintiffs had a solid case for alleging racial discrimination. In 1969, when the federal government began more aggressively enforcing desegregation, white attendance in public schools in the area plummeted from 771 to 28. The following year, exactly zero white students remained in the local public schools.

When the case of the black families went to court, the court granted a preliminary injunction and determined that *any* school— public or private—that discriminated on the basis of race could not hold the designation of "charitable" institution. In 1971, the Supreme Court upheld that decision in *Green v. Connally* and said that "racially discriminatory private schools are not entitled to Federal tax exemption provided for charitable, educational institutions."[37] This ruling threatened the financial solvency of any Christian school that could not demonstrate an integrated student body or show positive efforts to desegregate. The IRS, however, did not strictly pursue penalties against racial discrimination, so very few schools felt the effects.[38]

It only took one school, Bob Jones University, to bring the threat of government-enforced integration to the attention of Christian conservatives and to politically mobilize them. A poor white person in the South had few advantages. They typically had little schooling and not enough food, and the richer white people often looked down on them. The only advantage many felt they had was their whiteness. This was the context in which Bob Jones Sr. grew up. Born in rural Alabama in 1883, he adopted Jim Crow ideas of racial segregation even though his poverty likely gave him more in common with the black people around him than the wealthy whites. But Jones absorbed the cultural values of racism and eventually brought these ideas of racial hierarchy with him when he set out to found a new school.

Bob Jones Sr. ostensibly started what would become Bob Jones University (BJU) not out of any racial considerations but to stand as a bulwark against what he saw as the increasing secularization and liberalism in the public schools. He already had a prolific career as a traveling evangelist, and hundreds of thousands has heard him preach. Many more recognized his name. In the 1920s, Jones grew concerned about the Fundamentalist-Modernist controversy and more specifically about the way the theory of evolution had infiltrated public education, so Jones decided to start his own fundamentalist Christian college as an alternative to both public colleges and denominational schools that he felt had become too liberal. His friends prevailed upon him to use his own name in the school's title in order to transfer his fame as a preacher into the successful launch of a new institution.[39]

Classes commenced at Bob Jones College in 1927 with eighty-eight students. The south Florida school grew quickly but was forced to sell its property in Florida during the Great Depression. It relocated to Tennessee where a young preacher named Billy Graham enrolled in 1936, though Graham soon transferred as he chafed under the college's strict rules and fundamentalist doctrines. For those unfamiliar with the differences between fundamentalists and evangelicals, it is worth noting that while there are many similarities, the two are not identical. Historian George Marsden, in his book *Fundamentalism in American Culture*, writes: "Fundamentalists were evangelical Christians . . . who in the twentieth century militantly opposed both modernism in theology and the cultural changes that modernism endorsed."[40] Fundamentalists espoused separatism from the modernizing culture and even from other evangelical denominations and churches considered too liberal in their beliefs. Their strict rules for moral behavior alienated more moderate evangelicals who sought greater engagement with the world for the sake of evangelism.[41] In this case, the young Billy Graham was in the process of clarifying his own convictions as an evangelical and could not stomach the more restrictive culture of Bob Jones, a fundamentalist institution.

In 1947, the school moved to its current residence in Greenville, South Carolina, where it became a university. Politically and in his preaching and teaching, Bob Jones Sr. supported segregation as a biblical mandate and stood firm in his convictions all throughout the civil rights movement. He died before the issue of integration came knocking on the door of the university he founded, so it fell to his son, Bob Jones Jr., to defend his father's vision during one of the most tumultuous and notorious eras of the school's history.

The younger Jones continued the school's tradition of segregation, and during his tenure as president the younger Jones granted honorary degrees to notorious segregationists such as Strom Thurmond, George Wallace, and Lester Maddox.[42] The university did finally admit its first black students in 1971, but they were only allowed if they were married. The ages-old bugaboo of interracial marriage and miscegenation made the idea of having single black men on campus as potential suitors for young white ladies an unconscionable prospect for the leaders at Bob Jones University. In 1975, the school changed its policy and allowed unmarried black students to enroll, but as clearly outlined in the student handbook, the school prohibited interracial dating. Bob Jones III, who served as president from 1971 to 2005, stated in an interview: "There are three basic races—Oriental, Caucasian and Negroid. At BJU, everybody dates within those basic three races."[43] Anyone involved in an interracial relationship or those who promoted such pairings would face expulsion.

The Civil Rights Act and the IRS's newly adopted policies meant that Bob Jones University's stance on interracial dating placed it in violation of racial discrimination laws. The IRS revoked the school's tax-exempt status in 1976, but these financial penalties did not deter university officials. They sued the IRS and presented their case as an issue of religious freedom. "Even if this were discrimination, which it is not, though the government disagrees," Jones III said, "it is a sincere religious belief founded on what we think the Bible teaches, no matter whether anyone else believes it or not."[44] Similar to what some proponents of slavery had argued in the Civil War era, segregationists in the twentieth century considered it a "right" to separate people based on race. It was a religious belief with which the government had no right to interfere. Even as recently as 1998, Jonathan Pait, a spokesperson for the university, explained, "God has made people different from one another and intends those differences to remain. Bob Jones University is opposed to intermarriage of the races because it breaks down the barriers God has established."[45]

In recent years, Bob Jones University has officially changed its views on race and interracial relationships. In 2000, George W. Bush, who was the Republican candidate for president at the time, endured harsh criticism for speaking at BJU. In response to the controversy, the school's president, Bob Jones III, led the decision to officially change the rules and allow interracial dating. In 2008, Stephen Jones, the new leader of the school since 2005, issued a formal apology for Bob Jones University's past racial recalcitrance. The apology reads, "For almost two centuries American Christianity, including BJU in its early stages, was characterized by the segregationist ethos of American culture." Jones was finally able to see the connection between the American church's historic complicity with racism and the university's specific policies regarding race. He goes on to explain, "We conformed to the culture rather than providing a clear Christian counterpoint to it."[46] In other words, Stephen Jones acknowledged his Christian school's complicity in racism. Yet the damage had been done. Bob Jones University had intentionally indoctrinated generations of students with racist ideas about interracial relationships.

The IRS's guidelines about racial integration in 1978 sparked national outrage among many Christian conservatives. Department officials as well as members of Congress received tens of thousands of messages in protest. In an interview Weyrich explained, "What galvanized the Christian community was not abortion, school prayer, or the [Equal Rights Amendment]. . . . What changed their minds was Jimmy Carter's intervention against the Christian schools, trying to deny them tax-exempt status on the basis of so-called de facto segregation."[47] While it would be wrong to suggest that racist resistance to integration was the single issue that held the Religious Right together in these years, it clearly provided an initial charge that electrified the movement.

THE MORAL MAJORITY'S SUPPORT OF RONALD REAGAN

We've seen that the rise of the Religious Right represents a time when conservative Christians got more involved in politics. But what *exactly* did the Religious Right support in terms of specific policies and platforms? The era's most prominent Christian political organization—the Moral Majority—provides clear evidence that the new Christian Right tended to promote laws, practices, and ideas that limited or even sought to reverse the gains of the civil rights movement.

In the mid-1960s, Jerry Falwell, a well-known fundamentalist pastor of Thomas Road Baptist Church in Lynchburg, Virginia, would have seemed an unlikely candidate to shepherd conservative Christians into mainstream politics. In an oft-quoted sermon he gave in 1965 entitled "Ministers and Marches," Falwell declared, "Preachers are not called to be politicians, but soul winners."[48] Delivered during the height of the civil rights movement, most observers interpreted Falwell's sentiments as a critique of the movement in general and of Martin Luther King Jr. specifically. By 1976, Falwell had completely flipped his position and his stance against mixing religion and politics and embarked on an "I Love America" rally tour. In a sermon delivered on the Fourth of July, he made his new position crystal clear: "This idea of 'religion and politics don't mix' was invented by the devil to keep Christians from running their own country."[49]

In 1979, Falwell met with other members of the emerging "New Right," including Paul Weyrich, Edward McAteer, and Robert Billings, to strategize how to gather a coalition into a potent force for political influence. During the lengthy meeting Weyrich used the phrase "moral majority," and Falwell immediately halted the conversation to have Weyrich repeat the phrase. "That's it," he said. "That's what I'm going to call the organization, 'Moral Majority.'"[50] Falwell and his associates formed Moral Majority Inc. a month later. He explained their simple program in three steps: "Get 'em saved, get 'em baptized, get 'em registered."[51] According to the Moral Majority's founder, the platform was "pro-life, pro-family, pro-moral, and pro-America." The organization proved immensely popular with religious conservatives of all kinds. As an avowedly political organization, Falwell and other leaders of the Moral Majority courted people from across the religious spectrum including conservative Mormons, Jews, and Catholics as well as Pentecostals and a variety of Protestant denominations. Within a few years, the Moral Majority had an annual budget of $6 million, and its publication, *Moral Majority Report*, went to 840,000 households, with hundreds of Christian radio stations carrying their daily commentary.[52]

The Moral Majority organized just in time to support the man who would become the darling of the Religious Right, Ronald Reagan. Reagan, a divorced Hollywood actor-turned politician who supported a liberal pro-abortion law while governor of California, certainly did not scream out "champion of Christian conservatism." But Reagan's skilled campaigning and winsome speechmaking quickly endeared him to the Religious Right, and Reagan was quick to adopt the right talking points to win white evangelical voters. When asked what single book he would read if he could only read one for the rest of his life, Reagan soberly answered, "I [know] of only one book that could be read and re-read and continue to be a challenge: the Bible."[53] Reagan also recognized the political advantages of endearing himself to a voting bloc that numbered in the millions, and he did all he could to earn their favor. In a famous speech given at First Baptist Church in Dallas early in 1980, Reagan all but sealed the conservative Christian support for his bid for the presidency when he remarked: "I know this is a non-partisan gathering, so I know you can't endorse me, but I want you to know I endorse you and what you are doing."[54] In the 1980 presidential election, Reagan won the electoral college in a landslide of 489 to 49. He carried all the Sunbelt states and all the states in the former Confederacy except Georgia, the home state of his Democratic opponent, Jimmy Carter. The momentum of electing a GOP president helped other Republican politicians gain an additional thirty-five seats in the US House of Representatives and a majority in the Senate for the first time in over two decades. Jerry Falwell credited the Moral Majority for several of those victories and called that election night "my finest hour."[55]

What did conservative Christians support when they voted for Reagan? A brief glimpse of his actions and policies demonstrates that in throwing their electoral power behind this charismatic politician, they also bolstered several stances that could be perceived as antiblack. Reagan did not shy away from publicly aligning himself with racists or from using racially coded language in his appeals to white voters. As historian Joseph Crespino relates, Reagan began his 1980 presidential campaign at an annual fair in Neshoba County, Mississippi, where in 1964, three civil rights workers—James Chaney, Mickey Schwerner, and Andrew Goodman—had disappeared. After a search that lasted all summer and attracted national attention, an anonymous tip led investigators to an earthen dam where the bodies of the three young men were buried. They had each been shot by white supremacist members of the KKK and local law enforcement officers who were outraged by the presence of "outside agitators" during Freedom Summer, a movement to register black voters in Mississippi.[56] Even though it was years later, that infamous crime was still a fresh memory, yet Reagan chose to speak at the annual Neshoba County Fair and use words familiar to Mississippi segregationists, who believed the federal government should stop disrupting the social affairs of the states. Republicans assisting Reagan intentionally tailored his speech that day to appeal to "George Wallace inclined voters" (referring to the failed 1968 third-party presidential candidate who opposed black civil rights).[57] "I believe in state's rights," Reagan said. If elected, he promised to "restore to states and local governments the power that properly belongs to them."

Reagan also championed Bob Jones University even at a time when it refused to change its policies on interracial dating. In January of 1980, Ronald Reagan spoke in front of an enthusiastic crowd at Bob Jones University and called it a "great institution" despite its persistent refusal to change its stance on race. Reagan went still further in his attempts to appeal to the Religious Right by promising to zealously pursue a "limited government" approach. That same month, he led his administration to reverse the IRS's ruling against BJU and restored its tax-exempt status. Echoing a common argument against affirmative action, Reagan insisted, "You do not alter the evil character of racial quotas simply by changing the color of the beneficiary."[58] After this statement, a public furor erupted, and the president had to backtrack in what advisers called a "salvage operation." Reagan ended up submitting a bill to Congress that gave the IRS express permission to revoke the tax-exempt status of racially discriminatory schools, adding that racially discriminatory practices "are repugnant to all that our nation and its citizens hold dear, and I believe this repugnance should be plainly reflected in our laws," which he wrote in a note to Congress.[59] The Supreme Court officially upheld the IRS's position in a 1983 decision, and the university remained a taxable institution because of its racial stances.

Reagan was also known for popularizing the term *welfare queen*, which became an oft-used phrase by the president. He told the story of a black woman from Chicago with "80 names, 30 addresses, 12 Social Security cards," who gamed the social support system for $150,000 in annual tax-free income. The "welfare queen" became a stand-in for the president's criticism of an undeserving class of poor people, especially inner-city black women.[60] He, along with an all-too-willing national media, helped push the issue of crack cocaine use to the status of a national crisis. Even though rates of drug use between whites and blacks were about the same, the drug war intentionally focused on areas of high poverty where there were high concentrations of racial and ethnic minorities. Spending was increased to fund the drug war. In Reagan's first term, antidrug spending by the FBI went from $38 million to $101 million. The Drug Enforcement Agency's budget went from $86 million to over $1 billion. At the same time, the budget for the Department of Education's drug prevention programs dipped from $14 million to $3 million.[61]

Reagan's questionable politics regarding racial equality and his political appeals to racist sentiments may be just that—politics. After all, Reagan made several public overtures to the black community throughout his public career. As governor of California, he appointed several black people to executive positions. He met with black Republicans throughout the Republican National Convention in 1980 and spent nearly $1 million on African American outreach during his campaign.[62] He signed a bill that made Martin Luther King Jr. Day a national holiday. Of course, this only came about *after* his initial objections and only when its passage in Congress seemed inevitable. Yes, there were some positive signs, but overall Reagan's advocacy of black civil rights was less than enthusiastic. Whatever their intentions, when the Religious Right signed up to support Reagan and his views, they were also tacitly endorsing an administration that refused to take

strong stances toward dismantling racism. Here we see further complicity with institutional racism as conservative Christians chose to
support certain elements of the modern Republican platform.

The Religious Right's own statement of political objectives
also demonstrates its troubling compromise with racism by promoting policies that failed to advance or support black civil rights.
Anticommunism stood as a conspicuous pillar of the Religious Right's
platform, and while on the surface this aversion to communism as
a political philosophy and to the countries that espoused it appears
positive, at another level anticommunism could also signal an anti-
integrationist stance. A lay Christian from Macon, Georgia, voiced the
mentality of many conservative Christians when he said, "What are
we doing as Christians while this awful thing called integration, that
should be called communism, is destroying our way of life and our
entire race?"[63] Furthermore, Christian conservatives carefully coded
any change, especially those related to race, as "liberal," and they
perceived themselves as constantly under attack by liberal operatives
in the media and politics. In 1974, a Baptist churchgoer in Alabama
plainly stated his beliefs about liberalism and its relation to racial integration: "I firmly believe in each race having its own schools, social
organizations, and churches. . . . Of course, what I am suggesting will
be considered ridiculous and absurd by today's liberal and brainwashed
public and I will be labeled a dirty old racist and bigot."[64] In addition,
a stance against welfare led to stereotypes of black people and the
poor as lacking in initiative and having no work ethic. As historian
James German explains, "The welfare state, in the mind of the New
Christian Right, undermined the sense of individual responsibility in
which public morality rested."[65] Efforts to reduce funding to social
support systems functioned as a subtle judgment on welfare recipients
in general, but to the extent that welfare was associated with black
people, it also functioned as a judgment against "lazy blacks."

The flip side of what Falwell called "welfarism" was the promotion
of capitalism and the "free market." In his book *Listen, America*, Falwell
wrote, "The free enterprise system is clearly outlined in the Book of
Proverbs."[66] Drawing on the work of conservative economist Milton

Friedman, Falwell claimed that capitalism was the only Christian form of commerce and contended that a free enterprise system liberated from government constraints would lift black people out of poverty.[67] In terms of policy, the Religious Right supported GOP efforts to reduce funding for welfare programs and increase tax breaks for corporations. This contributed to the overall perception among black people that Christian conservatives did not care about the concerns of a historically oppressed group. Although their intentions may have been varied, in terms of political impact the Religious Right failed to demonstrate a clear commitment to black advancement.

The introduction to this chapter stated that racism never goes away; it just adapts. The growth of the Sunbelt and the white suburban ethos accompanying it meant that many politically and theologically conservative Christians strayed away from the use of explicitly race-based language and appeals. Yet those appeals did not disappear. Instead, they mobilized around the issue of taxation of private Christian schools, many of which remained racially segregated or made only token efforts at integration. They supported presidents and legal policies that disproportionately and negatively impacted black people. They accepted a color-blind rhetoric that still utilized racially coded messages.

Yet as we have seen in this brief historical tour, after more than three centuries of deliberate, systematic race-based exclusion, the political system that had intentionally disenfranchised black people continued to do so, yet in less overt ways. Simply by allowing the political system to work as it was designed—to grant advantages to white people and to put people of color at various disadvantages—many well-meaning Christians were complicit in racism. Of course, there are always unintended consequences for our political choices, and not all of them can be foreseen or even avoided. But when we examine our attitudes about race and consider them in light of the history of slavery and racism in America, we begin to see that Christians have a responsibility to, at the very least, consider how the political connections between theologically conservative evangelicalism and conservative politics, namely through the Republican Party, have supported racial inequities.

RECONSIDERING RACIAL RECONCILIATION IN THE AGE OF BLACK LIVES MATTER

The close of the twentieth century brought about many changes in the American church and race relations, changes that may have resulted in violence had they happened in earlier generations. The Southern Baptist Convention (SBC), the nation's largest Protestant denomination that had been founded to protect slaveholders within its ranks, finally apologized for its racist roots. They issued a resolution repenting of racism and slavery at their annual meeting on the 150th anniversary of the denomination, a statement which read in part, "We lament and repudiate historic acts of evil such as slavery from which we continue to reap a bitter harvest, and we recognize that the racism which yet plagues our culture today is inextricably tied to the past."[1] The resolution went on to ask forgiveness from African Americans and pledged to "eradicate racism in all its forms" from their denomination. In ages past such words of racial equality would have engulfed entire congregations in controversy.

New racial reconciliation movements arose in the final decade of the twentieth century as well, notably a movement begun by Bill McCartney. McCartney was a good athlete but an even better coach.

After graduating from the University of Missouri in 1962, he went on to coach high school football, and several years later, legendary University of Michigan football coach Bo Schembechler took notice of him and made the rare decision to hire a high school coach to work at the Division I college level. McCartney's talents landed him a head coaching job at the University of Colorado eight years later. His prowess eventually earned him a place in the College Football Hall of Fame. But McCartney is perhaps best known as the founder of the Promise Keepers movement.

In 1990, McCartney, a Roman Catholic who became a "born again" Protestant Christian, attended a Fellowship of Christian Athletes (FCA) banquet where he and a companion discussed the need for men's discipleship. McCartney pictured a stadium full of 50,000 men gathered to learn about what it means to be "godly men." Promise Keepers was incorporated in December of 1990 and held its first conference the following year. By 1993, McCartney's vision of tens of thousands of men filling a stadium had become a reality.

McCartney, who is white, cited his experience recruiting and working with black players as one of the reasons he made the decision to turn Promise Keepers toward racial reconciliation.[2] In 1996, organizers for the annual conference chose the theme of "Break Down the Walls" and Ephesians 2:14: "For he himself is our peace, who has made the two groups one and has destroyed the barrier, the dividing wall of hostility."[3] In what was touted as the "world's largest gathering of clergy," 39,000 pastors of varying races, ethnicities, and denominations who attended the Promise Keepers rally in Atlanta ended their time in tears and hugs. "Better than any other national or visible movement, Promise Keepers is not only preaching racial reconciliation, but they are doing something about it," said Silas Pinto, a Latino pastor who attended the rally.[4]

In addition to movements like Promise Keepers in the '90s, the start of the new millennium witnessed the growth of intentional, multiethnic churches. The historic dictum that 11:00 a.m. on Sunday is the most segregated hour in America has been challenged by the growth of these churches. A 2010 survey found that about 12.5 percent of churches could be considered multiethnic—meaning no single ethnic group comprises more than 80 percent of the congregation. Contemporary attitudes toward diversity in the church show a desire for even more integration. A 2014 study by Lifeway Research indicated that 85 percent of senior pastors in the Protestant churches surveyed said, "Every church should strive for racial diversity." Speaking about evangelical pastors and congregational diversity, Mark DeYmaz, founder of the multiethnic church network Mosaix, said, "Increasingly, their question is not, 'why should I,' but 'how can I?'"[5]

Yet beneath this apparent racial progress, divisions have lingered. Voters elected Barack Obama as the nation's first black president in 2008, and immediately talk began of a "postracial" society. Obama's election, however, stimulated racist backlash in some quarters, only to be followed by a slew of grisly videos depicting police officers slaying unarmed black women and men. The ensuing debate over "law and order" once again highlighted the stark racial divisions present in America today. In 2015, a white supremacist entered a Bible study at a historic black church and murdered nine worshipers, sparking divisive debates about monuments to and symbols of the Confederacy.[6] Amidst the furor of racist words and events, Christians today remain divided along racial lines.

One of the challenges we face in discussions of racism today is that the conversation about race has shifted since the civil rights era. Legislation has rendered the most overt acts of racism legally punishable. Hate crimes of various forms still occur, but most American Christians would call these acts evil. Yet the legacy of racism persists, albeit in different forms. Sociologists Michael Emerson and Christian Smith studied white evangelical ideas about race in their book *Divided by Faith*. To frame their study, they used the concept of a "racialized" society which they defined as a society "wherein race matters profoundly for differences in life experiences, life opportunities and social relationships." It is, as they say, "a society that allocates differential economic, political, social, and even psychological rewards to groups along racial lines; lines that are socially constructed."[7] Racialization functions differently from straightforward racism. Emerson and Smith go on to explain that discrimination in a racialized society is increasingly covert, embedded in the normal operations of institutions, and it avoids direct racial terminology, making it invisible to most white people. The relative invisibility of these racialized structures to white Christians often leads them to unknowingly compromise with racism.

This chapter examines the ongoing conflicts between black and white Christians today and offers some suggestions as to why racism remains a persistent problem—even in the twenty-first century. We will examine how the racial divide between Christians has, in some ways, become even starker in recent years. Through an analysis of the role of contemporary black activism, stubborn patterns of segregation, and political polarization (especially in the presidential election of 2016), we will take a closer look at why the American church is in the midst of a reevaluation and a reckoning about its identity and future.

THE WHITE EVANGELICAL CULTURAL TOOLKIT AND POLITICS

In *Divided by Faith*, Emerson and Smith introduce the notion of a "cultural tool kit." They explain that "culture creates ways for individuals and groups to organize experiences and evaluate reality. It does so by providing a repertoire or 'tool kit' of ideas, habits, skills, and styles."[8] The particular religio-cultural tools that white evangelicals use to understand race actually tend to perpetuate the very racial problems they say they want to ameliorate. A brief explanation of the white evangelical cultural tool kit will help explain how Christians from different racial backgrounds can have such different views of contemporary racial and political problems.

Accountable individualism means that "individuals exist independent of structures and institutions, have freewill, and are individually accountable for their own actions."[9] This belief promotes skepticism toward the idea that social systems and structures profoundly shape the actions of individuals. The white evangelical understanding of individualism has this effect, and it tends to reduce the importance of communities and institutions in shaping the ways people think and behave. Another belief in the cultural toolkit is *relationalism*, "a strong emphasis on interpersonal relationships."[10] According to relationalism, social problems are fundamentally due to broken personal relationships: "Thus, if race problems—poor relationships—result from sin, then race problems must largely be individually based."[11] And *anti-structuralism* refers to the belief that "invoking social structures shifts guilt away from its root source—the accountable individual."[12] In other words, systems, structures, and policies are not to blame for the problems in America; instead, the problems come from the harmful choices of individuals. "Absent from their accounts is the idea that poor relationships might be shaped by social structures, such as laws, the ways institutions operate, or forms of segregation. . . . They often find structural explanations irrelevant or even wrongheaded," Emerson and Smith explain.[13]

While black and white citizens in general exhibit vastly divergent views of American life and governance, these differences tend to be especially pronounced among American Christians. Speaking very broadly, black Christians tend to agree that a personal relationship with Jesus Christ is necessary for a saving faith. However, they also recognize that structures influence individuals and that addressing America's racial issues will require systemic change. In accounting for the black-white wealth gap, for instance, black and white Christians have remarkably different understandings of the problem and the solution. Sixty-two percent of white evangelicals attribute poverty among black people to a lack of motivation, while 31 percent of black Christians said the same. And just 27 percent of white evangelicals attribute the wealth gap to racial discrimination, while 72 percent of blacks cite discrimination as a major cause of the discrepancy.[14] The differing cultural tool kits applied by black and white Christians help illuminate some of the conflicts over racial justice at the dawn of the twenty-first century.

BLACK LIVES MATTER AND CHRISTIAN RESPONSES ACROSS THE COLOR LINE

On July 13, 2013, Alicia Garza, a black activist and writer in Oakland, California, sat down at her computer to pen what she called "a love note to black people." In the brief post she wrote, "Black people. I love you. I love us. Our lives matter." Her friend and fellow activist, Patrisse Cullors, responded to the post with the words, "Declaration: black bodies will no longer be sacrificed for the rest of the world's enlightenment. i am done. i am so done. trayvon, you are loved infinitely. #blacklivesmatter." Together with their friend Opal Tometi, these three black women started a hashtag that flowered into a movement that would significantly change the conversation about race and justice in America.[15]

The event that prompted Garza's initial post was the news that George Zimmerman, a Hispanic and multiracial man patrolling on neighborhood watch, had been acquitted of all charges in the killing of Trayvon Martin, a black seventeen-year-old high school student. On February 26, 2012, Martin had been walking back to his father's fiancée's townhouse, a place he had visited several times before, in a gated community of Sanford, Florida. He wore a "hoodie" sweatshirt and had Skittles and an iced tea in his hand. Zimmerman, who happened to be driving in the neighborhood at the time, called the police to report Martin as a suspicious person. A transcript of the call records him saying, "We've had some break-ins in my neighborhood, and there's a real suspicious guy." At some point, Martin started running. Zimmerman pursued him, even though the dispatcher told him that was not necessary. Zimmerman can be heard saying, "These assholes, they always get away."[16]

What happened next remains a mystery because only one person remains alive to tell the story. Somehow, Zimmerman and Martin got into a physical altercation. In the ensuing battle, Zimmerman, a licensed gun owner, shot Martin once in the chest. Zimmerman phoned police at 7:09 p.m., and paramedics pronounced Martin dead at 7:30 p.m. In the span of a few minutes an innocuous walk to the local convenience store for snacks had resulted in a homicide.

Police eventually arrested but then released Zimmerman, who claimed to have acted in self-defense. Florida's controversial "stand your ground" law permits the use of lethal force if citizens feel threatened in a given situation. A jury acquitted Zimmerman. Black and white citizens viewed the incident from drastically different perspectives.

A Pew Research poll found that 49 percent of whites were satisfied with the verdict that acquitted Zimmerman, while just 5 percent of black people surveyed agreed with the trial's outcome. When asked whether Trayvon Martin's death should spur further conversations about race, 28 percent of whites agreed that more discussions needed to take place compared to 78 percent of black people surveyed.[17] Trayvon Martin's death became a proxy for age-old debates about law enforcement, respectability, and criminal justice.

Just a year after Martin's homicide, Patrisse Cullors first used the #blacklivesmatter hashtag, but the phrase did not become ubiquitous until 2014 when another black teenager, Mike Brown, was killed. On August 9, Mike Brown and a friend, Dorian Johnson, were walking in the neighborhood of Ferguson, Missouri, near St. Louis. Video camera footage shows that a short time before, Brown had stolen a pack of cigarillos from a convenience store and forcefully shoved the clerk out of the way as he left. Darren Wilson, a white police officer, spotted Brown and Wilson walking in the middle of the street and ordered them to move. Wilson stopped his police SUV very close to the two youth. According to Wilson, Brown reached in the car and attempted to wrestle a sidearm away from the officer. Wilson fired the gun twice while in the car with one of the shots hitting Brown in the hand. Brown and Johnson then fled. At some point, Brown and Wilson faced each other again, and Wilson continued firing at Brown, hitting him several more times. The final shot entered the top of Brown's skull and killed him. Initial witness reports indicated that Brown had his hands up in a gesture of surrender when he was shot, prompting protestors to chant "Hands up! Don't shoot!" in the following days. A Department of Justice report released in March 2015 indicated, however, that all the shots had hit Brown from the front and that he likely did not have his hands up when this happened. After he died, the teenager's body lay in the street for several hours in the summer heat in front of an ever-growing crowd of community residents before officials finally removed him from the scene.[18]

After a highly atypical grand jury procedure, District Attorney Robert P. McCulloch announced that Officer Wilson would not be indicted. Black people and their allies across the nation responded in outrage. Protestors took to the streets in more than 150 cities. The reality that yet another unarmed black youth had been killed and no one would face legal penalties communicated a message that black lives could be extinguished with impunity.[19] Observers not only considered the isolated incidents that led to the deaths of Trayvon Martin and Mike Brown, they looked at the longer history of similar events, from the absolute power of life and death slaveowners had held over black slaves to the decades of lynching during the Jim Crow era, when few of the murderers had paid for their crimes against black people and their communities. Even in the past few years, the list of black human beings who have become hashtags has grown ever longer—Stephon Clark, Philando Castile, Freddie Gray, Walter Scott, Jamar Clark, Rekia Boyd, Eric Garner, Sandra Bland, Tamir Rice, to name just a few. Activists have deployed the phrase *black lives matter* because the cascade of killings indicated that black lives did not, in fact, matter.

Black lives matter served as a rallying cry for protests, but it also acted as an assertion of the image of God in black people. In Christian anthropology, saying that black lives matter insists that all people, including those who have darker skin, have been made in the image and likeness of God. *Black lives matter* does not mean that *only* black lives matter; it means that black lives matter too. Given the racist patterns of devaluing black lives in America's past, it is not obvious to many black people that everyone values black life. Quite the contrary, the existential equality of black people must be repeatedly and passionately proclaimed and pursued, even in the twenty-first century.

The words *black lives matter* also function as a cry of lament. Theologian Soong-Chan Rah explains in his book *Prophetic Lament* that in the Bible lament is "a liturgical response to the reality of suffering and engages God in the context of pain and suffering."[20] He goes on to say that it is a way "to express indignation and even outrage about the experience of suffering."[21] Racism has inflicted incalculable suffering on black people throughout the history of the United States, and in such a context, lament is not only understandable but necessary.

Black lives matter presents Christians with an opportunity to mourn with those who mourn and to help bear the burdens that racism has heaped on black people (Rom. 12:15).

CHRISTIAN RESPONSES TO BLACK LIVES MATTER

It may be helpful for Christians to distinguish between Black Lives Matter as an organization and *black lives matter* as a concept and movement. Many Christians, including some conservative black Christians, have rejected the concept or phrase *black lives matter* because of the Black Lives Matter organization. The organization that developed to channel passion into long-term change includes a strong platform advocating for gay, queer, and transgender rights, a position that is contrary to a conservative evangelical definition of marriage as between one man and one woman. The Black Lives Matter organization does not identify itself as a faith-based organization like the Southern Christian Leadership Conference and other organizations that formed during the civil rights movement of the 1950s and '60s. As a result, many evangelicals have distanced themselves from or even opposed both the Black Lives Matter organization and the phrase. But the American evangelical church has yet to form a movement as viable and potent that addresses the necessary concept that black lives do indeed matter. This is not to suggest that evangelicals have not responded to present-day racism but that the national presence and influence of Black Lives Matter, as both an organization and a concept, should prompt critical engagement rather than a reflexive rejection.

Although opinions about the organization vary widely, the phrase itself resonated at a deep level with numbers of Americans across the nation, and in particular it spoke to black people who sensed those words addressing a deep and painful longing—the longing for others to recognize their full, unqualified humanity. Sadly, many white Christians did not realize this, and they responded with opposition.

Many white Christians viewed the killings that made national headlines as isolated events, and they could not understand why black people and other keen observers had such strong reactions.

Evangelicals would agree that black people should be treated fairly and have all the civil rights other citizens have. But the root of the disagreement over racial issues lies deeper beneath the surface. It is a failure to acknowledge the subtler ways that racism operates today. Because their religious beliefs reinforce accountable individualism, relationalism, and antistructuralism, many white Christians wrongly assume that racism only includes overt acts, such as calling someone the "n-word" or expressly excluding black people from groups or organizations. It is good that black and white people generally can agree that racism of this type is wrong, and it usually elicits swift and unequivocal condemnation in public discourse. But the longer arc of American history reveals that Christian complicity with racism does not always require specific acts of bigotry. Being complicit only requires a muted response in the face of injustice or uncritical support of the status quo.

When Grammy-winning hip hop artist Lecrae, who is both Christian and black, began speaking up about Ferguson and *black lives matter*, the backlash from his white evangelical fans came swiftly. In response to his posts on social media outlets such as Twitter and Facebook, commenters said he was playing the "race card" and creating division.[22] And when Lecrae said he was praying for Ferguson, the first response in a long thread of replies reads "#Pray4Police" as if in rebuttal to the need to pray for the black people affected by the tragedy.[23]

After repeatedly using his platform as a famous artist to speak out against racialized injustice, Lecrae wrote an op-ed in the *Huffington Post* expressing the frustration he felt from battling the misperceptions of conservative Christians. "I hit a serious low on tour at one point. I was done with American Christian culture. No voice of my own. No authenticity. I was a puppet." He went on to explain that his difficulties in talking to white Christians about race in America even affected his relationship with God. "I'd seen so much fakeness from those who claimed to be my brothers and sisters that I didn't even know how to talk to my Heavenly Father."[24]

Early in 2016, while *black lives matter* and discussions of racial justice still inundated blogs and social media timelines, Thabiti

Anyabwile, a black pastor and writer living in Washington DC, expressed empathy for black people in the midst of the ongoing criminal justice crisis. Because of his comments, he lost support among some white evangelicals. In a blog post early in 2016, Anyabwile pointed out that his rejection came not as a result of changing his positions on the longstanding "culture war" issues of the Religious Right and evangelicals such as gay marriage, homosexuality, and abortion. Rather, the controversy began when he started talking about justice. "But mention 'justice' and that wall of evangelical troops splits like the Red Sea and turns against itself. Men who worked as fellow combatants in the traditional 'culture war' begin to suspect and even attack one another when 'justice' becomes the topic."[25] Anyabwile wrote his post in response to a message posted by another Christian, Phil Johnson, who served as the director of a prominent evangelical ministry. Johnson posted a video of Anyabwile at an evangelical conference in 2010 preaching a message called, "Fine-Sounding Arguments: How Wrongly 'Engaging the Culture' Adjusts the Gospel." Along with the video came Johnson's caption: "Before he became an agitator for the radical left wing #BlackLivesMatter movement, Thabiti Anyabwile was arguing for a more biblical, gospel-centered approach."[26] As Anyabwile pointed out in his blog post, Johnson's implication was that speaking about racial justice somehow indicated a drift away from the "true" gospel.

Some of the most pointed debates among Christians about *black lives matter* came in the wake of the triennial Urbana missions conference organized by the evangelical organization InterVarsity Christian Fellowship. On the second night of the conference, some of the staff members and hosts on stage wore t-shirts that read, "Black Lives Matter." The shirts were only a prelude to a firestorm of controversy about to be unleashed by the evening's next speaker, Michelle Higgins. Higgins is a black woman who leads the music during worship at her theologically conservative and multiethnic Presbyterian church in St. Louis. When the Ferguson uprisings took place, she got involved alongside other Christians from her church and throughout the city, and eventually she became director of outreach for an organization of Christians in the area called Faith for Justice.

Higgins's talk lasted only twenty-eight minutes, but that was plenty of time to spark heated disagreement over her remarks. "Black lives matter is not a mission of hate. It is not a mission to bring about incredible anti-Christian values and reforms to the world," she informed the audience of 16,000 college students. As if speaking about *black lives matter* head on was not enough, she went further still and criticized the primacy of abortion in the evangelical canon of sins. "We can wipe out the adoption crisis tomorrow," she said. "But we're too busy arguing to have abortion banned. We're too busy arguing to defund Planned Parenthood."[27]

This combination of an endorsement of *black lives matter* and a negative assessment of pro-life efforts to combat abortion resulted in a flood of condemnation. In a *New York Times* article, Greg Jao, a senior administrator for InterVarsity, said the organization "got blowback from just about every side." He spoke candidly about reactions from financial contributors to the organization. "Certainly we have donors and friends who have raised concerns and questions. They want to know how to interpret this [focus on *black lives matter*.]" Jao also mentioned that comments did not take on a universally negative tone. "And we've had friends and donors say 'Bravo, that was brave and courageous.'"[28]

Reactions to Lecrae, Anyabwile, and Higgins merely illustrate common attitudes that many white evangelicals have regarding issues of racial justice. A survey by the Barna Research Group revealed the mixed responses to *black lives matter* and how the responses often split along racial lines. When it came to *black lives matter*, just 13 percent of evangelicals said they supported the "message" compared to 27 percent of adults overall and 45 percent of millennials. On the same question only 7 percent of those who identified as Republicans supported the movement. Perhaps predictably, 94 percent of evangelicals thought the Christian church "plays an important role in racial reconciliation" as compared to 73 percent of all adults. In a summary of the survey's findings, researchers concluded, "If you're a white evangelical Republican, you are less likely to think race is a problem, but more likely to think you are *victim* of reverse racism." They further contended, "You are also less convinced that people of color are socially disadvantaged." Citing the importance evangelicals attribute to the church in racial reconciliation, the researchers said, "This dilemma demonstrates that those supposedly most equipped for reconciliation *do not see the need for it.*"[29]

Many Christians may agree with the principle that black lives matter, but they still wonder whether they should get involved with an organization that espouses beliefs contrary to his or her religious convictions. There is no single answer that will fit every person's situation. There should be efforts to critically engage rather than reflexively dismiss, and Christians should consider that the best way to start is to start local. Many national organizations are intentionally decentralized, so the character of individual groups varies. It helps to learn who is involved and what issues they prioritize. Contact the nearest Black Lives Matter chapter and speak with representatives. It may be that the people involved are people of faith. Countless ministers, Christians, and other religious adherents have been involved with the organization. Organizations sometimes host their meetings at churches or religious venues. Some people decide that they can participate in certain actions but not others. Ultimately, the organizations with which one chooses to affiliate in the cause of antiracism is a matter of conscience. The only wrong action is inaction.

The longstanding failure among many white Christians to acknowledge ongoing discrimination embedded in systems and structures means black and white Christians often talk past each other. One group focuses on isolated incidents; the other sees a pattern of injustice. To properly assess and move toward a solution to racism in America, both perspectives are needed. Every person makes choices and is accountable for the consequences. At the same time, injustice imposes limits on the opportunities and choices people have. In the church, conversations about injustice should include an examination of the circumstances of each incident, but Christians should also analyze the larger patterns—ones that can operate independent of malicious intent—to see the historic and systemic picture and advocate for more effective solutions.

THE 2016 PRESIDENTIAL ELECTION
AND THE 81 PERCENT

According to Franklin Graham, son of evangelical powerhouse Billy Graham, even Vice President Mike Pence thought he and his running mate, Donald Trump, had lost on election night in 2016. "[Pence] thought they had lost the election," said Graham. "I said, 'Listen buddy. If you guys win tonight, you make sure Donald understands that it's the Lord.'" When the results became official, Trump had, against the predictions of most pollsters and prognosticators, emerged as the forty-fifth president of the United States. In a text to Pence that night, Graham said, "Mike, look what God did tonight.' [Pence] said, 'Isn't it awesome?'"[30]

Graham serves as one of the faces of what historian John Fea calls the "court evangelicals," those who publicly and consistently support Donald Trump as president despite a string of decidedly non-evangelical character traits.[31] Trump, who had never held political office until he won the presidency in 2016, has been divorced and remarried. In 2017, a former adult-film actress with the stage name "Stormy Daniels" alleged that she had an affair with Trump several years earlier, just after his current wife, Melania, gave birth to their son. A month before the election, a tape obtained by the *Washington Post* recorded the presidential candidate making lewd comments about women, including kissing them and groping them without consent, while boasting that "And when you're a star they let you do it. They let you do anything."[32] Trump hardly fits the "family values" mold that conservative evangelicals had cast for their ideal candidate.

Trump traffics in harmful racial stereotypes as well. Long before he ran for president, Trump had a dubious record on race. In 1973, the US Department of Justice sued his company, Trump Management, for discrimination against potential black renters of his apartments. Under directions from their superiors, apartment managers refused to show certain apartments to black people or claimed that the rent was much higher in order to dissuade them. The company settled the case with no admission of guilt in 1975, but the Department of Justice reopened the case three years later, alleging that the discrimination, a violation of the 1968 Fair Housing Act, had continued.[33] In 1989, police accused five black and Latino teenagers of beating and raping a white woman in Central Park. In response, Trump paid $85,000 to place full-page ads in four New York City newspapers calling for a return of the death penalty. "Muggers and murderers should be forced to suffer and, when they kill, they should be executed for their crimes," he wrote. DNA evidence exonerated all five youth of the crime, but Trump never publicly changed his position.[34] In doing so, he perpetuated the assumption of criminality that many still hold toward black and brown people.

Trump gained political notoriety before the 2016 election with his comments about Barack Obama, who became the nation's first black president in 2008. Trump promoted a right-wing conspiracy theory that Obama, whose mother was white and from Kansas and whose father was a black Kenyan, was not actually born in the United States and was therefore ineligible for the presidency. In a series of interviews in 2011, Trump expressed his doubts about Obama's citizenship. "I'm starting to think that he was not born here," he told the hosts on NBC's *Today Show*.[35] Observers accused Trump of racism in questioning the American-ness of the country's first black president and of leading the charge to force Obama to reveal his long-form birth certificate to the public.

Trump's questionable stances on race have not been confined to black people. In a speech announcing his presidential candidacy in 2015, Trump promised to build a wall along the Mexico-US border because Mexicans entering the United States were "bringing drugs, they're bringing crime, they're rapists. And some, I assume, are good people."[36] In a meeting about immigration with top officials during his presidency, Trump asked why the United States should accept more immigrants from "shithole" countries such as Haiti and countries in Africa. In response, a United Nations representative said, "There is no other word one can use but 'racist.' . . . It is not just a story about vulgar language, it's . . . validating and encouraging racism and xenophobia."[37]

On August 12, 2017, America experienced a flashback to its racial past when white supremacists descended on Charlottesville, Virginia, to protest the possible removal of a monument to Confederate general Robert E. Lee from a local park. This time the protestors, who called their rally "Unite the Right," did not wear the white robes and hoods of the Ku Klux Klan; instead, they wore khaki pants and polo shirts and held tiki torches. During a counterprotest, a white supremacist rammed his car into a crowd of people and killed one woman, as well as injuring many others. In his first statement about the events that the Department of Justice labeled "domestic terrorism," Trump failed to unequivocally condemn the racist acts. Instead, he simply denounced "hatred, bigotry, and violence on many sides."[38] Many viewed his comments as creating a false equivalency between white supremacists and those who assembled to oppose them. Add to these incidents the support the president has received from white nationalist groups, his call for a ban on Muslim immigration, and his tendency to positively and uncritically quote from white nationalist media sources, and it's clear why Trump's actions have elicited repeated accusations of racism.

Black people recognized the pattern of prejudice from Trump, and they showed their distaste at the polls. Eighty-eight percent of black voters, including 94 percent of black women, supported the Democratic candidate Hillary Clinton. By contrast, 58 percent of white people voted for Trump. Breaking the 2016 voting numbers down even further reveals overwhelming support for Donald Trump among white evangelicals. According to a Pew Research report, 81 percent of voters who self-identified as white evangelicals pulled the lever for Trump. While white evangelical support for the Republican presidential candidate has regularly hovered around 75 percent or above, their support remained high in spite of his deplorable comments, especially concerning race.[39] Further reports demonstrate that during his presidency, Trump has maintained strong support from white evangelicals, especially more frequent church-goers. "Eight-in-ten white evangelical Protestants who attend church at least once a month approve of the way Trump is handling his job as president."[40]

Why did so many white evangelicals support Trump despite his obvious racist tendencies? First, it should be acknowledged that plenty of evangelicals did not support him. Many took a #NeverTrump stand and objected to his rhetoric and policies. They voted third party or refrained from voting altogether. Russell Moore, president of the Southern Baptist Convention's Ethics and Religious Liberty Commission, vocally opposed Trump during the primaries and the early part of the election campaign. He called evangelical support of Trump "illogical." He went on to suggest that evangelicals might risk losing credibility among black people by supporting Trump: "When evangelicals should be leading the way on racial reconciliation, as the Bible tells us to, are we really ready to trade unity with our black and brown brothers and sisters for this angry politician?"[41] Apparently plenty of white evangelicals did not mind trading unity with people of color, because they threatened Moore's job. In an episode reminiscent of Southern Baptist opposition to Martin Luther King Jr.'s visit decades prior, more than 100 Southern Baptist churches promised to withdraw their funding from the collective cooperative fund unless Moore changed his tone or was dismissed.[42]

Evangelical support for Donald Trump can be attributed to a combination of policy issues they thought he would champion as well as an intense dislike of Hillary Clinton. White evangelicals looked to Trump to support their pro-life stance. They wanted him to oppose gay marriage and, of vital importance, to appoint conservative Supreme Court justices who would protect and promote their policy interests. In addition, many evangelicals did not necessarily cast a vote for Donald Trump so much as vote against Hillary Clinton. Aside from being a Democrat, Clinton's public championing of abortion and alignment with Planned Parenthood, her relatively rare public expressions of her faith, her lack of outreach to conservative evangelicals, and her "emails" all combined into a mix that many white evangelicals found repugnant. But other Republican candidates in the primaries had more credible conservative bona fides than Trump and could have stood up for evangelical political priorities. Evangelical support of Trump and dislike of Clinton went beyond policy concerns.

Trump tapped into the latent sense among some evangelicals that they were losing their influence in American culture and politics.

Increasingly, evangelicals believe they are the ones experiencing persecution. That gay marriage is now the law of the land, the lasting effects of *Roe v. Wade*, the controversy over whether Christians can refuse certain services to gay and lesbian customers, and the general trend toward liberalism make some evangelicals feel like people without a home in the American political landscape. A Public Religion Research Institute survey found that the only religious group that thought Christians in America faced more discrimination than Muslims were white evangelicals: 57 percent of evangelicals thought Christians faced a lot of discrimination compared to 33 percent of Americans overall.[43] Trump's campaign slogan promised to "Make America Great Again." In the conservative Christian political mind, Trump, despite his, promised to "Make Evangelicals Great Again."

The impact of the 2016 election cannot be underestimated. In an interview for a *New York Times* article, Michael Emerson, coauthor of *Divided by Faith*, gave his assessment: "The election itself was the single most harmful event to the whole movement of reconciliation in at least the past 30 years," he said. "It's about to completely break apart."[44] The Trump campaign and presidency revealed just how tenuous the interracial coalition of Christians that had emerged in the past two and a half decades really was. The forty-fifth president did not produce the racial and political divide between black and white Christians, but he exposed and extended longstanding differences while revealing the inadequacy of recent reconciliation efforts.

THE COLOR OF COMPROMISE IN THE TWENTY-FIRST CENTURY

The never-ending struggle for black freedom has resulted in tangible gains for all Americans. Black people who once largely inhabited this country as slaves have become *Fortune* 500 CEOs, media moguls, award-winning academics, and even president. It has become more difficult, though not unheard of, for the American church to openly make racist statements and argue for the inferiority of black people. But racism has by no means disappeared from the headlines.

Examples abound. In a culturally obtuse move, a group of white professors at Southwestern Baptist Theological Seminary thought it would be funny to send off a retiring colleague by posting a posed picture of themselves in baggy pants, hoodies, and crooked caps. One professor even held a real gun.[45] The Presbyterian Church in America, a denomination founded in the 1970s but with connections to Southern Presbyterians, decided to deliberate for a year before passing a resolution about their complicity in racism during the civil rights movement.[46] The Southern Baptist Convention faced a public relations debacle when a committee refused to consider a proposal by a black minister to condemn the racism of the alt-right.[47] And while multiracial congregations have become more commonplace, many churches remain some of the most segregated places in America.

Plenty of white evangelicals have promoted reconciliation and have attempted to address the racism that has defined large portions of the American church in the past. Yet, spurred by evangelical support for Trump, many black Christians have distanced themselves from white evangelicals. In a widely circulated op-ed for the *New York Times*, black Baptist minister Lawrence Ware renounced his membership in the Southern Baptist Convention. "My reasoning is simple," he explained. "As a black scholar of race and a minister who is committed to social justice, I can no longer be part of an organization that is complicit in the disturbing rise of the so-called alt-right, whose members support the abhorrent policies of Donald Trump and whose troubling racial history and current actions reveal a deep commitment to white supremacy."[48] Ware articulated a keen sense that white evangelicals have continued to compromise with racism even in an age when the obvious racist actions of the past have been denounced. Chanequa Walker-Barnes, now a professor of theology in Atlanta, left her position on staff at a majority white church after the 2016 election. "We were willing to give up our preferred worship style for the chance to really try to live this vision of beloved community with a diverse group of people," she said. "That didn't work."[49]

Christian complicity with racism in the twenty-first century looks different than complicity with racism in the past. It looks like

Christians responding to *black lives matter* with the phrase *all lives matter*. It looks like Christians consistently supporting a president whose racism has been on display for decades. It looks like Christians telling black people and their allies that their attempts to bring up racial concerns are "divisive." It looks like conversations on race that focus on individual relationships and are unwilling to discuss systemic solutions. Perhaps Christian complicity in racism has not changed much after all. Although the characters and the specifics are new, many of the same rationalizations for racism remain.

Centuries of racism in the American church cannot be overcome by "pious irrelevancies and sanctimonious trivialities" that ignore the deep social, political, and cultural divides that persist across the color line.[50] If the church hopes to see meaningful progress in race relations during the twenty-first century, then it must undertake bold, costly actions with an attitude of unprecedented urgency. The solutions are simple though not easy. They are, in many cases, obvious though unpopular. No matter their difficulty or distastefulness, however, they are necessary in order to change the narrative of the American church and race.

THE FIERCE URGENCY OF NOW

Burdened by the brutality of racism in America, Martin Luther King Jr. stepped to the microphone near the Lincoln Memorial in Washington DC and delivered his "I Have a Dream" speech. Most people remember the line from his historic address where King expressed the desire for his children to be judged not by the color of their skin but by the content of their character. Just as important, though, is the restlessness he displayed in the speech. "We have also come to this hallowed spot to remind America of the fierce urgency of now," King explained. "This is no time to engage in the luxury of cooling off or to take the tranquilizing drug of gradualism. . . . Now is the time to rise from the dark and desolate valley of segregation to the sunlit path of racial justice."[1]

That was August 28, 1963. More than fifty years later, how far has the American church come in terms of race relations? The "Whites Only" and "No Negroes Allowed" signs have been taken down, but schools remain segregated. People of color are incarcerated at disproportionally high rates. Black unemployment remains double that of whites. Most poignantly, churches remain largely segregated. The reluctance to reckon with racism has led to a chasm between black and white Christians in theology, politics, and culture. This chasm only makes it harder to productively communicate and take effective action around racial issues. When it comes to opposing racism, have we as a nation overdosed on "the tranquilizing drug of gradualism"?[2]

In this book, I have provided a brief historical survey to illustrate the many ways the American church has been complicit in racism over several centuries. In some cases, they actively constructed ideological and structural impediments to equality. If the twenty-first century is to be different from the previous four centuries, then the American church must exercise even more creativity and effort to break down racial barriers than it took to erect them in the first place.

In spite of all the shortcomings highlighted in this examination of the American church, many of the solutions proposed, solutions that might actually prove effective in changing the status quo, are often dismissed as impractical. Effective remedies to the present state of racial injustice—a situation created by an unbending commitment to ideas of racial superiority and inferiority—are deemed too inconvenient to pursue. But studying the history of the American church's compromise with racism should teach us that action is necessary and long overdue. Pioneering black historian John Hope Franklin said, "I think knowing one's history leads one to act in a more enlightened fashion." He went on to state, "I cannot imagine how knowing one's history would not urge one to be an activist." Those who have humbly submitted to the tutelage of history cannot help but exclaim, "I have to do something!"[3]

This chapter presents practical ways to address the current state of racial injustice in America. Most of the solutions focus on structural and institutional methods to combat inequality. I understand that this approach may provoke resistance in some readers since the default way of thinking for many conservative Christians is to focus on the relational aspects of race. To be clear, friendships and conversations are necessary, but they are not sufficient to change the racial status quo. Christians must also alter how impersonal systems operate so that they might create and extend racial equality.

Many of these suggestions have been or are being practiced by a small but committed number of people, but some Christians consider them too risky or impractical to seriously consider. My hope is that as people learn about how deep and far reaching the problem of racism is, these "radical" solutions will start to seem more reasonable. This list is far from exhaustive. It is an initial attempt to offer a few actions that I believe can actually impact race relations for the better. Perhaps my suggestions will inspire additional ideas. Many of the methods of addressing racism highlighted here pertain to white Christians, but people of all races and ethnicities play a role in bringing about racial justice.

THE ARC OF RACIAL JUSTICE

The most frequent question I get when presenting about racial justice is, What do we do? People who ask this agree that the American church has compromised with racism and that racism continues to be a problem. Their next impulse is to want to do something about the problem, so they ask me what they should do. After years of listing random action items, I have now grouped them into three broad categories.

The ARC (Awareness, Relationships, Commitment) of racial justice helps distinguish different types of antiracist actions. They are not formulaic; they can happen nonsequentially and simultaneously. Nor should this process ever be considered complete. Even the most seasoned racial justice activists constantly learn, question, and reform their own attitudes and actions. Though not the final word on antiracism, the ARC of racial justice provides a useful framework for taking decisive action against discrimination.

To increase your capacity to fight your own complicity in racism, you can start by increasing your awareness of the issues and the people involved. Although you can expand your awareness in many ways, one particularly fruitful place to start is by reading and learning more about the racial history of the United States. I am concerned that our knowledge about racial justice in this country tends to extend no further than one chapter in a high school social studies textbook. History is about context, so studying history remains vital. It teaches us how to place people, events, and movements within the broader scope of God's work in the world.

Context is something Bible-believing Christians should understand better than anyone. In our passionate pursuit of biblical interpretation, we know that we must always look at the context. We want to know the historical-grammatical situation of the text so that we can accurately explain and apply it. It's no different with racial justice. We have to develop an awareness of the context to properly exegete the times and apply biblical solutions.

Some action steps to increase your awareness include the following:

- Watch documentaries about the racial history of the United States.[4]
- Diversify your social media feed by following racial and ethnic minorities and those with different political outlooks than yours.
- Access websites and podcasts created by racial and ethnic minorities.
- Do an internet search about a particular topic instead of always asking your black friend to explain an issue to you.[5]

But awareness isn't enough. No matter how aware you are, your knowledge will remain abstract and theoretical until you care about the people who face the negative consequences of racism. The problem is that it is hard to make friends with people from different racial and ethnic backgrounds. A Public Religion Research Institute study revealed that in a one-hundred-friend scenario, white people had just one black friend, one Latinx, and one Asian friend. In that same scenario, black people had eight white friends, two Latinx friends, and zero Asian friends.[6] The long history of racial segregation in this country coupled with the tendency to associate with those most like ourselves has left all of us in mostly homogenous social networks.

Some action steps to develop interracial relationships include:

- Start with the people you know. Most of us know someone of a different race or ethnicity. Have you talked with them specifically about their experiences and perspectives of race and justice? These individuals cannot merely be projects or sources of information. They are real people with whom to pursue a meaningful friendship. Still, it takes intentionality to diversify our social networks, and we should start with those nearest us.

- Find new places to hang out. We are creatures of habit and convenience. We go to particular places simply because they are familiar. A purposeful effort to develop relationships with people from diverse backgrounds will carry you to different restaurants, grocery stores, and hangouts. If you strategically organize your spatial habits, the mundane places where you enact your regular routines can become the richest sites to encounter those who are different from you.

- Join a sport, club, or activity with people who are different. In my experience, other than people who have been involved with the military, those who have the most diverse networks of friends have participated in some sort of activity that brought them into frequent contact with people of other races and ethnicities. You may have to engineer these opportunities, but they can lead to organic friendships that cross traditional lines of social division.

Committing to concrete action may be the hardest part of pursuing racial justice. Commitment to the ARC model requires a total shift in disposition so that antiracist activity is a way of life, not simply a topic to which you give occasional and superficial attention. Developing awareness and relationships may create a burden for the struggles of others, but does that burden move you to act? Are you willing to set aside preferences and prestige to take the side of the marginalized and despised? More to the point, are you willing to address the systemic and institutional aspects of racism rather than solely work on an interpersonal level?

Action steps for developing a lifelong commitment to racial justice include:

- Create something. Write a blog post. Write a book. Write a sermon. Do a Sunday School class. Host a forum. Write a song or a poem. Create something that speaks to racial justice.

As you do it, though, remember it always helps to get feedback from person from a different racial or ethnic background who is willing to help.[7]

- Join an organization that advocates for racial and social justice.
- Donate money to organizations that advocate for racial and social justice.
- Speak with candidates for elected office in your area and ask them about their views of racial justice and the policies they advocate.
- Vote.

The ARC of racial justice provides an entry point for anyone who may be new to the journey for racial equity. After a survey of the American church's complicity in racism, though, Christians must undertake courageous and urgent action to correct historic wrongs and their ongoing ramifications. The following suggestions may seem extreme to some, but they are merely proportional to the effort and intentionality that many Christians in America lent to building racial divisions in the first place.

REPARATION(S)

Perhaps the only other "r-word" more controversial to American Christians than racism is reparations. The idea goes against politically conservative ideas of small government and low taxes. It raises all kinds of questions about practicality, such as how to determine which black people are actually descendants of slaves and who counts as black in a socially constructed paradigm? These and other concerns present valid obstacles to the implementation of reparations, but they should not halt the conversation altogether. The fact remains that enslaved black people labored for centuries without pay. They tilled the soil, picked crops until their fingers bled, raised other people's children, and performed many other valuable forms of labor even as they endured abuse, rape, murder, and family separations. But reparations pertain not only to the problems that attended slavery. The opportunities lost due to legalized segregation during the Jim Crow era also demand redress. Segregation denied black people opportunities for education, employment, and asset accumulation, all of which contribute to the wealth gap between black and white citizens.

The wealth gap between black and white citizens is colossal, and there is no end in sight. A 2011 study revealed that a typical white household had sixteen times the wealth of a black one.[8] According to a 2014 report, for every dollar in a white household, a black household has less than seven cents. Black people comprise about 13 percent of the population but hold less than 3 percent of the nation's total wealth. Even among the richest people, the wealthiest 1 percent of black families have about $1.6 million compared to $12 million for the wealthiest 1 percent of white families.[9] The reasons for these gaps include redlining in real estate, denying bank loans to people of color, and higher unemployment rates among black people, just to name a few. These gaps will persist unless a broad-based reform effort takes hold. One facet of these reforms could include reparations.

Presbyterian minister Duke Kwon distinguishes between reparation and reparations.[10] The former refers to the principle, and the latter refers to the practice. In terms of the principle, reparation simply means repair. Injustice obligates reparation. Reparation is not a matter of vengeance or charity; it's a matter of justice. The concept of reparation has biblical precedence. Under Old Testament law if a person wrongs another person, the wrongdoer should confess the sin. But saying "I'm sorry" is not enough. Expressing remorse may begin the process of healing, but somehow that which was damaged must be restored. The law goes on to state that the wrongdoer "must make full restitution for the wrong they have done, add a fifth of the value to it and give it all to the person they have wronged" (Num. 5:7). In the New Testament, when the Jewish tax collector Zacchaeus accepted Jesus as Lord, he gave away half his possessions and repaid those he had cheated "four times the amount" (Luke 19:8).

Some might object that the concept of reparation applies only to interactions among individuals, not societal or institutional issues. The prophet Daniel prayed for forgiveness not only for himself, not only for the people of Israel, but also for "our princes and our ancestors" who were "covered with shame" (Dan. 9:8). Daniel made the petition in light of both present injustice and that of his forebears. Within Christianity, then, is a sense of corporate and communal participation. The injustices of the past continue to affect the present, and it is up to the current generation to interrupt the cycle of racial compromise and confront it with courage.

Reparations, on the other hand, can take many forms. Kwon distinguishes between "civic reparations" and "ecclesiastical reparations."[11] Civic reparations come through the state. These reparations originate from government policies, laws, and institutions that can begin to repair the damages done. Germany has paid about $50 billion to Holocaust survivors and their families. Japanese-Americans confined to internment camps during World War II received an apology from the government and $20,000 per victim. Although far too few received far too little, some Native American nations received some recompense for the land stolen from them. But any conversation about reparations must necessarily include discussions about how to enact justice toward the original inhabitants of this land.[12] For black people, no serious attempt at the civic level has ever been sustained, and the material and financial injustices remain.

According to Kwon, ecclesiastical reparations occur mainly from and within Christian churches. These pertain to the obligations that the faithful have to one another in light of historic injustices. Even apart from political attempts at reparations, the church should be willing to consider some talk about reparations. Jesus taught his disciples that if they are at the altar and remember their brother or sister has something against them, they should leave their gift. "First go and be reconciled to them; then come and offer your gift" (Matt. 5:24). Black people have endured innumerable offenses at the hands of white people in the American church. Injuries to the church body, as Jesus teaches, are so important that one should interrupt worship to go address the problem. Much of the American church has not yet considered racism to be a serious enough sin to interrupt their regularly scheduled worship, at least not much beyond conversations and symbolic gestures, to repair the relationship.

Churches could lead society by independently declaring a literal or figurative "year of Jubilee" for black people. They could pool resources to fund a massive debt forgiveness plan for black families. Or they could invest large amounts into trust funds for black youth, who now experience disproportionate rates of poverty in America. These monies could fund educational opportunities or down payments on houses. Funds could be used for financial investments. Another way churches could also help immediately is by funding black-led church plants and religious nonprofit organizations. Black Christians have an abundance of innovative ideas for evangelism, apologetics, discipleship, media, and the arts. What they often lack is funding. In an attempt at reparations, churches could decide to funnel significant resources into promising Christian enterprises that have the talent and vision to be successful but lack financial stability. Further, countless pastors in the urban core and rural areas diligently labor in bivocational ministry. They attend to the spiritual needs of a congregation in a storefront or small building while attempting to make a living through some other occupation that pays more. Wealthier churches could fund a salary sufficient for a pastor to work full time in the church and exponentially increase the minister's capacity to serve in the local community.[13] Additionally, Christian churches and schools could partner to make sure black students pay no tuition to Christian colleges and grad schools. The tuition relief would directly address some of the damage caused by the racially discriminatory tactics that some Christian schools employed in the past. Churches could also invest money in local public schools that predominately serve black students so they have the books, technology, and teachers they need for an adequate education.

TAKE DOWN CONFEDERATE MONUMENTS

More than 150 years after Union and Confederate forces laid down their guns, America is still fighting the Civil War. Instead of firing canons and muskets, the combatants fire off blog posts and petitions to either take down or preserve monuments to the Confederacy. If the American church wants to make a clear break with the racial compromise that has characterized its past, then believers must agree that it is time to take down the Confederate monuments.

The white supremacist "Unite the Right" rally in Charlottesville, Virginia, in 2017 brought back memories of similar events throughout US history, a past that many thought the nation had moved beyond. Photos of Dylan Roof, the white man who killed nine black churchgoers at Mother Emanuel Church in Charleston, posing with a Confederate flag also helped ignite an energetic debate about what to do with Confederate monuments, statues, and symbols. The statues and flags stand both as a message that America is the "white man's country" and as a way to redeem the Confederacy in the eyes of southerners and the nation.

Removing Confederate statues and symbols from public places will not eradicate racism. Indeed, even some black people express indifference at the endeavor. But statues and symbols are supposed to represent the community. Symbols of the Confederacy only represent a part of the community, a part that stood for the preservation of slavery. Those who declare that Confederate symbols represent "heritage not hate" must recognize that part of that heritage was hate in the form of slavery and white supremacy.

Given the racist roots of Confederate iconography in public places, Christians should stand against their continued presence as an act of racial solidarity. One Christian woman, Bree Newsome, illustrated her opposition in dramatic fashion and cut through the stalling tactics of politicians by climbing a flagpole in front of the state house in South Carolina and removing the Confederate flag. Holding the flag aloft she declared, "You come against me with hatred, oppression, and violence. I come against you in the name of God. This flag comes down today."[14] In the name of God, will other Christians stand against the visible symbols of racism promoted in America's public places?

LEARN FROM THE BLACK CHURCH

Part of the pernicious effects of white supremacy in the church has been the devaluing of black theology—the biblical teachings that arise from and are informed by the experience of racial suffering, oppression, and perseverance by black people in America. In many white Christian contexts, theology produced by racial minorities comes with an assumption of heresy and heterodoxy. The implicit message from many conservative white pastors and professors is that black Christians have theological integrity to the degree they adopt the teachings that come from approved European and white American sources. This should not be so. Rather, the body of believers should commit themselves to valuing and learning from the distinct contributions that come from marginalized groups such as black people in America.

For example, the American church can learn from the black church what it means to lament. Many church traditions have allowed triumphalism to creep into the pulpit and the pews. Just as citizens can sometimes presume the ascendancy and inevitability of American economic and global power, so the church can presume its own favor and privilege by imagining itself as God's chosen nation and people. Soong-Chan Rah studied popular Christians songs and found that most of them focus on victory and joy.[15] This canon of sacred songs, however, exhibits a dearth of lament and sorrow. Much of Christian history has been characterized by persecution and rejection, and black Christians intimately and experientially know the reality of ongoing suffering that comes from the bigotry of others and by no fault of their own. In the midst of marginalization, they have learned how to dwell with sadness and transform it into strength.

The musical genre of the Negro spiritual exemplifies the ability of black Christians to theologize their suffering in song. They moaned, "Hold on just a little while longer," in order to make it through one more day. They knew that earth was not their only stop, and they welcomed the "sweet chariot coming forth to carry me home." The Negro spiritual put black lamentations into songs that soared upward as prayers for God to save them and grant them the perseverance to exist and resist. Through their understanding of Scripture, black Christians sang, "His eye is on the sparrow, and I know he watches me." They looked to the book of Exodus and saw God saving the Israelites from slavery. In the white slaveowners they saw "old Pharaoh" and knew they could pray, "Let my people go." They saw Daniel saved from the fiery furnace and asked, "Didn't my Lord deliver Daniel? Then why not every man?" Black people have somehow found a way to flourish because of faith. It is a faith that is vibrant and still inspires black Christians to endure and struggle against present-day forms of racism. The entire church can learn from believers who have suffered yet still hold onto God's unchanging hand.

Black theology can teach the American church not just how to lament but how to rejoice as well. The exuberant vocal and bodily expressions common in much of black worship represent a faith that celebrates God's goodness in equal measure with lament over humanity's sinfulness. Those who have suffered much find much joy in God's salvation. After laboring all week under the dehumanizing conditions of slavery, black Christians celebrated on Sunday. They thanked God for giving them life and breath and the full functioning of their faculties. They worshiped God as an outlet for the creativity and vitality that had been suppressed all week. Shouts of "Amen" and "Hallelujah" punctuated every part of the service. Generations of black Christians have inherited a tradition of unashamed praise for God. The rest of American churches may well discover a new sense of God's goodness when they engage their full selves in worship.

The pleasant byproduct of learning theology from the black church is that some of the assumptions of suspicion will start to fall away. Christians will learn that people from different nations and ethnicities have dwelled in different contexts that cause them to approach the Bible with different questions and emphases. As the church learns to value the unique applications of eternal biblical principles across people groups, it will grasp more of God's truth than ever before.

START A NEW SEMINARY

Existing seminaries, especially theologically conservative ones, often lack the institutional knowledge to properly train Christians for effective ministry in an increasingly pluralistic and diverse society. While many schools have made admirable efforts to change this

reality—offering full-ride scholarships for minorities, adjusting some
course offerings and required readings to reflect more diversity, adding
black faculty and staff—it simply may not be possible to tweak existing
structures enough to adequately educate their students in a culturally
responsive way. New seminaries that have incorporated antiracist ideas
from their inception may be required. This is not to say that racially
responsive seminaries do not already exist, just that we need more
of them.

A new seminary would begin with a diverse Board of Trustees,
faculty, and staff. Rather than trying to add diversity, racial and ethnic
variety would be there from the start. This team would compose the
curriculum in such a way that students gain exposure to a slate of
theologians, both male and female, from all kinds of races and nation-
alities. The courses and readings would incorporate themes of justice,
not simply focusing on conversion and relegating issues of culture
and context exclusively to "missions" classes. Courses would have a
renewed focus on theological anthropology, and professors would dedi-
cate more of their time to researching and teaching new applications
of the image of God doctrine. History would form a critical part of
the curriculum with entire courses dedicated to black history in theological context. The variety of representation among the visible leaders
of the institution and in the curriculum would then make it easier to
recruit a diverse student body.

The delivery method of education would be sensitive to the needs
of black students, who often work bivocationally as pastors and are only
available to take classes on nights and weekends. Classroom content
would come through intensive weekend, evening, or online courses.
A structured internship and mentoring component in churches and
other ministries would replace the "practical theology" classes many
seminaries now require. Critically, this seminary would need endow-
ment and large upfront contributions to lower the cost of tuition for the
students, many of whom may come from lower income backgrounds.

A new seminary would present the opportunity to embed racial
equality into the identity of the institution. Unfortunately, many
conservative Christian schools have existed with racially insensitive

policies and cultural myopia for so long that substantive changes may take generations to realize, if they can occur at all. Swaying donors, alumni, faculty, staff, and current students may cause even the most impassioned reformer to give up. Instead of expending valuable energy transforming a school whose personnel may resist the very idea of antiracism, that energy could go toward starting a new seminary that is already racially aware and responsive.

HOST FREEDOM SCHOOLS AND PILGRIMAGES

Education must lead to liberation. The acquisition of knowledge should not result only in personal enlightenment but also the allevi- ation of oppression. Freedom schools and pilgrimages would employ experiential education to bend minds and hearts toward compassion and activism.

In the 1960s, activists started Freedom Schools to teach people at the grassroots level about civil rights and methods of protesting for change. Freedom Schools in the new millennium would have a similar purpose. In-depth teaching about America's racial history would reveal the ways racism has operated and changed over time. These lessons would go deeper than the simplistic narratives many textbooks and schools teach. They would include lessons about nations in Africa and their achievements because black history did not start with slavery. At the same time, in the North American context, Freedom Schools would describe the daily dehumanization of slavery, the terror of lynching, and the strength and limitations of previous freedom movements.

New Freedom Schools would also teach everyday Christians how to get involved in activism. They would discuss current systemic injustices such as mass incarceration, police brutality, underfunded schools, and healthcare inequality. But they would go further. Freedom Schools would also highlight organizations that are already doing the work of reform. They would bring in speakers and analyze case studies for methods that work in bringing about justice. Christians would be encouraged to get involved in the current civil rights movement when- ever and however they can—as marchers, writers, artists, financial contributors. Some motivated and resourceful individuals may even start their own new organizations and groups to join the movement for justice and freedom.

These schools would be geared primarily toward adults, but youth curricula could be developed as well. Attendees would come for a series of workshop sessions over the course of a few days or a week. By the end they will have gained valuable information to equip them for effective antiracist action. The Freedom School experience could be augmented by partnerships with colleges, universities, and seminaries to earn classroom credit. This education could also be coupled with some sort of organizational certification that attests to the participants' skills to lead racial justice efforts in a Christian organization or church. This is not a brand-new idea. What might be different from similar programs is the explicit effort to recruit Christians from conservative theological traditions into the schools.

Pilgrimages serve as another method of transformative education. Reading books and listening to presentations serve a purpose, but they cannot replicate the experience of visiting the sites and seeing the places where historical events happened. Christians should visit Emanuel AME Church in Charleston and touch the white walls that have stood for decades and seem to breathe with life. They should travel to the National Civil Rights Museum in Memphis and see the wreath hung on the balcony of the Lorraine Motel in the exact spot where Martin Luther King Jr. stood when an assassin's bullet stole his life. Christians should look into the history of their communities to explore significant sites to develop an appreciation for the black past and present that exists in their own vicinity.[16]

Pilgrimages would take place over the course of several days or weeks. Such journeys would be appropriate for all kinds of people, including Bible study groups, the staffs of Christian ministries, pastors, teachers, professors, and laypeople in the church. Many pilgrimages could explore several sites in one journey. This is not a sightseeing excursion though. Pilgrimages are spiritual ventures that challenge the participants to make sense of their surroundings and what they are learning from a spiritual standpoint. They include prayer, journaling,

Scripture readings, and humble listening to individuals who have experienced suffering or who have conducted in-depth research on relevant topics. A pilgrimage makes abstract concepts of racism real through physical, sensible encounters that evoke visceral and emotional responses. The result of such pilgrimages would be the kind of transformative encounter that leads to an ongoing commitment to working against racism in all its forms.

MAKE JUNETEENTH A NATIONAL HOLIDAY

The demise of what many have called America's "original sin" would seem to be a likely candidate for frequent, even annual, commemoration nationwide. The moment when millions of black people finally gained the liberation they had been fighting for since at least 1619 deserves space in the calendar to help people remember who America truly is and how much effort it takes to overcome the racism that often characterizes life in this nation. At present, the most logical occasion to mark the abolition of slavery, Juneteenth, is marked at the state but not the national level.

Juneteenth, a mash-up of the words June and nineteenth, remembers the day in 1865 when slaves in Texas finally learned about their emancipation. It is the oldest-known celebration of black freedom from slavery. While over forty states currently recognize Juneteenth as a state holiday or observance, it should become a national one.

Making Juneteenth a national holiday would serve several purposes. First, it would highlight freedom. While Confederate monuments should come down, that's only part of what healing from the racial wounds of slavery and racism entails. Positive reminders of the struggle for freedom must be created. Second, it would commemorate one of the most important historical events in US history. The Emancipation Proclamation opened the way for further legislation designed to grant black people their civil and human rights such as the thirteenth, fourteenth, and fifteenth amendments. Emancipation is a singular moment in US history, and making Juneteenth a national holiday would help solidify the reality that black history *is* American history. Third, celebrating Juneteenth as a national holiday would remind us how far we've come and how far we have left to go. This commemoration would both amplify the agency of black people in securing the end of race-based chattel slavery while also motivating present-day activism for securing the full independence and equality of all people.

Full freedom has not been achieved for all Americans. Too many people still struggle to break all kinds of gender, racial, ethnic, and economic bonds. The fight for the full equality and freedom of all Americans persists. The time is now and long overdue for the nation to memorialize Juneteenth as a day that marks liberty as both a reality and an aspiration.[17]

PARTICIPATE IN THE MODERN-DAY CIVIL RIGHTS MOVEMENT

Reverend William J. Barber Jr., a pastor and activist from North Carolina, has called for a third reconstruction. The first reconstruction occurred immediately after the Civil War when newly freed slaves joined in a flowering of black political, economic, and social participation. The second reconstruction happened during the civil rights movement of the 1950s and 1960s when activists assailed the stronghold of Jim Crow segregation. The third reconstruction is happening right now.

Careful observers agree that the nation is in the midst of another wave of the civil rights movement. People across the nation from all kinds of backgrounds increasingly recognize entrenched injustice and are mobilizing for change. People are marching in the streets. They are staging sit-ins in state capitols and allowing themselves to be arrested for nonviolent civil disobedience. New organizations have formed to combat specific forms of oppression and recruit others to their cause. The national news reports daily on the individual and public outcry about issues such as the poisoned water in Flint, Michigan, the separation of immigrant children from their parents, and the racism still present in politics as well as business, entertainment, and the church.

Some may have missed the fact that a civil rights movement is afoot. Part of the reason is that the modern movement looks different. Although male pastors garnered most of the media attention during the civil rights movement of the twentieth century, women have always been an indispensable force in resistance movements. This fact is demonstrated in the modern-day freedom struggle through the continued leadership of dynamic women such as Kimberly Bryant who started "Black Girls Code" to give young girls the opportunity to learn technical skills and computer programming.[18] Erica Garner, the daughter of Eric Garner, whose father's death at the hands of police sparked the #Icantbreathe hashtag, became an advocate for police reform until her death in 2017 at the age of twenty-seven.[19] Tarana Burke founded the #MeToo movement to advocate for the dignity of sexual abuse survivors, especially black women.[20]

One aspect of the civil rights movement that has remained critical is the role of people of faith. While it is true that the civil rights movement of the mid-twentieth century had a clearly church-based core of activists, Christians are still involved in today's black freedom struggle. Leaders such as Brittany Packnett, Bryan Stephenson, and Bernice King often speak publicly about their faith. Pastors and laypeople alike populate the marches and fill the churches where rallies still take place. The question is whether the broader American church will recognize and participate in today's civil rights movement.

The movement of the twenty-first century is happening along several vectors. First, mass incarceration and criminal justice reform have become priorities for thousands of Americans. The entrance to the Legacy Museum: From Enslavement to Mass Incarceration, which opened in 2018 in Montgomery, Alabama, has the words *slavery evolved* at the beginning of an exhibit showing how slavery morphed into modern-day mass incarceration. Spurred by police-related shootings of unarmed black people, more citizens have become aware of the skyrocketing levels of incarceration among black and brown people. New scholarships, organizations, and movements have cropped up to combat overcriminalization.

Another aspect of today's civil rights movement attempts to combat ongoing segregation. Despite the *Brown v. Board of Education* ruling, schools and residential areas remain as segregated as ever, sometimes even more so. Nikole Hannah-Jones, an award-winning investigative journalist, has committed her research to exploring segregation in public education. She finds that "most black and Latino students today are segregated by both race and class, a combination that wreaks havoc on the learning environment."[21] Christians need to pay attention to how their educational choices for their own children reinforce racial and economic segregation in schools.

The new civil rights movement continues to fight for voting rights for poor people and racial minorities. In 2013, a five to four vote in the Supreme Court struck down a key component of the 1965 Voting Rights Act. The component stipulated that certain states that had historically practiced voter suppression had to request federal permission to change their state voting laws. Many saw the court's ruling as a step back toward the days of Jim Crow when white supremacists routinely barred black people and others from their right to exercise the vote. Strict voter identification laws, hyperpartisan gerrymandering, and the lifetime loss of voting privileges for the formerly incarcerated have all become targets of renewed attention and cries for reform. Christians, whether Republican or Democrat, should be able to agree on ways to ensure a truly democratic political process and work together for change.

Many Christians today say they would have been active participants in the civil rights movement fifty years ago. Now, in the midst of a new civil rights movement, is their chance to prove it.

PUBLICLY DENOUNCE RACISM

Public offense calls for public opposition. Too many Christian leaders refuse to use their platforms to publicly speak against racism. Those who do tend to speak in generalities. "Racism is wrong," they say, but they refrain from naming individuals or situations in which racism is at play. Moreover, they use euphemisms like "racial tension" or "racially charged" instead of simply naming words or actions "racist." More Christians, particularly people with large platforms, must be willing to take the criticism that comes with taking a prominent stance against bigotry. The effort to exercise due diligence and gather accurate information may delay a response, but it should not preclude one. In addition, the reticence to call out specific sins specifically poses a problem. If a particular person has done something that violates the spirit of racial equality, then that person should be cited no matter how famous that person is. Confronting the shortcomings of powerful and respected people has never been easy, but it has always been necessary.

Publicly denouncing racism should also include disassociating with racists. If someone has been called out for racism, and they refuse to accept responsibility for the harm they caused—whatever their intent—then that person should not enjoy continued credibility and attention. Refuse to go to their conferences, buy their books, quote them on social media, or share their work. All of this can be done without rancor but with conviction.

START A CIVIL RIGHTS MOVEMENT . . . TOWARD THE CHURCH

Large segments of the American church have lost all moral authority to speak prophetically against racism because they continue to practice it. This tends to happen in subtle ways—sharing the works of people who practiced slavery without any context or criticism; continually hosting panels, conferences, and other events that feature only white men; Christian schools making peace with the presence of buildings named after racists or featuring their statues on campus grounds; harboring an uncritical opinion that Republicans represent the "Christian political party" in spite of increasingly overt racist rhetoric from the party's elected officials and other leaders. The list goes on.

In light of ongoing complicity with racism in the church, what is to be done? Shall we hold another conference? Form another panel? Write another book like this one? At what point will Christians who are fed up with racism take more decisive action?

Perhaps the American church should be the object of a mass movement for justice. Maybe a mass march for racial justice in our congregations is called for. Or Christians could conduct pray-ins in the administrative offices of Christian organizations and institutions that refuse to take meaningful action to eliminate racism. Additionally, Christ followers could boycott specific events, publications, or organizations until they concede to demands for a more racially inclusive environment.

Conducting nonviolent direct action protests toward other Christians and their institutions may seem offensive to some. They may decry such activism as divisive, disrespectful of the law, and militant. Those objections echo the ones antiracist activists have heard throughout American history. Change must come to the American church. It is up to Christians who comprise the church to end compromise with racism within the church.

FAITH WITHOUT WORKS IS DEAD

This much is clear—the American church has compromised with racism. Countless Christians have ignored, obscured, or misunderstood this history. But the excuses are gone. The information cannot be hidden. The only question that remains is what the church will do now that its complicity in racism has been exposed.

In the Bible, James 4:17 says, "If anyone, then, knows the good they ought to do and doesn't do it, it is sin for them." This chapter has given some suggestions for what to do about racism in the church. The church today must practice the good that ought to be done. To look at this history and then refuse to act only perpetuates racist patterns. It is time for the church to stand against racism and compromise no longer.

Conclusion

BE STRONG AND COURAGEOUS

After Moses died, God called Joshua to lead the people of Israel into the promised land. Joshua understandably experienced trepidation at the prospect of leading a throng of people into a land filled with enemies and succeeding Moses, the leader of Israel who spoke face-to-face with God. Sensing the fear that threatened to paralyze Joshua, God exhorted him. Three times in the first nine verses of the book of Joshua, God tells Joshua to be strong and courageous (Josh. 1: 6–7, 9). The words "be strong and courageous" came in the form of a command, not a suggestion. In the face of the most difficult role of his life, God ordered Joshua to have strength and courage so that Joshua could faithfully execute his calling. In much the same way, the church today must receive God's command to show strength and courage to combat racism.

When it comes to racism, the American church does not have a "how to" problem but a "want to" problem. Given ten minutes, a pen, and paper, most American Christians could come up with a list of ways to increase racial equity in our congregations and communities. We know that we need a more diverse leadership, that we should develop relationships across racial and ethnic lines, that people who continue to peddle prejudice should be opposed. Though solutions abound, racism remains. In my experience of talking to hundreds of Christians—black and white, men and women, young and old—I have observed one primary reason more of us do not exhibit the strength and courage required to root out racism: *fear*.

The second chapter of Galatians illustrates how fear can sabotage interracial solidarity. The apostle Peter had been eating with the gentiles, an act forbidden by Old Testament Jewish law. Christ had broken down the "dividing wall of hostility" between Jew and gentile (Eph. 2:14). Yet the old prejudices remained. At a certain point, Peter withdrew from fellowship with the gentiles, and the Bible explains why. A certain group from James came to meet Peter, and "he began to draw back and separate himself from the Gentiles because he was afraid of those who belonged to the circumcision group" (Gal. 2:12). There it is again. Fear. Paul withdrew from the gentiles because he feared human beings more than the Lord who sits on high.

I am convinced that a fear of other people—what they will say, think, and do if we stand against racism—holds the church back from more aggressive action to bring about justice. Indifference certainly plays a role. Apathy has its part. But when confronted with a choice to oppose racism or to acquiesce to business as usual, people of God too often shrink back. This goes for Christians of all colors. Even minorities fear causing too much of a stir over racism for fear they will lose their job, money, status, or opportunities (and with good reason!). Fear affects us all.

Another type of fear that may affect some of us is the fear of getting it wrong. We worry that we do not know enough yet, that our good intentions may have unintended negative consequences, or that the very people we seek to serve will rebuke us for our ignorance or missteps. I cannot say this will not happen. Standing for racial justice involves risk. But effective advocacy is a skill just like any other, and skills can be learned. Ultimately, though, you cannot read your way, listen your way, or watch your way into skillful advocacy. At some point you must act. Go forth not in fear but in faith that even your mistakes will increase your capacity to disrupt racism.

As the American church considers facing racism, we must remember that God's command for Joshua to be strong and courageous also came with a promise. "Do not be afraid; do not be discouraged, for the

Lord your God will be with you wherever you go" (Josh. 1:9). The guarantee that God's people can do what God commands is the promise of God's presence. For Christians God's promise is a person—Jesus Christ. Immanuel, which means "God with us," took on flesh to make God's presence real among us.

Jesus crossed every barrier between people, including the greatest barrier of all—the division between God and humankind. He is our peace, and because of his life, death, resurrection, and coming return, those who believe in Jesus not only have God's presence *with* us but *in* us through the Holy Spirit. Therefore, we have the power, through God, to leave behind the compromised Christianity that makes its peace with racism and to live out Christ's call to a courageous faith. The time for the American church's complicity in racism has long past. It is time to cancel compromise. It is time to practice courageous Christianity.

ACKNOWLEDGMENTS

One of the best reasons to write a book is that it gives you an opportunity to thank the many people who have positively influenced your life and work. In this area, I have an embarrassment of riches.

First, it is a privilege to thank my wife, Janeé. Her patience and diligent work on behalf of our family created the space for me to undertake this project, and along the way she endured far too many of my rants about racism and the church. My little boy kept me grounded and reminded me that no matter how significant it may seem to write a book, it's nothing if you can't do a backflip on the trampoline. My family has been there for me when I was an even more awkward and undeveloped person than I am now. I thank my brother and sister, who never let me forget that I am both the youngest sibling and abundantly loved. I offer my eternal appreciation to my parents, Jim and Sharese, who both instilled in me the value of education and a love of learning. Their simple message, "We're proud of you," made me feel invincible.

I thank Christina, Ekemini, and Tyler, whose love, humor, empathy, and intelligence kept me grounded and motivated in the midst of nonstop brokenness in the world. This book was also made possible by The Witness and Pass the Mic team—although we are colleagues, more than that, we are a community. It is in large part due to my friend Otis Pickett that I discovered how powerful the past can be in changing the present. His knowledge of history, love of people, and love for the church gave me a vision for advocacy through education. I thank Robby Luckett, whose class on the New South at Jackson State University introduced me to the academic study of history at the graduate level and helped spur me on to doctoral studies. I have learned so much from my professors, especially Dr. Shennette Garrett-Scott, who educated me and encouraged me to pursue not just an education but a mission. The team at Zondervan gave me the chance to write my first book, and their insights, editing, and encouragement made this an inestimably better project and an incredibly positive experience. Heath Carter made time to give feedback from a historian's perspective and helped me add essential information to provide a more robust narrative. I am also indebted to the meticulous work of dozens of historians, whose endless hours in archives and grueling journey from concept to manuscript provided much of the material for this book.

Finally, I strive to be part of the centuries-long legacy of black Christians who put their faith in action in the cause of freedom. Their joyful pursuit of justice has helped provide a template for me as we continue the stride toward freedom.

NOTES

CHAPTER 1: THE COLOR OF COMPROMISE

1. Taylor Branch, *Parting the Waters: The King Years, 1954–1963* (New York: Simon & Schuster, 1998), 890.
2. Diane McWhorter, *Carry Me Home: Birmingham, Alabama; The Climactic Battle of the Civil Rights Revolution* (New York: Simon & Schuster, 2000), 525–27.
3. United Press International, "Six Dead After Church Bombing," *Washington Post*, September 16, 1963.
4. The funeral was for three of the four girls killed in the bombing. Carole Robertson's service had been held the previous day at St. John's Missionary Baptist Church at the request of her mother. See Branch, *Parting the Waters*, 892.
5. Andrew Cohen, "The Speech That Shocked Birmingham the Day after the Church Bombing," *The Atlantic*, September 13, 2013, https://www.the atlantic.com/national/archive/2013/09/the-speech-that-shocked-birmingham -the-day-after-the-church-bombing/279565/.
6. Cohen, "The Speech That Shocked Birmingham."
7. Cohen, "The Speech That Shocked Birmingham."
8. Cohen, "The Speech That Shocked Birmingham."
9. Martin Luther King Jr., "Letter from a Birmingham Jail," April 16, 1963.
10. Beverly Daniel Tatum, *Why Are All the Black Kids Sitting Together in the Cafeteria? And Other Conversations About Race* (New York: Basic Books, 1997).
11. Carolyn Renée DuPont, *Mississippi Praying: Southern White Evangelicals and the Civil Rights Movement* (New York: New York University Press, 2013), 5.
12. As a survey, *The Color of Compromise* relies mainly on secondary literature. I am indebted to the dozens of historians whose work I cite in this book and many others who have labored countless hours in archives and offices writing invaluable narratives of the past.
13. I acknowledge that this is a more "top down" approach to history rather than a "bottom up" approach. My hope is that nonhistorians and people new to the history of race in the American church might understand an outline of major events and people, which then can lead to a more detailed study. This is

not an academic history text. I avoided historiographical discussions in the main body of the book, but I have included the occasional counterpoint or further context of interest to historians in various footnotes.

14. See Nancy Maclean, *Freedom Is Not Enough: The Opening of the American Workplace* (Cambridge, MA: Harvard University Press, 2006).

15. King, "Letter from a Birmingham Jail."

16. David Masci, "Five Facts about the Religious Lives of African Americans," *Pew Research Center*, February 7, 2018, http://www.pewresearch.org/fact -tank/2018/02/07/5-facts-about-the-religious-lives-of-african-americans/.

17. See, for example, Austin Channing Brown, *I'm Still Here: Black Dignity in a World Made for Whiteness* (New York: Convergent, 2018); Christena Cleveland, *Disunity in Christ: Uncovering the Hidden Forces that Keep Us Apart* (Downers Grove, IL: Intervarsity Press, 2013); Christopher S. Collins and Alexander Jun, *White Out: Understanding White Privilege and Dominance in the Modern Age* (New York: Peter Lang, 2017); and Ijeoma Oluo, *So You Want to Talk about Race* (New York: Seal, 2018).

CHAPTER 2: MAKING RACE IN THE COLONIAL ERA

1. The terms *Native American*, *American Indian*, and *indigenous* find various usage in contemporary thought and literature. To my knowledge, no consensus has been reached. Many now prefer to employ tribe names to resist the homogenizing effects of exogenous terms.

2. Eric Weiner, "Coming to America: Who Was First?," interview with Russell Freedman, NPR Books, October 8, 2007, https://www.npr.org/templates/ story/story.php?storyId=15040888.

3. Christopher Columbus, *The Journal of Christopher Columbus (during His First Voyage, 1492–93) and Documents Relating the Voyages of John Cabot and Gaspar Corte Real*, trans. Clements R. Markham (London: Hakluyt Society, 1893), 109. Available from the Hathi Trust Digital Library.

4. Columbus, "October 11, 1492," in *The Journal of Christopher Columbus*, 38.

5. Richard White, *The Middle Ground: Indians, Empires, and Republics in the Great Lakes Region, 1650–1815*, 20th anniv. ed. (Cambridge: Cambridge University Press, 2011), loc. 491, Kindle.

6. The difference between slavery as practiced among tribes in Africa and that which was practiced in North America cannot be overstated. When African tribes took prisoners of war and enslaved them, they often used them as household servants. Although they were ripped from their home and family, they had considerably more freedom than the enslaved in America. They performed chores alongside other members of the household and were allowed to marry. Nor was slavery in Africa based on skin color or race. For a summary, see "Catherine Ancholou on the difference between African slavery

and American slavery," in *Africa in the Americas*, PBS, https://www.pbs.org/wgbh/aia/part1/1i3018.html.

7. Darlene Clark Hine, William C. Hine, and Stanley C. Harrold, *African American Odyssey*, vol. 1, 7th ed. (Boston: Pearson, 2016), 33–46.

8. Some historians now think it is possible that Equiano was born in North America and gathered memories of the middle passage from other slaves who actually made the journey. In either case, his description of the conditions is accurate.

9. Olaudah Equiano, *The Interesting Narrative of the Life of Olaudah Equiano, or Gustavus Vassa, the African* (Public Domain Books, 2006), 29–30, Kindle.

10. Equiano, *The Interesting Narrative*, 77.

11. Equiano, *The Interesting Narrative*, 32.

12. John Newton, *Thoughts upon the African Slave Trade* (London: J. Buckland, 1788), 2.

13. Hine, Hine, and Harrold, *African American Odyssey*, 47.

14. Hine, Hine, and Harrold, *African American Odyssey*, 48–49.

15. Christians today can easily romanticize or overemphasize the role Christians had in abolition. Very few Christians actively opposed slavery, and they did so amid sharp resistance from other Christians.

16. Joyce Appleby, *The Relentless Revolution: A History of Capitalism* (New York: Norton, 2010), 152.

17. Michael Guasco notes the dangers of overemphasizing the 1619 date for the arrival of African slaves. He writes, "The most poisonous consequence of raising the curtain with 1619 is that it casually normalizes white Christian Europeans as historical constants and makes African actors little more than dependent variables in the effort to understand what it means to be American." Guasco, "The Fallacy of 1619: Rethinking the History of Africans in Early America," *Black Perspectives* (blog), September 4, 2017, https://www.aaihs.org/the-fallacy-of-1619-rethinking-the-history-of-africans-in-early-america/.

18. Gregory O'Malley, *Final Passages: The Intercolonial Slave Trade of British America, 1619–1807* (Chapel Hill: University of North Carolina Press, 2014), 88.

19. Hine, Hine, and Harrold, *African American Odyssey*, 31–32.

20. Steven Mintz, "Historical Context: American Slavery in Comparative Perspective," in *The Gilder Lehrman Institute of American History: History Now*, https://www.gilderlehrman.org/content/historical-context-american-slavery-comparative-perspective.

21. Joseph B. Ingle, *Slouching Toward Tyranny: Mass Incarceration, Death Sentences, and Racism* (New York: Algora, 2015), 17.

22. Edmund S. Morgan, *American Slavery, American Freedom: The Ordeal of Colonial Virginia* (repr., New York: Norton, 2003), 155.

23. Morgan, *American Slavery, American Freedom*, 299–301.

24. Rebecca Anne Goetz, *The Baptism of Early Modern Virginia: How Christianity Created Race* (Baltimore: Johns Hopkins University Press, 2012), 3.

25. Goetz, *The Baptism of Early Modern Virginia*, 162.

26. For a notable exception in the eighteenth century, see the Shekomeko Mohicans, who converted to Christianity through the ministry of the Moravians. The Shekomeko Mohicans differentiated between the Moravians and the British colonists because the former "generally shied away from associating particular cultural traits with the Christian life." See Rachel Wheeler, *To Live Upon Hope: Mohicans and Missionaries in the Eighteenth-Century Northeast* (Ithaca, NY: Cornell University Press, 2013).

27. Albert J. Raboteau, *Slave Religion: The "Invisible Institution" in the Antebellum South*, rev. ed. (New York: Oxford University Press, 2004), 16. See also Thomas C. Oden, *How Africa Shaped the Christian Mind: Rediscovering the African Seedbed of Western Christianity* (Downers Grove, IL: IVP Academic, 2010).

28. Travis Glasson, "The Society for the Propagation of the Gospel in Foreign Parts," Oxford Bibliography, May 29. 2015, http://www.oxfordbibliographies.com/view/document/obo-9780199730414/obo-9780199730414-0067.xml.

29. Frank J. Klingberg, ed., *The Carolina Chronicle of Dr. Francis Le Jau, 1706–1717*, University of California Publications in History 53 (Berkeley: University of California Press, 1956).

30. Michael O. Emerson and Christian Smith, *Divided by Faith: Evangelical Religion and the Problem of Race in America* (New York: Oxford University Press, 2000), 24.

31. Martin Luther King Jr., "I Have a Dream," speech, Washington DC, August 28, 1963, during the "March on Washington."

CHAPTER 3: UNDERSTANDING LIBERTY IN THE AGE OF REVOLUTION AND REVIVAL

1. Mitch Kachun, *The First Martyr of Liberty: Crispus Attucks in American Memory* (New York: Oxford University Press, 2017), 3.

2. John Locke, *Two Treatises of Government* (London: Whitmore and Fenn, and C. Brown, 1821), 191.

3. Locke, *Two Treatises of Government*, 317.

4. Darlene Clark Hine, William C. Hine, and Stanley C. Harrold, *African American Odyssey*, vol. 1, 7th ed. (Boston: Pearson, 2016), 93.

5. Hine, Hine, and Harrold, *African American Odyssey*, 97.

6. By contrast, Jon Butler contends that in Africa slaves experienced "an African spiritual holocaust that forever destroyed African religious systems as *systems* in North America and that left slaves remarkably bereft of traditional collective religious practice before 1760" (Butler, *Awash in a Sea of Faith: Christianizing the American People* [Cambridge: Harvard University Press,

1990], 132). For a helpful overview and other viewpoints see Jason Young, "African Religions in the Early South," *Journal of Southern Religion* 14 (2012), http://jsr.fsu.edu/issues/vol14/young.html.

7. Allan Gallay, "The Origins of Slaveholders' Paternalism: George Whitefield, the Bryan Family, and the Great Awakening in the South," *Journal of Southern History* 53, no. 3 (August 1987): 377.

8. Albert J. Raboteau, *Slave Religion: The "Invisible Institution" in the Antebellum South*, rev. ed. (New York: Oxford University Press, 2010), 133.

9. Paul Harvey, *Through the Storm, Through the Night: A History of African American Christianity* (Lanham, MD: Rowman & Littlefield, 2011), 32.

10. Thabiti Anyabwile, *The Faithful Preacher: Recapturing the Vision of Three Pioneering African-American Pastors* (Wheaton, IL: Crossway), 18.

11. Anyabwile, *The Faithful Preacher*, 43.

12. "Slave Code of South Carolina, Articles 34–37 (1740)," Duhaime Law Museum, http://www.duhaime.org/LawMuseum/LawArticle-1501/1740 -Slave-Code-of-South-Carolina-Articles-34-37.aspx.

13. Heath Carter and Laura Romniger Porter, eds., *Turning Points in the History of American Evangelicalism* (Grand Rapids: Eerdmans, 2017), 6.

14. Gallay, "The Origins of Slaveholders' Paternalism," 381.

15. Thomas Kidd, *George Whitefield: America's Spiritual Founding Father* (New Haven, CT: Yale University Press, 2014), 42.

16. Stephen J. Stein, "George Whitefield on Slavery: Some New Evidence," *Church History* 42, no. 2 (June 1973), 245.

17. Kidd, *George Whitefield*, 209.

18. Stein, "George Whitefield on Slavery," 246.

19. George Whitefield, *A Continuation of the Reverend Mr. Whitefield's Journal, from His Arrival at Savannah, to His Return to London*, vol. 2 (London: Strahan, 1740), 78.

20. Harry Stout, "What Made the Great Awakening Great?," in *Turning Points in the History of American Evangelicalism*, ed. Carter and Porter, 10.

21. Jonathan Edwards, *Edwards on Revivals: Containing a Faithful Narrative of the Surprising Work of God in the Conversion of Many Hundred Souls in Northampton, Massachusetts, A.D. 1735: Also Thoughts on the Revival of Religion in New England, 1742, and the Way in Which It Ought to Be Acknowledged and Promoted* (New York: Dunning & Spalding, 1832), 38, Kindle.

22. Kenneth P. Minkema, "Jonathan Edwards on Slavery and the Slave Trade," *The William and Mary Quarterly* 54, no. 4, Religion in Early America (October 1997): 823–34.

23. Mark A. Noll, *The Rise of Evangelicalism: The Age of Edwards, Whitefield and the Wesleys* (repr., Downers Grove, IL: InterVarsity Press, 2018), 254.

24. Kenneth P. Minkema and Harry S. Stout. "The Edwardsean Tradition and

the Antislavery Debate, 1740–1865," *The Journal of American History* 92, no. 1 (June 2005): 47–74.

25. Monica Najar, "'Meddling with Emancipation': Baptists, Authority, and the Rift over Slavery in the Upper South," *Journal of the Early Republic* 25, no. 2 (Summer 2005): 163.

26. Najar, "Meddling with Emancipation," 163.

27. Najar, "Meddling with Emancipation," 165.

28. "Richard Allen, Bishop, AME's First Leader," African American Registry, https://aaregistry.org/story/richard-allen-bishop-ames-first-leader/.

29. Richard Allen, *The Life, Experience, and Gospel Labours of the Rt. Rev. Richard Allen, To Which is Annexed the Rise and Progress of the African Methodist Episcopal Church in the United States of America. Containing a Narrative of the Yellow Fever in the Year of Our Lord 1793: With an Address to the People of Colour in the United States Written by Himself* (Philadelphia: Martin & Boden, 1833), 13.

30. Allen, *The Life, Experience, and Gospel Labours of the Rt. Rev. Richard Allen*, 13.

31. "It was Rev. Richard Allen (1760–1831) who founded the first *permanent* black denomination in the country, the historic African Methodist Episcopal Church of 1816." Douglas A. Sweeney, *The American Evangelical Story: A History of the Movement* (Grand Rapids: Baker, 2005), 121.

32. Raboteau, *Slave Religion*, 294.

CHAPTER 4: INSTITUTIONALIZING RACE IN THE ANTEBELLUM ERA

1. Craig D. Townsend, *Faith in Their Own Color: Black Episcopalians in Antebellum New York City* (New York: Columbia University Press, 2005), 1–3.

2. Townsend, *Faith in Their Own Color*, 132.

3. David Waldstreicher, *Slavery's Constitution: From Revolution to Ratification* (New York: Farrar, Straus and Giroux, 2010), 3.

4. Walter Johnson, *Soul by Soul: Life Inside the Antebellum Slave Market* (Cambridge, MA: Harvard University Press, 1999), 19.

5. Johnson, *Soul by Soul*, 25.

6. Johnson, *Soul by Soul*, 22.

7. Olaudah Equiano, *The Interesting Narrative of the Life of Olaudah Equiano, or Gustavus Vassa, the African* (Public Domain Books, 2006), 23, Kindle.

8. See Melton A. McLaurin, *Celia, A Slave: A True Story of Violence and Retribution in Antebellum Missouri* (Athens, GA: University of Georgia Press, 1991).

9. Harriet Ann Jacobs, *Incidents in the Life of a Slave Girl*, ed. L. Maria Child (Boston, 1861), 83.

10. Henry Louis Gates Jr., "Did African-American Slaves Rebel?," PBS.org, http://www.pbs.org/wnet/african-americans-many-rivers-to-cross/history/did-african-american-slaves-rebel/.

11. "The Confessions of Nat Turner," *Africans in America*, PBS.org, https://www
    .pbs.org/wgbh/aia/part3/3h500.html.

12. Justin Fornal, "Inside the Quest to Return Nat Turner's Skull to His Family,"
    National Geographic, October 7, 2016, https://news.nationalgeographic.
    com/2016/10/nat-turner-skull-slave-rebellion-uprising/.

13. Charles F. Irons, *The Origins of Proslavery Christianity: White and Black
    Evangelicals in Colonial and Antebellum Virginia* (Chapel Hill: University of
    North Carolina Press, 2008), 1.

14. Darlene Clark Hine, William C. Hine, and Stanley C. Harrold, *African
    American Odyssey*, vol. 1, 7th ed. (Boston: Pearson, 2016), 248.

15. Irons, *The Origins of Proslavery Christianity*, 97–98.

16. Henry Noble Sherwood, "The Formation of the American Colonization
    Society," *Journal of Negro History* 2, no. 3 (July 1917): 214.

17. Roger Joseph Green, "Charles Grandison Finney: The Social Implications of
    His Ministry," *Asbury Theological Journal* 48, no. 2 (Fall 1993), 17.

18. Charles G. Finney and James Harris Fairchild, *Charles G. Finney's Systematic
    Theology* (repr., Grand Rapids: Eerdmans, 1951), 312.

CHAPTER 5: DEFENDING SLAVERY AT THE ONSET OF THE CIVIL WAR

1. Mark A. Noll, *The Civil War as a Theological Crisis* (Chapel Hill: University
   of North Carolina Press, 2006).

2. Noll, *The Civil War as a Theological Crisis*, 89–90.

3. Abraham Lincoln, "Second Inaugural Address," Washington DC, May 4, 1865.

4. J. David. Hacker, "A Census-Based Count of the Civil War Dead," *Civil War
   History* 57, no. 4 (December 2011): 307–48.

5. "Civil War Casualties," American Battlefield Trust, https://www.battlefields
   .org/learn/articles/civil-war-casualties.

6. Roger Taney, "The Dred Scott Decision," Library of Congress, 1857, https://
   www.loc.gov/item/17001543/.

7. Abraham Lincoln, "Fourth Debate," presidential debate with Stephen
   Douglas, September 18, 1858, Charleston, IL. For a transcript of the debate,
   see https://www.nps.gov/liho/learn/historyculture/debate4.htm.

8. Henry Louis Gates Jr. "Was Lincoln a Racist?," *The Root*, February 12, 2009,
   https://www.theroot.com/was-lincoln-a-racist-1790868802.

9. Confederate States of America, "Declaration of the Immediate Causes Which
   Induce and Justify the Secession of South Carolina from the Federal Union,"
   adopted December 24, 1860. Available at the Avalon Project: Documents
   in Law, History, and Diplomacy, http://avalon.law.yale.edu/19th_century/
   csa_scarsec.asp.

10. Confederate States of America, "A Declaration of the Immediate Causes
    which Induce and Justify the Secession of the State of Mississippi from the

Federal Union," adopted January 9, 1861, *The Avalon Project: Documents in Law, History, and Diplomacy.*

11. John Wesley, *Thoughts Upon Slavery* (London: Joseph Crukshank, 1778), 56, http://docsouth.unc.edu/church/wesley/wesley.html.

12. Benjamin Hill, quoted in the "Minutes of the Meetings of the American Baptist Home Mission Society and of Its Executive Committee," October 7, 1844, in Joseph Early, *Readings in Baptist History: Four Centuries of Selected Documents* (Nashville: B&H Academic, 2008), 101.

13. Daniel Sharp, *Baptist Missionary Magazine*, vol. 25, August 1845, p. 220, as cited by Joseph Early Jr., *Readings in Baptist History: Four Centuries of Selected Documents* (Nashville: B&H Academic, 2008), 103.

14. Joseph Early Jr., *Readings in Baptist History: Four Centuries of Selected Documents* (Nashville: B&H, 2008), 115.

15. "Obituary: Re. Gardiner Spring, D.D.," *New York Times*, August 20, 1873, p. 4.

16. Bradley J. Longfield, *Presbyterians and American Culture: A History* (Louisville: Westminster John Knox, 2013), 106.

17. Frank J. Smith, *The History of the Presbyterian Church in America: The Continuing Church Movement* (Manassas, VA: Reformation Educational Foundation, 1985), 3.

18. Noll, *The Civil War as a Theological Crisis*, 19.

19. Robert Lewis Dabney, *A Defence of Virginia (and through Her, of the South) in Recent and Pending Contests against the Sectional Party* (New York: E. J. Hale, 1867), 281.

20. Dabney, *A Defence of Virginia*, 281.

21. Dabney, *A Defence of Virginia*, 281.

22. George D. Armstrong, *The Christian Doctrine of Slavery* (New York: Scribner, 1857), 111.

23. Alexander H. Stephens, "Doc. 48—Speech of A. H. Stephens," in *The Rebellion Record: A Diary of American Events*, ed. Frank Moore (New York: Putnam, 1861), 46.

24. Dabney, *A Defence of Virginia*, 104.

25. Stephen R. Haynes, *Noah's Curse: The Biblical Justification of American Slavery* (New York: Oxford University Press, 2002), loc. 2737, Kindle.

26. Noll, *The Civil War as a Theological Crisis*, 40–41.

27. James Henley Thornwell, "Relation to the Church on Slavery," in *The Collected Writings of James Henley Thornwell*, vol. 4, *Ecclesiastical* (Richmond: Presbyterian Committee of Publication, 1873), 383.

28. Thornwell, "Relation to the Church on Slavery," 381.

29. Sean Michael Lucas, "Own Our Past: The Spirituality of the Church in History, Failure, and Hope," *Reformed Faith and Practice* 1, no. 1 (May 2016): 25–38.

CHAPTER 6: RECONSTRUCTING WHITE SUPREMACY IN THE JIM CROW ERA

1. Eric Foner, *A Short History of Reconstruction, 1863–1877* (New York: Harper & Row, 1990), 31.
2. Heather Andrea Williams, *Help Me to Find My People: The African American Search for Family Lost in Slavery* (Chapel Hill, NC: University of North Carolina Press, 2012), 166.
3. "Reconstruction," *The American Yawp*, http://www.americanyawp.com/text/15-reconstruction/#identifier_10_92.
4. Foner, *A Short History of Reconstruction*, 111–13.
5. Charles Regan Wilson, *Baptized in Blood: The Religion of the Lost Cause, 1865–1920* (Athens, GA: University of Georgia Press, 2009).
6. Wilson, *Baptized in Blood*, 16.
7. Wilson, *Baptized in Blood*, 49.
8. "Whose Heritage: Public Symbols of the Confederacy," Southern Poverty Law Center, updated 2016, pp. 4–7, 9–10, 14, https://www.splcenter.org/sites/default/files/com_whose_heritage.pdf.
9. W. Fitzhugh Brundage, "I've Studied the History of Confederate Memorials. Here's What to Do about Them," *Vox*, August 18, 2018, https://www.vox.com/the-big-idea/2017/8/18/16165160/confederate-monuments-history-charlottesville-white-supremacy.
10. Wilson, *Baptized in Blood*, 33–34.
11. Foner, *A Short History of Reconstruction*, 244–45.
12. See C. Vann Woodward, *The Strange Career of Jim Crow* (New York: Oxford University Press, 2002) for a thorough discussion of how Jim Crow segregation developed through a series of missed opportunities to form different patterns of social interaction between the races.
13. Henry B. Brown, "Opinion," Plessy v. Ferguson, May 18, 1896, Legal Information Institute, Cornell Law School, law.cornell.edu/supremecourt/text/163/537.
14. "Achilles V. Clark to Judith Porter and Henrietta Porter, April 14, 1864," *The Civil War: The Final Year by Those Who Lived It*, ed. Aaron Sheehan-Dean (New York: Literary Classics, 2014).
15. Michael Newton, *White Robes and Burning Crosses: A History of the Ku Klux Klan from 1866* (Jefferson, NC: McFarland, 2014), 6–7.
16. Newton, *White Robes and Burning Crosses*, 18.
17. Michael Newton, *The Ku Klux Klan in Mississippi: A History* (Jefferson, NC: McFarland, 2010), 36.
18. Kelly J. Baker, *The Gospel According to the Klan: The KKK's Appeal to Protestant American, 1915–1930* (Lawrence, KS: University Press of Kansas, 2011), 6, italics original.
19. Mark E. Benbow, "Birth of a Quotation: Woodrow Wilson and 'Like Writing

History with Lightning,'" *Journal of the Gilded Age and Progressive Era* 9, no. 4 (October 2010): 509.

20. George Robertson, "We . . . and Our Fathers Have Sinned (Daniel 9:8)," *First Presbyterian Augusta*, June 26, 2015, https://firstpresaugusta.org/resource/we -and-our-fathers-have-sinned-daniel-98/.

21. Juan O. Sanchez, *Religion and the Ku Klux Klan: Biblical Appropriation in Their Literature and Songs* (Jefferson, NC: McFarland, 2016), 14.

22. Kenneth T. Jackson, *The Ku Klux Klan in the City, 1915–1930* (New York: Oxford University Press, 1967), xv.

23. Linda K. Gordon, *The Second Coming of the KKK: The Ku Klux Klan of the 1920s and the American Political Tradition* (New York: Liveright, 2017), 1–3.

24. Olivia B. Waxman, "How the KKK's Influence Spread in Northern States," *Time*, October 24, 2017, http://time.com/4990253/kkk-white-nationalists-history/.

25. Jackson, *The Ku Klux Klan in the City*, 7.

26. Waxman, "How the KKK's Influence Spread in Northern States."

27. James W. Loewen, *Sundown Towns: A Hidden Dimension of American Racism* (New York: New Press, 2005), 3–11.

28. Danielle L. McGuire, *At the Dark End of the Street: Black Women, Rape, and Resistance—A New History of the Civil Rights Movement from Rosa Parks to the Rise of Black Power* (New York: Knopf, 2010), xv–xvii.

29. McGuire, *At the Dark End of the Street*, xviii.

30. Theodore Bilbo, *Take Your Choice: Separation or Mongrelization* (Poplarville, MI: Dream House, 1947), 88, in the US Archive, https://archive.org/stream/ TakeYourChoice/TakeYourChoice_djvu.txt; see also Ian Millhiser, "When 'Religious Liberty' Was Used To Justify Racism Instead Of Homophobia," *Think Progress*, February 27, 2014, https://thinkprogress.org/when-religious -liberty-was-used-to-justify-racism-instead-of-homophobia-67bc973c4042/.

31. Douglas A. Blackmon, *Slavery by Another Name: The Re-Enslavement of Black Americans from the Civil War to World War II* (New York: Doubleday, 2008), 1–10.

32. Chris Myers Asch, *The Senator and the Sharecropper* (Chapel Hill: University of North Carolina Press, 2008).

33. "Most Horrible: Details of the Burning at the Stake of the Holberts," *Vicksburg Evening Post*, February 13, 1904.

34. "Most Horrible," *Vicksburg Evening Post*.

35. Walter White, "The Work of a Mob," *The Crisis* 16, no. 5 (September 1918): 221.

36. White, "The Work of a Mob," 222.

37. Darlene Clark Hine, William C. Hine, and Stanley C. Harrold, *African American Odyssey*, vol. 1, 7th ed. (Boston: Pearson, 2016), 386.

38. Stephen Ward Angell, *Bishop Henry McNeal Turner and African-American Religion in the South* (Knoxville, TN: University of Tennessee Press, 1992), 1–5.

39. Angell, *Bishop Henry McNeal Turner*, 1.

40. Angell, *Bishop Henry McNeal Turner*, 90–91.

41. James H. Cone, *The Cross and the Lynching Tree* (Maryknoll, NY: Orbis, 2011), 158.

42. Cone, *The Cross and the Lynching Tree*, xviii.

43. Ezra Klein, "Bryan Stevenson Explains How It Feels to Grow up Black amid Confederate Monuments," *Vox*, May 24, 2017, https://www.vox.com/2017/5/24/15675606/bryan-stevenson-confederacy-monuments-slavery-ezra-klein.

CHAPTER 7: REMEMBERING THE COMPLICITY IN THE NORTH

1. Darlene Clark Hine, William C. Hine, and Stanley C. Harrold, *African American Odyssey*, vol. 1, 7th ed. (Boston: Pearson, 2016), 421.

2. Patrick T. Reardon, "The World's Columbian Exposition at the 'White City,'" *Chicago Tribune*, n.d., http://www.chicagotribune.com/news/nationworld/politics/chi-chicagodays-columbianexposition-story-story.html.

3. Hine, Hine, Harrold, *African American Odyssey*, 421.

4. Frederick Douglass, introduction to *The Reason Why the Colored American Is Not in the World's Columbian Exposition: The Afro-American's Contribution to Columbian Literature*, by Ida B. Wells, with contributions by Frederick Douglass, Irvine Garland Penn, and Ferdinand Lee Barnett (1893), https://www.loc.gov/item/mfd.25023.

5. Thomas Sugrue, *Sweet Land of Liberty: The Forgotten for Civil Rights in the North* (New York: Random House, 2008), xv.

6. John T. McGreevy, *Parish Boundaries: The Catholic Encounter with Race in the Twentieth Century Urban North* (Chicago: University of Chicago Press, 1996), 33. See also David R. Roediger, *The Wages of Whiteness: Race and the Making of the American Working Class*, rev. ed. (London: Verso, 1999).

7. James and Patrick Healy were ordained as Roman Catholic priests and were biracial, but they "passed" as white and refused to be identified as *colored*.

8. C. Vanessa White, "Augustus Tolton: Pioneer Pastor," *U. S. Catholic* 79, no. 2 (February 2014): 55–56.

9. Vinson Synan, "Pentecostalism: William Seymour," *Christianity Today*, no. 65 (2000), https://www.christianitytoday.com/history/issues/issue-65/pentecostalism-william-seymour.html.

10. Synan, "Pentecostalism: William Seymour."

11. Vinson Synan, *The Holiness-Pentecostal Tradition: Charismatic Movements in the Twentieth Century*, 2nd ed. (Grand Rapids, MI: Eerdmans, 1997), loc. 1063, Kindle.

12. Frank Bartleman, *Azusa Street: An Eyewitness Account* (Alachua, FL: Bridge-Logos, 1980), 59.

13. Synan, *The Holiness-Pentecostal Tradition*, loc. 1919.

14. Synan, *The Holiness-Pentecostal Tradition*, loc. 1937.

15. Paul B. Rauschenbusch, foreword to *Christianity and the Social Crisis in the 21st Century: The Classic That Woke up the Church*, by Walter Rauschenbusch (New York: HarperCollins, 2017), loc. 7620, Kindle.

16. David R. Swartz, *Moral Minority: The Evangelical Left in an Age of Conservatism* (Philadelphia: University of Pennsylvania Press, 2012), loc. 227, Kindle.

17. Charles R. Erdman, "The Church and Socialism," in *The Fundamentals: A Testimony to the Truth*, ed. R. A. Torrey and A. C. Dixon, vol. 12 (Harrington, DE: Delmarva, 2013), loc. 19862, Kindle.

18. It must be noted, however, that Fundamentalist abstention from the political arena was selective. For instance, they decried the teaching of evolution in schools and sought to pass laws against it.

19. Mary Beth Swetnam Mathews, *Doctrine and Race: African American Evangelicals and Fundamentalism Between the Wars* (Tuscaloosa, AL: University of Alabama Press, 2017), 2.

20. Mathews, *Doctrine and Race*, 45.

21. Glenda E. Gilmore and Thomas J. Sugrue, *These United States: A Nation in the Making, 1890 to the Present* (New York: Norton, 2015), 106–8.

22. Hine, Hine, and Harrold, *African American Odyssey*, 458–60.

23. W. E. B. Du Bois, "Returning Soldiers," *The Crisis* 18 (May 1919): 13.

24. Ethan Michaeli, *The Defender: How the Legendary Black Newspaper Changed America from the Age of the Pullman Porters to the Age of Obama* (Boston: Mariner, 2016), 80.

25. Michaeli, *The Defender*, 80.

26. "Red Summer of 1919," *Equal Justice Initiative*, https://eji.org/reports/online/lynching-in-america-targeting-black-veterans/red-summer.

27. Gilmore and Sugrue, *These United States*, 143.

28. Tony Martin, *Race First: The Ideological and Organizational Struggles of Marcus Garvey and the Universal Negro Improvement Association* (repr., Dover, MA: First Majority, 1986), 359–60.

29. Alison Collis Greene, *No Depression in Heaven: The Great Depression, the New Deal, and the Transformation of Religion in the Delta* (New York: Oxford University Press, 2016), 2.

30. Thomas Sugrue, *Sweet Land of Liberty: The Forgotten Struggle for Civil Rights in the North* (New York: Random House, 2008), xvii.

31. Pope Pius XI, *Quadragesimo Anno: On Reconstruction of the Social Order*, May 15, 1931, 25, http://w2.vatican.va/content/pius-xi/en/encyclicals/documents/hf_p-xi_enc_19310515_quadragesimo-anno.html.

32. Heath W. Carter, *Union Made: Working People and the Rise of Social Christianity in Chicago* (New York: Oxford University Press, 2015), 179.

33. Carter, *Union Made*, 180.

34. Darren Dochuk, *From Bible Belt to Sunbelt: Plain-Folk Religion, Grassroots and the Rise of Conservative Evangelicalism* (New York: Norton, 2012), 69–70.

35. Dochuk, *From Bible Belt to Sunbelt*, 67–69.

36. Dochuk, *From Bible Belt to Sunbelt*, 70, 81. For a discussion of how Christian colleges in the South inculcated their students with a faith in the free-market see Bethany Moreton, *To Serve God and Wal-Mart: The Making of Christian Free Enterprise* (Cambridge, MA: Harvard University Press, 2009).

37. Ira Katznelson, *When Affirmative Action Was White: An Untold History of Racial Inequality in Twentieth-Century America* (New York: Norton, 2005), x.

38. Katznelson, *When Affirmative Action Was White*, 22.

39. Katznelson, *When Affirmative Action Was White*, 84.

40. Richard Rothstein, *The Color of Law: The Forgotten History of How Our Government Segregated America* (New York: Norton, 2017), 167.

41. Rothstein, *The Color of Law*, 64.

42. Thomas Sugrue, *The Origins of the Urban Crisis: Race and Inequality in Postwar Detroit*, rev. ed. (Princeton, NJ, Princeton University Press, 2005), 193–94.

43. Sugrue, *Sweet Land of Liberty*, loc. 3751, Kindle.

44. Joshua Ruff, "Levittown: The Archetype for Suburban Development," *American History Magazine*, October 4, 2007, http://www.historynet.com/levittown-the-archetype-for-suburban-development.htm.

45. Ruff, "Levittown."

46. Sugrue, *The Origins of the Urban Crisis*, 231–33.

47. Sugrue, *The Origins of the Urban Crisis*, 232–33.

48. Sugrue, *The Origins of the Urban Crisis*, 233.

49. Rachael A. Woldoff, *White Flight/Black Flight: The Dynamics of Racial Change in an American Neighborhood* (Ithaca, NY: Cornell University Press, 2011), 3, 13.

50. Kriston Capps, "How Real-Estate Brokers Can Profit from Racial Tipping Points," *City Lab*. March 3, 2015, https://www.citylab.com/equity/2015/03/how-real-estate-brokers-can-profit-from-racial-tipping-points/386674/.

51. Mark T. Mulder, *Shades of White Flight: Evangelical Congregations and Urban Departure* (New Brunswick, NJ: Rutgers University Press, 2015), loc. 127, Kindle.

52. Mulder, *Shades of White Flight*, Loc. 235.

53. Martin Luther King Jr., *"Thou, Dear God": Prayers that Open Hearts and Spirits*, ed. Lewis V. Baldwin (Boston: Beacon, 2012), 171.

54. David Garrow, *Bearing the Cross: Martin Luther King, Jr., and the Southern Christian Leadership Conference*, (repr., New York: HarperCollins, 2004), 431–33.

55. Garrow, *Bearing the Cross*, 427.

56. Taylor Branch, *At Canaan's Edge: America in the King Years, 1965–1968* (New York: Simon & Schuster, 2006), 510.

57. Branch, *At Canaan's Edge*, 511.

58. Matthew J. Countryman, *Up South: Civil Rights and Black Power in Philadelphia* (Philadelphia: University Pennsylvania Press, 2006), 3.

CHAPTER 8: COMPROMISING WITH RACISM DURING THE CIVIL RIGHTS MOVEMENT

1. Carolyn Bryant in 2007 confessed to historian Timothy Tyson that the most sensational part of her testimony in court about Till touching her was "not true." See Sheila Webber, "How Author Timothy Tyson Found the Woman at the Center of the Emmett Till Case," *Vanity Fair*, January 26, 2017, https://www.vanityfair.com/news/2017/01/how-author-timothy-tyson-found-the-woman-at-the-center-of-the-emmett-till-case.

2. Timothy Tyson, *The Blood of Emmett Till* (New York: Simon & Schuster. 2017), loc. 1041–60, Kindle.

3. Tyson, *The Blood of Emmett Till*, loc. 3609; Lily Rothman and Arpita Aneja, "You Still Don't Know the Whole Rosa Parks Story," *Time*, November 30, 2015, http://time.com/4125377/rosa-parks-60-years-video/.

4. See Jeanne Theoharis's *The Rebellious Life of Mrs. Rosa Parks* (Boston, MA: Beacon Press, 2013) for a fresh reinterpretation of the civil rights activist's life.

5. David Garrow, *Bearing the Cross: Martin Luther King, Jr., and the Southern Christian Leadership Conference* (New York: William Morrow, 1986), 22.

6. Emanuella Grinberg, Sheena Jones, and Amir Vera, "Linda Brown, Woman at Center of Brown v. Board Case, Dies," *CNN*, March 26, 2018, https://www.cnn.com/2018/03/26/us/linda-brown-dies/index.html.

7. "Transcript of Brown v. Board of Education (1954)," ourdocuments.gov, https://www.ourdocuments.gov/doc.php?flash=false&doc=87&page=transcript.

8. G. T. Gillespie, "A Christian View of Segregation," speech, November 4, 1954, University of Mississippi Archives "Citizens' Council" Collection, p. 5.

9. Gillespie, "A Christian View of Segregation," 10.

10. Carey L. Daniel, "God the Original Segregationist," pamphlet, 1955, electronic version, McCain D. Williams Pamphlet Collection, University of Mississippi Libraries.

11. David Chappell argues in *A Stone of Hope: Prophetic Religion and the Death of Jim Crow* (Chapel Hill: University of North Carolina Press, 2005) that part of the reason the Christian case for segregation failed is that white ministers and theologians could not marshal the same level of biblical sanction for the practices of segregation. Their rationale withered amid the prophetic messaging of civil rights activists.

12. Steven P. Miller, *Billy Graham and the Rise of the Republican South* (Philadelphia: University of Pennsylvania Press, 2009), 28.

13. Miller, *Billy Graham and the Rise of the Republican South*, 31.

14. Miller, *Billy Graham and the Rise of the Republican South*, 16.

15. Howell Raines, "The Birmingham Bombing," *New York Times*, July 24, 1983,

https://www.nytimes.com/1983/07/24/magazine/the-birmingham-bombing.html.

16. Garrow, *Bearing the Cross*, 229.
17. A Group of Clergymen, "Letter to Martin Luther King," April 12, 1963, TeachingAmericanHistory.org, https://teachingamericanhistory.org/library/document/letter-to-martin-luther-king/.
18. A Group of Clergymen, "Letter to Martin Luther King."
19. A Group of Clergymen, "Letter to Martin Luther King."
20. Taylor Branch, *At Canaan's Edge: America in the King Years, 1965–1968* (New York: Simon & Schuster, 2006), 262.
21. Branch, *At Canaan's Edge*, 262.
22. Kay Mills, *This Little Light of Mine: The Life of Fannie Lou Hamer* (Lexington: University Press of Kentucky 2009), 238.
23. Martin Luther King Jr., "I Have a Dream," speech, Washington DC, August 28, 1963, during the "March on Washington."
24. "Civil Rights Movement Timeline," History, https://www.history.com/topics/civil-rights-movement-timeline.
25. "Civil Rights Act of 1964," The Martin Luther King Jr. Research and Education Institute, Stanford University, https://kinginstitute.stanford.edu/encyclopedia/civil-rights-act-1964.
26. William Martin, *A Prophet with Honor: The Billy Graham Story*, rev. ed. (Grand Rapids: Zondervan, 2018), 319.
27. Martin Luther King Jr., interview with Mike Wallace, *CBS Reports*, September 27, 1966.
28. Miller, *Billy Graham and the Rise of the Republican South*, 129.
29. Taylor Branch, *At Canaan's Edge: America in the King Years, 1965–1968* (New York: Simon & Schuster, 2006), 284.
30. "The Civil Rights Movement Moves North," *Digital History*, http://www.digitalhistory.uh.edu/disp_textbook.cfm?smtid=2&psid=3332.
31. Martin, *A Prophet with Honor*, 320–21.
32. Martin Luther King Jr., *Where Do We Go from Here: Chaos or Community?* (Boston: Beacon, 2010), loc. 481, Kindle.
33. Aram Goudsouzian, *Down to the Crossroads: Civil Rights, Black Power, and the Meredith March Against Fear* (New York: Farrar, Straus, and Giroux, 2014), 142–43.
34. Jonathan Eig, "The Real Reason Why Muhammad Ali Converted to Islam," *Washington Post*, October 26, 2017, https://www.washingtonpost.com/news/acts-of-faith/wp/2017/10/26/the-real-reason-muhammad-ali-converted-to-islam/?utm_term=.b83ef354fe22.
35. Kevin M. Kruse, *White Flight: Atlanta and the Making of Modern Conservatism* (Princeton, NJ: Princeton University Press, 2005), 88.

36. Kruse, *White Flight*, 92.

37. Kruse, *White Flight*, 89.

38. Joseph P. Williams, "Segregation's Legacy," *US News and World Report*, April 20, 2018, https://www.usnews.com/news/the-report/articles/2018-04-20/us-is-still-segregated-even-after-fair-housing-act.

39. Alabama Council on Human Relations, "It's Not Over in the South: School Desegregation in Forty-Three Southern Cities Eighteen Years after Brown," May 1972, p. 142, https://files.eric.ed.gov/fulltext/ED065646.pdf.

40. Timothy Tyson, *Blood Done Sign My Name: A True Story* (New York: Three Rivers, 2004), 71–72.

41. Tyson, *Blood Done Sign My Name*, 16.

42. Tyson, *Blood Done Sign My Name*, 73.

43. Edward J. Blum and Paul Harvey, *The Color of Christ: The Song of God and the Saga of Race in America* (Chapel Hill: University of North Carolina Press, 2014), 211.

44. Blum and Harvey, *The Color of Christ*, 208.

45. Blum and Harvey, *The Color of Christ*, 210.

46. Blum and Harvey, *The Color of Christ*, 215.

47. Angela D. Dillard, "Religion and Radicalism: The Reverend Albert B. Cleage, Jr., and the Rise of Black Christian Nationalism in Detroit," *Freedom North: Black Freedom Struggles Outside the South, 1940–1980*, ed. Jeanne Theoharis and Komozi Woodard (New York: Palgrave Macmillan, 2003), 153.

48. Jacquelyn Dowd Hall, "The Long Civil Rights Movement and the Political Uses of the Past," *Journal of American History* 91, no. 4 (March 2005): 1234.

49. Taylor Branch, *The King Years: Historic Moments in the Civil Rights Movement* (New York: Simon & Schuster, 2013), 40.

50. Curtis J. Evans, "White Evangelical Protestant Responses to the Civil Rights Movement," *Harvard Theological Review* 102, no. 2 (April 2009): 258.

51. See Christin Scheller, "Billy Graham Helped Give White Evangelicals a Pass on Civil Rights," *Religion News Service*, March 1, 2018, https://religionnews.com/2018/03/01/billy-graham-helped-give-white-evangelicals-a-pass-on-civil-rights-scholars/. Portions of this section originally appeared in my article in *The Washington Post*, "Why So Many White Churches Resisted Martin Luther King Jr.'s Call," January 15, 2018, https://www.washingtonpost.com/news/acts-of-faith/wp/2018/01/15/why-so-many-white-churches-resisted-martin-luther-king-jr-s-call/?utm_term=.502d7275b45a.

52. Curtis W. Freeman, "'Never Had I been So Blind' W. A. Criswell's 'Change' on Racial Segregation," *Journal of Southern Religion* 10 (2007): 1.

53. Edward Gilbreath, "Catching Up with a Dream: Evangelicals and Race 30 Years After the Death of Martin Luther King, Jr." *Christianity Today*, January 1, 2000, https://www.christianitytoday.com/ct/2000/januaryweb-only/15.0b.html.

CHAPTER 9: ORGANIZING THE RELIGIOUS RIGHT AT THE END OF THE TWENTIETH CENTURY

1. Michael Oreskes, "Lee Atwater, Mast of Tactics for Bush and G.O.P., Dies at 40," *The New York Times*. March 30, 1991.

2. Oreskes, "Lee Atwater."

3. Rick Perlstein, "Lee Atwater's Infamous 1981 Interview on the Southern Strategy," *The Nation*, November 13, 2012, https://www.thenation.com/article/exclusive-lee-atwaters-infamous-1981-interview-southern-strategy/.

4. Perlstein, "Lee Atwater's Infamous 1981 Interview."

5. Glenda E. Gilmore and Thomas J. Sugrue, *These United States: A Nation in the Making, 1890 to the Present* (New York: Norton, 2015), 549.

6. David W. Bebbington, *Evangelicalism in Modern Britain: A History from the 1730s to the 1980s* (London: Routledge, 1989).

7. Hannah Butler and Kristin Du Mez, "The Reinvention of 'Evangelical' in American History: A Linguistic Analysis," *The Anxious Bench* (blog), May 31, 2018, http://www.patheos.com/blogs/anxiousbench/2018/05/the-reinvention-of-evangelical-in-american-history-a-linguistic-analysis/.

8. J. Brooks Flippen, *Jimmy Carter, the Politics of Family, and the Rise of the Religious Right*, Since 1970: Histories of Contemporary America (Athens: University of Georgia Press, 2011).

9. Gary Wills, "'Born-Again' Politics," *New York Times*, August 1, 1976, https://www.nytimes.com/1976/08/01/archives/born-again-politics-born-again.html.

10. Lisa McGirr, *Suburban Warriors: The Origins of the New American Right* (Princeton, NJ: Princeton University Press, 2001).

11. Daniel K. Williams, *God's Own Party: The Making of the Christian Right* (New York: Oxford University Press, 2010), 4–6.

12. William Martin, *A Prophet with Honor: The Billy Graham Story*, rev. ed. (Grand Rapids: Zondervan, 2018), 212.

13. Martin, *A Prophet with Honor*, 356.

14. Martin, *A Prophet with Honor*, 102; Lyman Kellstedt et al. "Faith Transformed: Religion and American Politics from FDR to George W. Bush," in *Religion and American Politics from the Colonial Period to the Present*, ed. Mark Noll and Luke E. Harlow (New York: Oxford University Press, 2007), 272–73.

15. Rick Perlstein, *Nixonland: The Rise of a President and the Fracturing of America* (New York: Scribner, 2008), loc. 2666, Kindle.

16. Ian Haney-Lopez, *Dog-Whistle Politics: How Coded Racial Appeals Have Reinvented Racism and Wrecked the Middle Class* (Oxford: Oxford University Press, 2014), 1.

17. Elizabeth Hinton, *From the War on Poverty to the War on Crime: The Making of Mass Incarceration in America* (Cambridge, MA: Harvard University Press, 2016), 2–5. Hinton argues that the trend toward a more punitive criminal

justice system began under Lyndon B. Johnson with the passage of the Law Enforcement Assistance Act of 1965. John Pfaff makes the point that the uptick in US incarceration rates had much more to do with harsher attitudes and practices at the local and state level rather than the federal level. Pfaff, *Locked In: The True Causes of Mass Incarceration and How to Achieve Real Reform* (New York: Basic Books, 2017), 5–7, 26–30. Also see Anthony Bradley, *Ending Overcriminalization and Mass Incarceration: Hope from a Civil Society* (Cambridge University Press, 2018).

18. Matthew Lassiter, *The Silent Majority: Suburban Politics in the Sunbelt South* (Princeton, NJ: Princeton University Press. 2006), 3–10. Lassiter argues that a top-down "Southern strategy" thesis is incorrect. It was instead a suburban or "Sunbelt strategy" that spanned regions far beyond the South and was constructed by grassroots organizers, not federal-level politicians.

19. Lassiter, *The Silent Majority*, 3–10.

20. Haney-Lopez, *Dog-Whistle Politics*, 1.

21. Darren Dochuk, *From Bible Belt to Sunbelt: Plain-Folk Religion, Grassroots and the Rise of Conservative Evangelicalism* (New York: Norton, 2012), 329.

22. For more on the conservative suburban ethos, see especially Lassiter, *The Silent Majority*.

23. Dochuk, *From Bible Belt to Sunbelt*, xviii.

24. Dochuk, *From Bible Belt to Sunbelt*, xiii.

25. McGirr, *Suburban Warriors*, 3.

26. McGirr, *Suburban Warriors*, 6.

27. Williams, *God's Own Party*, 99.

28. Haney-Lopez, *Dog-Whistle Politics*, 24.

29. Michelle Alexander, *The New Jim Crow: Mass Incarceration in the Age of Colorblindness*, rev. ed. (New York: New Press, 2012), 44.

30. Kellstedt et al., "Faith Transformed," 272–73.

31. Lassiter, *The Silent Majority*, 4.

32. See Thomas Kidd, "Were Evangelicals Really Silent about Roe v. Wade?," *Gospel Coalition*, September 25, 2018, https://www.thegospelcoalition.org/blogs/evangelical-history/evangelicals-really-silent-roe-v-wade/.

33. "Resolution on Abortion," St. Louis, MO, 1971, http://www.sbc.net/resolutions/13/resolution-on-abortion.

34. Steven P. Miller, *Billy Graham and the Rise of the Republican South* (Philadelphia: University of Pennsylvania Press, 2009), 54.

35. David Roach, "How Southern Baptists Became Pro-Life," *Baptist Press*, January 16, 2015, http://www.bpnews.net/44055/how-southern-baptists-became-prolife.

36. Randall Balmer, "The Real Origins of the Religious Right," *Politico*

Magazine, May 27, 2014, https://www.politico.com/magazine/story/2014/05/religious-right-real-origins-107133.

37. Green v. Connally, section 1, June 30, 1971. Available online at http://dc.find acase.com/research/wfrmDocViewer.aspx/xq/fac.19710630_0000050.DDC .htm/qx.

38. Balmer, "The Real Origins of the Religious Right."

39. JBHE Foundation, "Bob Jones University Apologizes for Its Racist Past," *Journal of Blacks in Higher Education*, no. 62 (Winter, 2008/2009): 22–23.

40. George Marsden, *Fundamentalism and American Culture*, 2nd ed. (New York: Oxford University Press, 2006), 4.

41. Sean M. Lucas, *For a Continuing Church: The Roots of the Presbyterian Church in America* (Phillipsburg, NJ: R&R Publishing, 2015), 321.

42. Lucas, *For a Continuing Church*, 321.

43. Lelia C. Albrecht, "Should a Discriminatory School Be Tax-Free? Reagan Says Yes, Then No; Bob Jones Cries Foul," *People Magazine*, February 15, 1982, https://people.com/archive/should-a-discriminatory-school-be-tax-free -reagan-says-yes-then-no-bob-jones-cries-foul-vol-17-no-6/.

44. Albrecht, "Should a Discriminatory School Be Tax-Free?"

45. JBHE Foundation, "Bob Jones University Apologizes for Its Racist Past," 23.

46. JBHE Foundation, "Bob Jones University Apologizes for Its Racist Past," 23.

47. Frances Fitzgerald, *The Evangelicals: The Struggle to Shape America* (New York: Simon & Schuster, 2017), 304.

48. Frederick Lane, *The Court and the Cross: The Religious Right's Crusade to Reshape the Supreme Court* (Boston: Beacon, 2008), 44.

49. Lane, *The Court and the Cross*, 44.

50. "Rise of the Religious Right 1 of 2," and "Rise of the Religious Right 2 of 2," videos, posted by PlanoProf, April 16, 2015, YouTube, https://www.youtube.com/watch?v=PqE6WnIc8Rw, and https://www.youtube.com/watch?v=3WsREKJCx2s.

51. Randall Balmer, "God in America," interview by PBS, May 10, 2010, https://www.pbs.org/wgbh/pages/frontline/godinamerica/interviews/randall-balmer.html.

52. Angela Fritz, "Moral Majority," in *Religion and Politics in America: An Encyclopedia of Church and State in American Life*, 2 vols., ed. Frank J. Smith (Santa Barbara, CA: ABC-CLIO, 2016), 496.

53. Ronald Reagan, "National Affairs Campaign Address on Religious Liberty," speech, August 22, 1980, Dallas, Texas.

54. Williams, *God's Own Party*, 187.

55. Fitzgerald, *The Evangelicals*, 317.

56. John Dittmer, *Local People: The Struggle for Civil Rights in Mississippi* (Urbana, IL: University of Illinois Press, 1994), 247.

57. Joseph Crespino, *In Search of Another Country: Mississippi and the Conservative Counterrevolution* (Princeton, NJ: Princeton University Press, 2007), 1.

58. Joseph Crespino, "Civil Rights and the Religious Right," *Rightward Bound: Making America Conservative in the 1970s*, ed. Bruce J. Schulman and Julian E. Zelizer (Cambridge, MA: Harvard University Press, 2008), 104.

59. Seven R. Weisman, "Reagan Acts to Bar Tax Break to Schools in Racial Bias Cases," *New York Times*, January 19, 1982, https://www.nytimes.com/1982/01/19/us/reagan-acts-to-bar-tax-break-to-schools-in-racial-bias-cases.html.

60. Alexander, *The New Jim Crow*, 49. See also Kenneth Neubeck and Noel Cazenave, *Welfare Racism: Playing the Race Card Against America's Poor* (New York: Rutledge, 2001).

61. Haney-Lopez, *Dog-Whistle Politics*, 52.

62. Leah Wright Rigueur, *The Loneliness of the Black Republican: Politics and the Pursuit of Power* (Princeton, NJ: Princeton University Press, 2016), 284–85.

63. Paul Harvey, *Freedom's Coming: Religious Culture and the Shaping of the South from the Civil War through the Civil Rights Era* (Chapel Hill: University of North Carolina Press, 2005), 235. For a discussion of how anticommunist sentiment affected the civil rights movement, see Robert Korstad, *Civil Rights Unionism: Tobacco Workers and the Struggle for Democracy in the Mid-Twentieth-Century South* (Chapel Hill: University of North Carolina Press, 2003).

64. Harvey, *Freedom's Coming*, 246.

65. James German, "Economy," in *Themes in Religion and American Culture*, ed. Philip Goff and Paul Harvey (Chapel Hill: University of North Carolina Press, 2004), 289.

66. Jerry Falwell, *Listen, America!* (New York: Doubleday, 1980), 13.

67. Fitzgerald, *The Evangelicals*, 306.

CHAPTER 10: RECONSIDERING RACIAL RECONCILIATION IN THE AGE OF BLACK LIVES MATTER

1. "Resolution on Racial Reconciliation on the 150th Anniversary of the Southern Baptist Convention," SBC.net, Atlanta, GA, June 1995, http://www.sbc.net/resolutions/899/resolution-on-racial-reconciliation-on-the-150th-anniversary-of-the-southern-baptist-convention.

2. Laurie Goodstein, "A Marriage Gone Bad, Struggles for Redemption," *New York Times*, October 29, 1997, https://www.nytimes.com/1997/10/29/us/a-marriage-gone-bad-struggles-for-redemption.html.

3. "PK History," PromiseKeepers.org, https://promisekeepers.org/pk-history.

4. Gayle White, "Clergy Conference Stirs Historic Show of Unity," *Christianity Today*, April 8, 1996, https://www.christianitytoday.com/ct/1996/april8/6t4088.html.

5. Bob Smietana, "Research: Racial Diversity at Church More Dream Than

Reality," LifeWay Research, January 17, 2014, https://lifewayresearch.com/2014/01/17/research-racial-diversity-at-church-more-dream-than-reality/.

6. Christopher Dean Hopkins, "9 Dead in Shooting at Charleston, S.C., Church," *NPR*, June 18, 2015, https://www.npr.org/sections/thetwo-way/2015/06/18/415345850/reports-eight-dead-in-shooting-at-charleston-s-c-church.

7. Michael O. Emerson and Christian Smith, *Divided by Faith: Evangelical Religion and the Problem of Race in America* (New York: Oxford University Press, 2000), 9.

8. Emerson and Smith, *Divided by Faith*, 75.

9. Emerson and Smith, *Divided by Faith*, 76–77.

10. Emerson and Smith, *Divided by Faith*, 77.

11. Emerson and Smith, *Divided by Faith*, 78.

12. Emerson and Smith, *Divided by Faith*, 79.

13. Emerson and Smith, *Divided by Faith*, 78.

14. Michael O. Emerson and J. Russel Hawkins, "Viewed in Black and White: Conservative Protestantism, Racial Issues, and Oppositional Politics," in *Religion and American Politics: From the Colonial Period to the Present*, ed. Mark A. Noll and Luke E. Harlow, 2nd ed. (Oxford: Oxford University Press, 2007), 335.

15. Linda Steiner and Silvio Waisbord, eds., *News of Baltimore: Race, Rage and the City* (New York: Rutledge, 2017), 123.

16. John H. Richardson, "The Quote That Should End the Trayvon Trial," *Esquire*, June 24, 2013, https://www.esquire.com/news-politics/news/a23217/trayvon-martin-trial-quote-police-interview/.

17. "Big Racial Divide over Zimmerman Verdict," *Pew Research*, July 22, 2013, http://www.people-press.org/2013/07/22/big-racial-divide-over-zimmerman-verdict/.

18. "Department of Justice Report Regarding the Criminal Investigation into the Shooting Death of Michael Brown by Ferguson, Missouri Police Officer Darren Wilson," Department of Justice, March 4, 2015, pp. 5–8.

19. Dashiell Bennett and Russell Berman, "No Indictment," *The Atlantic*, November 24, 2014, https://www.theatlantic.com/national/archive/2014/11/ferguson-verdict-grand-jury/383130/.

20. Soong-Chan Rah, *Prophetic Lament: A Call for Justice in Troubled Times* (Downers Grove, IL: InterVarsity Press, 2015), 21.

21. Rah, *Prophetic Lament*, 44.

22. Carol Kuruvilla, "Rapper Has Choice Words for Christians Who Don't Want Him to Talk About Race," *Huffington Post*, July 12, 2016, https://www.huffingtonpost.com/entry/lecrae-rapper-christian-black-lives-matter_us_5783ff28e4b0344d51508a2e.

23. Joey Butler (@rapidcop109), "#Pray4Police," Twitter, November 24, 2014,

reply to Lecrae (@lecrae), "Praying for #Ferguson, https://twitter.com/lecrae/status/537064378638422016.

24. Lecrae Moore, "The Pains of Humanity Have Been Draining Me," *Huffington Post*, October 201, 2016, https://www.huffingtonpost.com/entry/i-declare-black-lives-matter_us_5808be36e4b0dd54ce385412?ke5s3ye0cxmwmte29.

25. Thabiti Anyabwile, "I'm Happy to Talk with Dr. Phil," *The Gospel Coalition*, February 11, 2016, https://www.thegospelcoalition.org/blogs/thabiti-anyabwile/im-happy-to-talk-with-dr-phil/.

26. Anyabwile, "I'm Happy to Talk with Dr. Phil."

27. Michelle Higgins, *Urbana 15*, video, https://vimeo.com/150226527.

28. Mark Oppenheimer, "Some Evangelicals Struggle with Black Lives Matter Movement," *New York Times*, January 22, 2016, https://www.nytimes.com/2016/01/23/us/some-evangelicals-struggle-with-black-lives-matter-movement.html.

29. "Black Lives Matter and Racial Tension in America," *Barna*, May 5, 2016, https://www.barna.com/research/black-lives-matter-and-racial-tension-in-america/, italics original.

30. Elizabeth Dias, "The Evangelical Fight to Win Back California," *New York Times*, May 27, 2018, https://www.nytimes.com/2018/05/27/us/politics/franklin-graham-evangelicals-california.html.

31. John Fea, "The Court Evangelicals," *The Way of Improvement Leads Home* (blog), May 6, 2017, https://thewayofimprovement.com/2017/05/06/the-court-evangelicals/.

32. David A. Fahrenthold, "Trump Recorded Having Extremely Lewd Conversation about Women in 2005," *Washington Post*, October 8, 2016, https://www.washingtonpost.com/politics/trump-recorded-having-extremely-lewd-conversation-about-women-in-2005/2016/10/07/3b9ce776-8cb4-11e6-bf8a-3d26847eeed4_story.html?utm_term=.a519eadf4e0f.

33. Josh Gerstein, "FBI Releases Files on Trump Apartments' Race Probe in '70s," *Politico*, February 15, 2017, https://www.politico.com/blogs/under-the-radar/2017/02/trump-fbi-files-discrimination-case-235067.

34. Sarah Burns, "Why Trump Doubled Down on the Central Park Five," *New York Times*, October 17, 2016, https://www.nytimes.com/2016/10/18/opinion/why-trump-doubled-down-on-the-central-park-five.html.

35. "Donald Trump on a Potential Presidential Run," *Today Show*, New York, NBC Universal, April 7, 2017, https://archives.nbclearn.com/portal/site/k12/browse/?cuecard=52817.

36. Michelle Ye Hee Lee, "Donald Trump's False Comments Connecting Mexican Immigrants and Crime," *Washington Post*, July 8, 2015, https://www.washingtonpost.com/news/fact-checker/wp/2015/07/08/donald-trumps-false-comments-connecting-mexican-immigrants-and-crime/?utm_term=.f7e0feb508fb.

37. "'Sh*thole Countries' Respond to Trump's Rhetoric," *CBS News*, January 12, 2018, https://www.cbsnews.com/news/donald-trump-shthole-countries -response-from-haiti-africa-el-salvador/.

38. Dan Merica, "Trump Condemns 'Hatred, Bigotry, and Violence on Many Sides' in Charlottesville," *CNN*, August 13, 2017, https://www.cnn.com/ 2017/08/12/politics/trump-statement-alt-right-protests/index.html.

39. Gregory A. Smith and Jessica Martinez, "How the Faithful Voted: A Preliminary 2016 Analysis," *Pew Research Center*, November 9, 2016, http:// www.pewresearch.org/fact-tank/2016/11/09/how-the-faithful-voted-a -preliminary-2016-analysis/.

40. Gregory A. Smith, "Among White Evangelicals, Regular Churchgoers Are the Most Supportive of Trump," *Pew Research Center*, April 26, 2017, http:// www.pewresearch.org/fact-tank/2017/04/26/among-white-evangelicals -regular-churchgoers-are-the-most-supportive-of-trump/.

41. Russell Moore, "Have Evangelicals Who Support Trump Lost Their Values?," *New York Times*, September 17, 2015, https://www.nytimes.com/2015/09/17/ opinion/have-evangelicals-who-support-trump-lost-their-values.html.

42. Sarah Pulliam Bailey, "Could Southern Baptist Russell Moore Lose His Job? Churches Threaten to Pull Funds after Months of Trump Controversy," *The Washington Post*, March 13, 2017, https://www.washingtonpost.com/news/ acts-of-faith/wp/2017/03/13/could-southern-baptist-leader-russell-moore-lose -his-job-churches-threaten-funding-after-months-of-trump-controversy/ ?utm_term=.cadf3cb73d80.

43. Emma Green, "White Evangelicals Believe They Face More Discrimination Than Muslims," *The Atlantic*, March 10, 2017, https://www.theatlantic.com/ politics/archive/2017/03/perceptions-discrimination-muslims-christians/519135/.

44. Campbell Robertson, "A Quiet Exodus: Why Black Worshipers Are Leaving White Evangelical Churches," *New York Times*, March 9, 2018, https://www .nytimes.com/2018/03/09/us/blacks-evangelical-churches.html.

45. See Jemar Tisby, "Why a Racially Insensitive Photo of Southern Baptist Seminary Professors Matters," *Washington Post*, April 27, 2017, https://www .washingtonpost.com/news/acts-of-faith/wp/2017/04/27/why-a-racially -insensitive-photo-of-southern-baptist-seminary-professors-matters/?utm _term=.2c4a097dfd4c.

46. "OC Recommends: Refer Civil Rights Resolution to 44th Assembly," *By Faith*, June 10, 2015, http://byfaithonline.com/oc-recommends-refer-civil -rights-resolution-to-44th-assembly-2/.

47. Emma Green, "A Resolution Condemning White Supremacy Causes Chaos at the Southern Baptist Convention," *The Atlantic*, June 14, 2017, https://www.theatlantic.com/politics/archive/2017/06/the-southern-baptist -convention-alt-right-white-supremacy/530244/.

48. Lawrence Ware, "Why I'm Leaving the Southern Baptist Convention," *New York Times*, July 17, 2017, https://www.nytimes.com/2017/07/17/opinion/why-im-leaving-the-southern-baptist-convention.html.

49. Robertson, "A Quiet Exodus."

50. Martin Luther King Jr., "Letter from a Birmingham Jail," April 16, 1963.

CHAPTER 11: THE FIERCE URGENCY OF NOW

1. Martin Luther King Jr., "I Have a Dream," speech, Washington DC, August 28, 1963, during the "March on Washington."

2. King, "I Have a Dream."

3. Naomi Nelson, "The John Hope Franklin Papers: A Historian Becomes History," *Huffington Post*, October 17, 2012, https://www.huffingtonpost.com/naomi-nelson/african-american-history_b_1973636.html.

4. For example, *The African Americans: Many Rivers to Cross*, PBS, https://www.pbs.org/show/african-americans-many-rivers-cross/.

5. This is not to say you can never ask a racial or ethnic minority any questions, but it does mean that we all have to take ownership for our own knowledge and not burden others with the responsibility of providing answers we can easily find ourselves, especially when conversation about race can prove so exhausting to those who live through racial discrimination on a daily basis.

6. Christopher Ingraham, "Three Quarters of Whites Don't Have Any Non-White Friends," *Washington Post*, August 25, 2014, https://www.washingtonpost.com/news/wonk/wp/2014/08/25/three-quarters-of-whites-dont-have-any-non-white-friends/?utm_term=.26fa7aa03dee.

7. Andy Crouch's *Culture Making: Recovering Our Creative Calling* (Downers Grove, IL: InterVarsity Press, 2009) offers an entire theology of how to change the culture by creating "cultural artifacts."

8. Laura Shin, "The Racial Wealth Gap: Why a Typical White Household Has 16 Times the Wealth of a Black One," *Forbes*, March 26, 2015, https://www.forbes.com/sites/laurashin/2015/03/26/the-racial-wealth-gap-why-a-typical-white-household-has-16-times-the-wealth-of-a-black-one/#7d3d267c1f45.

9. William Darity Jr., Darrick Hamilton, Mark Paul, Alan Aja, Anne Price, Antonio Moore, and Caterina Chiopris, "What We Get Wrong About Closing the Racial Wealth Gap," *Samuel DuBois Cook Center on Social Equity* (April 2014), 1, https://socialequity.duke.edu/sites/socialequity.duke.edu/files/site-images/FINAL%20COMPLETE%20REPORT_.pdf.

10. "Reparations NOW: Ecclesiastical Reparations with Duke Kwon," *Truth's Table* (podcast), interview, March 2018.

11. "Reparations NOW: Ecclesiastical Reparations with Duke Kwon."

12. William A. Darity Jr., "Reparations," *Encyclopedia of African-American*

Culture and History, ed. Colin A. Palmer, vol. 5, 2nd ed. (Detroit: Macmillan Reference, 2006), 1924–28.

13. An argument could certainly be made for pursuing bivocational ministry regardless of salary because it allows ministers to serve the community in other ways that go beyond the church walls, and these jobs provide access to people who may not otherwise visit a church.

14. Lottie Joiner, "Bree Newsome Reflects on Taking Down South Carolina's Confederate Flag 2 Years Ago," *Vox*, June 27, 2017, https://www.vox.com/ identities/2017/6/27/15880052/bree-newsome-south-carolinas-confederate-flag.

15. Soong-Chan Rah, *Prophetic Lament: A Call for Justice in Troubled Times* (Downers Grove, IL: InterVarsity Press, 2015), 21–22.

16. See, for example, Lisa Sharon Harper, "Freedom Road Pilgrimages," https:// freedomroad.us/what-we-do/freedom-road-pilgrimages/.

17. Portions of this section originally appeared in an article entitled "Why Juneteenth Should Be a National Holiday," *The Witness*, June 19, 2018. It is used here with permission. See https://thewitnessbcc.com/why-juneteenth -should-be-a-national-holiday/.

18. "About Our Founder," BlackGirlsCode, http://www.blackgirlscode.com/ about-bgc.html.

19. Vivian Wang, "Erica Garner, Activist and Daughter of Eric Garner, Dies at 27," *New York Times*, December 20, 2017, https://www.nytimes.com/2017/ 12/30/nyregion/erica-garner-dead.html.

20. Elizabeth Wagmeister, "How Me Too Founder Tarana Burke Wants to Shift the Movement's Narrative," *Variety*, April 10, 2018, https://variety.com/2018/ biz/news/tarana-burke-me-too-founder-sexual-violence-1202748012/.

21. Nikole Hannah Jones, "Choosing a School for My Daughter in a Segregated City," *New York Times*, June 9, 2016, https://www.nytimes.com/2016/06/12/ magazine/choosing-a-school-for-my-daughter-in-a-segregated-city.html.

INDEX